Environmental Melancl

CW01512351

In this groundbreaking book, Renee Lertzman applies psychoanalytic theory and psychosocial research to the issue of public engagement and public apathy in response to chronic ecological threats. By highlighting unconscious and affective dimensions of contemporary ecological issues, Lertzman deconstructs the idea that there is a gap between what people care about and what is actually carried out in policy and personal practice. In doing so, she presents an innovative way to think about and design engagement practices and policy interventions.

Based on key qualitative fieldwork and in-depth interviews conducted in Green Bay, Wisconsin, each chapter provides a psychosocial, psychoanalytic perspective on subjectivity, affect and identity and considers what this means for understanding behaviour in relation to environmental crises and climate change. The book argues for a theory of environmental melancholia that accounts for the ways in which people experience profound loss and disruption caused by environmental issues and yet may have trouble expressing or making sense of such experiences.

Environmental Melancholia offers a fresh perspective to the field of environmental psychology that until now has been largely dominated by research in cognitive, behavioural and social psychology. It will appeal to academics, researchers and postgraduate students in the fields of psychoanalysis, psychosocial studies and sustainability, as well as policy makers and educators internationally.

Renee Lertzman teaches Psychology of Environmental Education and Communication in the MA programme at Royal Roads University, British Columbia, Canada, and is a psychosocial researcher. She has a PhD in psychosocial studies from Cardiff University, UK, and actively speaks and teaches internationally. She currently works with environmental organizations in the public, private and governmental sectors, as a strategic communications and engagement consultant and as an applied researcher.

Psychoanalytic Explorations series

Environmental Melancholia

Psychoanalytic dimensions of engagement

Renee Lertzman

Routledge
Taylor & Francis Group

LONDON AND NEW YORK

First published 2015
by Routledge
2 Park Square, Milton Park, Abingdon, Oxon OX14 4RN

and by Routledge
711 Third Avenue, New York, NY 10017

*Routledge is an imprint of the Taylor & Francis Group,
an informa business*

First issued in paperback 2016

British Library Cataloguing in Publication Data
A catalogue record for this book is available from the British
Library

Library of Congress Cataloging-in-Publication Data
Lertzman, Renee.
    Environmental melancholia : psychoanalytic dimensions of
engagement / Renee Lertzman.
       pages cm
    Includes bibliographical references and index.
    1. Environmental psychology.   I. Title.
    BF353.L47 2015
    155.9′1—dc23
    2014049096

ISBN: 978-0-415-72799-0 (hbk)
ISBN: 978-1-318-73779-2 (pbk)

Typeset in Bembo
by Apex CoVantage, LLC

Dedicated to . . .

Jonathan Wege, for believing in me and making this project possible
  The memories of my grandfather Albert (Mandy) Mandelbaum and Uncle Melvin Lertzman, for sharing with me the joy of intellectual pursuits
  And to my parents for teaching me the meaning of תקון עולם (tikkun olam)

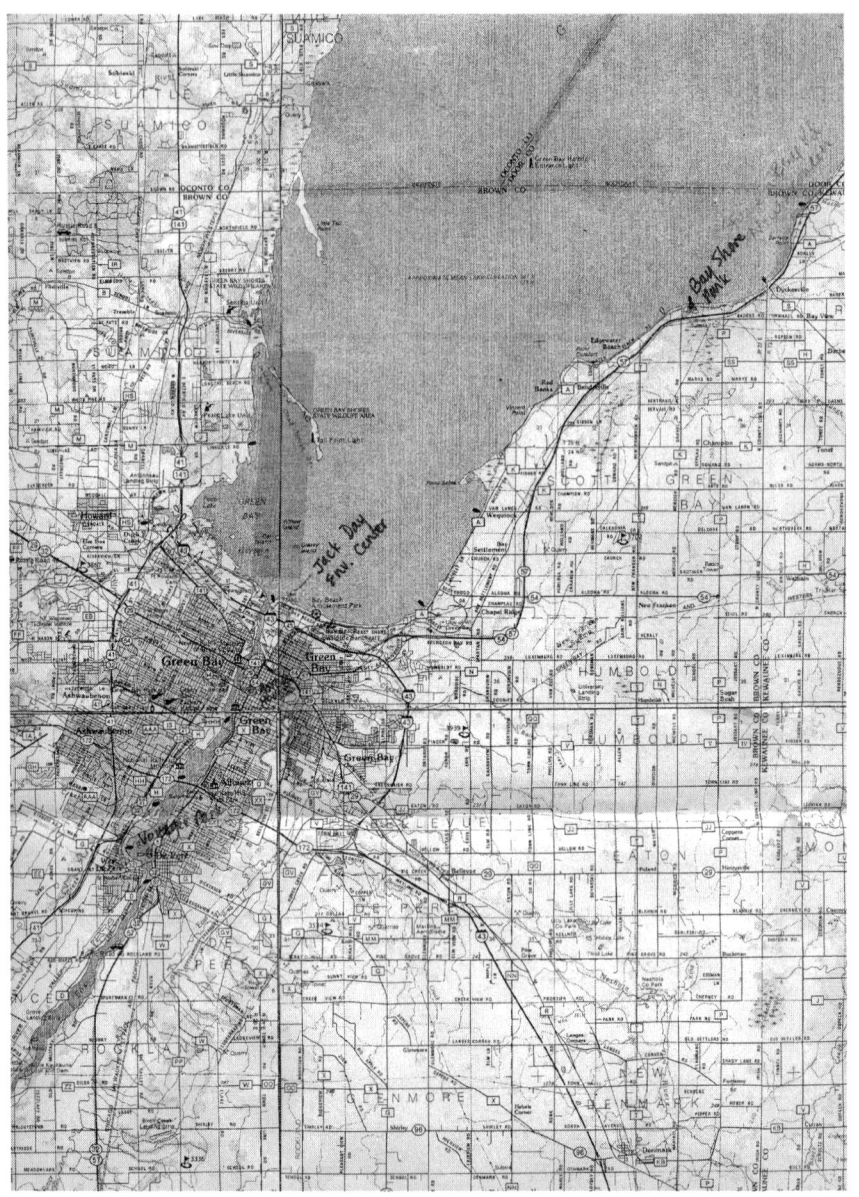

Figure 0.1 Map of Green Bay. (© 2007 DeLorme (www.delorme.com) | Wisconsin Atlas and Gazetteer.)

Contents

Appendices   155

Figures

Tables

Preface

In 1992, a group of psychoanalysts and environmental activists convened at the Freud Museum in London. There was, as it turned out, plenty to talk about (see Ward, 1993, for his review of the event). The group discussed and debated topics such as denial, projection, anxiety and loss in relation to how people relate with our most serious ecological threats. Perhaps not surprisingly, a subtext of these discussions concerned the relevance and practicality of psychoanalytic work. Associated with the cozy, rug-adorned confines of the consulting room, psychoanalytic work is hardly perceived as relevant for the busy and often frantic front line of environmental activism.

However, psychoanalytic work, as this book argues, is one of our greatest untapped resources when it comes to meeting our ecological crises more effectively. This is because we must understand on the deepest levels possible the workings of human behaviour, including unconscious processes such as denial, projection, splitting, disavowal and apathy. All of which, it must be noted, are roundly recognized as writ large in our contemporary responses to urgent ecological threats. Psychoanalytic work, based on its fine-grained attention to how humans strategize to defend and avoid distressing and painful experiences – as well as what facilitates creativity and repair – is uniquely positioned to serve and inform work in environmental advocacy sectors. However, in order for this to come into being, we must first overcome our biases and presumptions when it comes to unconscious dimensions of human life. We must be willing to rethink and challenge our assumptions about subjectivity, engagement and consciousness. We must be open to different epistemic orientations and what constitutes as 'data' and 'metrics'. And we must be willing to take methodological risks and innovate how we do research. This book is an invitation to do so.

Psychoanalytic researchers have an abundance of theoretical, clinical and conceptual resources to help us address the increasingly urgent ecological threats we are collectively facing. One of the most notable and significant attributes of psychoanalytic work as it pertains to ecological crisis is the recognition of how unconscious processes drive our individual and social behaviors. Notably, psychoanalytic work has historically explored the strategies engaged to manage anxieties and distressing experiences, regardless of the particular schools of thought or traditions. For example, Kleinian and Bionian perspectives may speak directly to the capacity for splitting, both internal splitting and compartmentalizing, including splitting off awareness of our dependence on earth systems (e.g. Segal, 1973; Mishan, 1996; Nicholsen, 2009). This capacity for dissociation is related to issues of vulnerability and anxiety, evoked in dependency contexts and exemplified by our relationship with nature and the ecological systems we need to survive (Searles, 1960; Worthy, 2013). Some psychoanalytic thinkers may focus on how this relationship is negotiated in fantasies of omnipotence, patterns of consumption as "spurious satisfactions" (Mishan, 1996, p. 62) or substitutes (Randall, 2005) and compulsive forms of activism (Žižek, 1992).

More recently, psychoanalytic analyses of greed, consumption and climate change are being addressed (e.g. Weintrobe, 2009; Rust & Totten, 2012), as well as issues of grief and loss in the face of the implications of environmental destruction (e.g. Randall, 2009). Relational psychoanalytic work is well situated for thinking through issues of human–nonhuman *relationality* and, more broadly, how relationships with ecological contexts may be more constructive and reality based. The application of psychoanalytic work to these relations, however, is far from straightforward. As others have noted, the 'portability' of clinical work to the biotic sphere requires thoughtful consideration and creativity (Randall, 2005). This book is an expression of my engagement with psychoanalytic concepts – notably, melancholia, ambivalence and reparation – to address the most urgent needs for addressing our ecological crises.

During my first year in college at University of California at Santa Cruz in 1986, I took an environmental studies class. We learned about a different environmental issue each week: deforestation, toxic contamination, species loss, the race to protect ancient agricultural practices, ozone depletion, a warming atmosphere. After class, I would make my way to my social psychology course with Eliot Aronson. We studied cognitive dissonance, aggression and prejudice. The next day, I attended a cultural studies seminar where we discussed postmodern theory, the mutable nature of human identities and deconstructed notions of the self. By the end of term, I was in an existential crisis. While we were clearly facing severe planetary ecological threats, no one was addressing how this information was impacting us. Away from home for the first time, we learned about how severely threatened our ecological systems are, on which human and nonhuman life depend. And yet, we were not discussing implications of this for us as individuals and social beings. While we learned about social psychology, we did not address how we interact with our ecological systems and the curious way in which humans degrade the very systems we depend on and the habitats of creatures which we supposedly value.

I left the classroom for a two-month immersion environmental field study course with Sierra Institute. We backpacked through Death Valley, the high Sierra Nevada, along the Eel River and by the Pacific Ocean, reflecting on our relationship with our biosphere and our communities. We read deep ecologists, emerging ecofeminism, nature writers and the transcendentalists. We hiked mountains and swam icy rivers and pools. Inspired by wilderness psychology pioneer Robert Greenway, we were encouraged to leave behind the "front country" and explore a more direct relationship with the natural world and ourselves. During this immersion and the re-entry back to civilization, I realized we needed radically different ways of addressing the *lived experience* of ecological degradation. That is, to go beyond whatever values, opinions or attitudes we may have and to appreciate the messier, complicated negotiations that can come with an environmental awareness. Rather than viewing our acute environmental predicaments through a lens of whether or not people 'care' or 'value' our environment, I discovered it is the places where people get stuck and "tangled" between conflicting desires and motivations that matter. Such negotiations are usually private, inchoate and not available through the administering of a survey, structured interview or tightly facilitated focus group. The grief, mourning, anger, confusion and overwhelm that can accompany awareness of environmental issues remain largely unaddressed, private and professionally and socially taboo.

Over the past two decades, I have worked actively as an environmental communications professional. I've interviewed leading environmental professionals and consulted with dozens of organizations across governmental, public and private sectors. I've designed and taught new courses on the psychological dimensions of environmental communications education internationally. Over these decades of experience, I have become aware of a singular question at the heart of our work: how do we engage the public and mobilize effective environmental action to stem the tides of ecological degradation and long-term consequences for all life on the planet? More specifically, how can we effectively mobilize the scale of response required to avoid further ecological travesties? Even when this was articulated differently according to campaign or initiative, the underlying impetus remained the same. The task was not to enlist those already 'on-board' but to persuade, cajole, scare or otherwise plea for some sort of response from a larger group on behalf of our environment.

In this book, I suggest that vast reserves of creative potential for engaging and addressing ecological challenge are available but 'tied up' in complex psychic negotiations. Namely, I argue that a form of melancholia, *environmental melancholia* – an arrested, inchoate form of mourning – is at the heart of much of the inaction in response to ecological degradation. Melancholia is deeply connected with the ways in which industry is negotiated as both beneficent and brutal. Understanding these dynamics profoundly informs how we practice engaging individuals and communities in the constructive responses to ecological challenges. This understanding offers new resources, tools and processes for engaging more constructively with various publics in the issues that arguably matter to us all. As I argue here and in my work as a researcher and practitioner, understanding these processes, particularly *anxiety* – and its relation to loss, whether actual or anticipated – is our greatest resource when it comes to environmental engagement and reparation. This may seem counterintuitive.

Anxiety, as well as sadness, loss or despair, is often seen as antithetical to a meaningful environmental engagement strategy. However, understanding anxiety can reveal how people often avoid what is most painful, which ecological threats arguably are, even when it is counterproductive in the long run.

As this book argues, this conceptual framework and use of psychoanalytically informed social science research methods – which I refer to as psychosocial research – has the potential to reframe environmental engagement, present new opportunities for how we research how people relate with chronic and acute ecological issues near and far and encourage the use of more dialogic, conversational platforms and modes for both investigations and engagement strategies.

The following material draws from fieldwork conducted in 2007 and 2008 in Green Bay, Wisconsin. During 2006–2009, I was awarded a research fellowship with the Biodiversity Project, a not-for-profit environmental communications organization based in Madison, Wisconsin. This fellowship afforded the opportunity to design a research project exploring how people experienced and made sense of issues impacting the Great Lakes, drawing on work Biodiversity Project had conducted with their partner, the then newly formed Healing Our Waters Coalition (now branded Healthy Lakes, Healthy Lives). I organized a field visit to Green Bay and was introduced to the region's industrial, ecological and cultural contexts, thanks to several generous and committed local ecologists and environmental professionals. I chose to conduct my fieldwork in Green Bay based on its proximity and ecological significance to the Great Lakes systems, as well as its history of ecological degradation. I also chose this as a field site because of the presence of a small but committed community of environmental scientists and researchers, in addition to the overall perception from the environmental community of a political and civic inertia when it comes to actively protecting, restoring and advocating for stricter regulations to protect its natural resources.

The heart of this approach is the design of what I call Relational, Dialogic Interviews, drawing from related practices used by psychoanalytic social science researchers. I interviewed 10 participants three times each, used an opening prompt, and established a relational style of interviewing to support rapport and trust. I also administered a survey via a local marketing research firm in Green Bay, which enabled me to both select participants and contrast survey data with the interview material. The use of these in-depth, psychosocially informed research interviews was critical for the discussion that follows here. As with psychoanalytic work, there was keen interest in narrative, specifically how we convey meanings indirectly through our stories, memories, associations and experiences. I spent three months in Green Bay in 2007 and conducted the interviews during that time. Their names and identifying details have been changed to protect their anonymity.

Understanding how people manage and negotiate potentially distressing information – such as industrial degradation (and destruction) of the natural environment – we can develop particular strategies and mechanisms to enable different modes of being and engaging with serious environmental problems. For example, we may be able to design more opportunities for people to access their creativity and specific skills, or we may create contexts for people to simply talk with one another and process their confusion or issues. Engagement may look very different from what we imagine, as more of a collaborative and participatory process and less as a 'selling and telling' approach. We may discover that people do experience painful dilemmas with regard to threats to natural environments but have devised complex strategies for negotiating such dilemmas, such as denial, disavowal, splitting or projection (all of which will be discussed). Or we may find that 'wilful forgetting' can sometimes be the most psychically coherent response to a distressing environmental situation.

The insights I experienced through my conversations with participants in Green Bay are presented in this book and deeply informed my work as an environmental communications and engagement practitioner. I was moved by the stories and accounts of loss related by my participants – many instances of profound care for their beloved Great Lakes and favorite watersheds, but with a lack of clarity as to how to best connect with this care.

In what follows is an account of what I learned throughout this process, specifically how our frameworks of the psychological dimensions of environmental issues can change. I present an analysis informed by an interest in how people may care deeply about our planet, our precious places and lakes and rivers, our air and forests and oceans, and the beings we share this place with – and find themselves unable to act on this care and concern. We begin with rethinking our assumptions about human subjectivity – that in fact we are capable of great contradiction and ambivalence and that we are also capable of profound reparation if we can access our capacities for creative engagement with our world.

I have organized the book into two parts. Part I establishes the context of taking a psychoanalytic approach and argument for why we need to look beyond our behavior change and attitudinal frameworks and explore the underpinnings of environmental engagement. Intrinsic to this argument is the need to rethink how we design and conduct our research methodologies. Part II explores the three core thematic affective components of this form of environmental research: Melancholia, Ambivalence and Reparation. As psychoanalytically informed theoretical concepts, they are mutually influencing and in actuality interrelated. However, for the purposes of this book, I have presented them as disparate affective themes to focus our attention. I conclude with a call to radically reframe how we are accustomed to thinking about the ways in which people engage with our most serious ecological threats facing our species and our planet – from one of an absence of care or concern to one that presumes intolerable levels of anxiety and ambivalence, which can thwart our aspirational capacities.

Renee Lertzman
Point Reyes Station, California
Spring 2014

References

Mishan, J., 1996. Psychoanalysis and environmentalism: First thoughts, *Psychoanalytic Psychotherapy* 10, pp. 59–70.

Nicholsen, S. W., & Doherty, J., 2009. Shierry Weber Nicholsen: The Ecopsychology Interview, *Ecopsychology* 1 (3), pp. 110–117.

Randall, R., 2005. A new climate for psychotherapy? *Psychotherapy and Politics International* 3, pp. 165–179.

Randall, R., 2009. Loss and climate change: The cost of parallel narratives, *Ecopsychology* 3, pp. 118–129.

Rust, M. J., & Totten, N., eds., 2012. *Vital Signs: Psychological Responses to Ecological Crisis.* London: Karnac.

Searles, H., 1960. *The Nonhuman Environment in Normal Development and in Schizophrenia.* New York City: International Universities Press.

Segal, H., 1973. *Introduction to the Work of Melanie Klein.* London: Karnac.

Ward, I., 1993. Ecological madness, a Freud Museum conference: Introductory thoughts, *British Journal of Psychotherapy* 10, pp. 178–187.

Weintrobe, S., 2009. On runaway greed and climate change denial: A psychoanalytic perspective, Lecture Series, Psychotherapy in the 21st Century. 25 April, Lincoln Clinic & Centre for Psychotherapy, London, UK.

Worthy, K. 2013. *Invisible Nature: Healing the Destructive Divide Between People and the Environment.* New York: Pantheon.

Žižek, S., 1992. *Looking Awry: An Introduction to Jacques Lacan Through Popular Culture.* Cambridge, MA: MIT Press.

Acknowledgements

This project is both a culmination of a journey and the beginning of a new one. Over the past two decades, I have been fortunate to know and work with inspiring individuals and groups who have encouraged my commitment to understanding the experience of contemporary environmental issues and who have also demonstrated the possibilities of thoughtful, graceful scholarship. This book would simply not exist without my knowing these individuals.

First, I wish to thank Jonathan Wege for believing in the project and making this possible. Without his support, it simply would not have happened. Jonathan has demonstrated that miracles *do* happen.

In Green Bay, Janice Galt offered a perfect base near the Fox River Trail during my fieldwork, and the people at Kavarna Coffeehouse in Green Bay offered excellent coffee and a friendly place to work. Paul Wozniak was selfless with his time and energy and an invaluable cultural and historical resource during my time in Green Bay. Kendra Axness provided tours of Green Bay and the surrounding farmlands and was unceasingly generous in her sharing of resources over the past three years. (Her maps grace the pages of this book.) Victoria and Bud Harris devoted an afternoon to showing me the Bay and various restoration projects they had worked on, and they continued to be invaluable resources. Heather Herdmann of Matousek & Associates was an *angel* in partnering for the survey research. Biodiversity Project provided excellent insights, particularly Jeffrey Potter, and helpfully administered my fellowship. And of course, I am deeply appreciative of and honored by the participants who generously shared their time, energy and experiences with me.

I would also like to thank Valerie Walkerdine, Steven Stanley, Paul Hoggett, Rosemary Randall, Hillary Britten, Joseph Dodds, Sally Weintrobe, Ivan Ward, Duncan Cartwright, Shierry Nicholsen, Marianne Stefancic, Kirstin Greene, Martin Tull, Charlie Weiss and the many others whom I have been fortunate to know who have provided collegial support and are pioneering this emerging field of research and practice. I am grateful to Hilary Britten for her consistent encouragement and support during my time in the UK. I am eternally grateful to Petra Shenk, Athena Wisotsky, Faith Kearn and Mark Brown for providing insightful input on earlier drafts.

Part I

Why psychoanalysis matters

Fox River, January 2008. (Photo: Ned Dorff.)

We lived right on the river. I have a tendency to be emotionally attached to the seasons as far as the river goes. I will, when the springtime comes, I will be in a better mood, when I see the river ice is off. When it's open. Because it opens from the center out, and that was, an old girlfriend told me that. She says, you know how much happier you get when the river is open? I know when you have seen the river is open, because you are in such a better mood. And I'm like, oh, that would make sense . . . I never been one to think it's better in some other place than what is here. Because I think it's got a lot of great things around here.

— Howard, Interview 1

Chapter 1

Introduction

Over the past two decades, working as an environmental communications professional across government, public and private sectors, the question of how to mobilize the public to effective environmental action has been ever present. It is often articulated differently according to campaign or initiative, but the underlying assumption that people do not care enough to act remains the same. So the quandary persists: how do we motivate people to care more? Nonetheless, to date, no sector has produced an effective method for changing people's behaviour toward environmental conservation, protection and restoration. This study, therefore, begins with an alternative premise for framing this foundational problem. Rather than trying to motivate and inspire people to act, which sets us up to push against a tide and which frames our work as persuasion, I take as a starting point that people already care a lot but may be caught up in complicated dilemmas or 'tangles' that make action hard to take. Thus, our job becomes recognizing the care and concern that exists and creating conditions to optimally support the expression of such care. As Aldo Leopold has written, "One of the penalties of an ecological education is that one lives alone in a world of wounds" (Leopold, 1949). Psychoanalytic insight combined with psychosocial research offers us this capacity and set of tools.

In this book, I propose that there are vast reserves of creative potential for addressing ecological challenges but that they are 'tied up' in complex psychic negotiations. Rather than positing a gap between affect and environmental action, I show how unconscious processes, such as ambivalence, loss, overwhelm and sorrow are missing factors in much of environmental communications, advocacy and campaign work. Moreover, the assumption that what people care about will naturally translate into actions is erroneous. On the contrary, studies show that how much we may care about something does not necessarily translate into our actions, particularly in the newly emerging behavioral change fixation (Pink, 2011; Heath & Heath, 2010; Kahnemann, 2011). Furthermore, underlying drivers of behavior are not isolated to the individual. We produce, share and co-construct our unconscious negotiations of highly charged issues through our conversations, stories, advertising, intimate dialogues and public media discourses (Norgaard, 2011; Lertzman, 2012b; Shove, 2010; Kahan, 2009; Billig, 2002).

A critical place to start is by investigating how loss and mourning, when unattended to and unresolved, contribute to what I call *environmental melancholia*. Environmental melancholia is a condition in which even those who care deeply about the well-being of ecosystems and future generations are paralyzed to translate such concern into action. Applying psychoanalytic understandings of the workings of ambivalence and loss can be one of our greatest resources when examining environmental engagement and reparation. This may seem counterintuitive because emotions like sadness, loss or despair are often seen as antithetical to fostering environmental advocacy and political action in general. In fact, environmental educators and advocates often worry that people will become immobilized by despair and are consequently often torn between transmitting the 'real story' to people or inspiring them through an array of solutions. In a climate increasingly fixated on discourses of hope, we tend to avoid difficult emotions and instead provide people with possible solutions and feel-good stories. However, psychoanalytic thought recognizes that ambivalence, loss and anxiety can impede our capacities for concern and repair. Rather than an exclusive focus on solutions, a psychoanalytic approach views loss and ambivalence as psychosocial 'achievements' not to be avoided but integrated for more authentic modes of engagement with a dynamic, uncertain world. This includes our collective capacities for generating the solutions needed. However, we must begin with the fundamental recognition of how ecological threats, including climate change, occasion unprecedented psychological and social tensions, conflicts and emotions.

A psychoanalytically inspired orientation to subjectivity and human experience addresses (and presumes) the capacity to tolerate multiple, competing desires, drives and wishes. This suggests by implication that *any* attempt to understand how people are making sense of ecological crises must take into account the probable misalignment between values and actions. To label misalignments as a 'gap' both perpetuates a myth of individual action devoid of social influence and perpetuates a (unitary) rational actor model of subjectivity. Based on decades of clinical practice and research, psychoanalytic thought offers a nuanced lens into how actual and anticipatory loss is managed and how individuals often defend against such loss by retreating into denial, projection and other related defense mechanisms. I argue that such topics clearly map onto contemporary environmental engagement and communications practices.

Environmental melancholia

Ecological degradation poses profound implications for all life on earth. Despite warnings from specialists and the tireless efforts of environmental organizations, a lack of engagement commensurate with the threats we face remains. Whether the focus is on political will, neurological circuits or consumer behaviour, theories regarding why humans are slow to respond to ecological problems abound. One of the most prevalent suggests that the greatest barrier to engagement with ecological threats is a lack of concern, care or interest. "People just can't be bothered" is a phrase often heard in environmental advocacy circles.

This book is an argument against this common line of thinking and instead claims that most people care very deeply about the quality of life on the planet and the desire for future generations to enjoy a vital world. It argues this by showing that what people care about does not unproblematically translate into action. In fact, people can care a whole lot and still do very little because a deep sense of fear and anxiety underlie our concern for the future. And what we learn from psychoanalytic research and practice are the ways in which fear and anxiety can contribute to paralysis, defensive mechanisms such as denial, projection, splitting and dissociation. I argue that these insights are invaluable for our work in environmental communications, strategy, policy and engagement. For example, in specific regions like Green Bay where this study takes place, social identities emerge from industrial practices. Our economic stability and livelihoods, our cars, clothes, homes and food depend upon a largely environmentally degrading industry. A psychosocial approach – in contrast to a focus on values, attitudes or beliefs – addresses how people manage and negotiate conflicts, particularly concerning the things that matter most and which may be viewed as threatened. The question is not about a 'lack of care' but rather, as I explore in my interviews, where does the care or concern go? How it is channelled and expressed? Where does it live inside of us? In so doing, this inquiry sheds light on a complex and arguably richer picture than a myth of apathy can provide. This helps illuminate and deconstruct denial, political polarization and avoidance of coming to terms with how humans have severely impacted the planet – and what steps are required to restore, repair and create new futures. Coming to terms with how these issues are *experienced and lived* is a fundamental reframe that a psychoanalytic and psychosocial orientation can offer and arguably vastly expands our field of inquiry, investigation and what is knowable about the human engagement with our ecologically degraded world and selves.

What follows is an account of my exploration of these affective dimensions and how focusing the inquiry on sites of conflict, confusion, incoherence and inchoate loss can reframe how we understand environmental engagement (and the lack thereof). The study investigates how people may care deeply about the planet and its precious places, lakes and rivers, about the quality of air, forests and oceans, as well as about the other beings with whom we share such places, yet find themselves unable to act on this care and concern. I begin by rethinking certain assumptions about human subjectivity and foreground our capacity for contradiction and ambivalence, as well as our capacity for profound reparation when we access our creative engagement with our world.

This book argues that in order to facilitate a viable, pragmatic politics of environmental advocacy, complicated psychological dimensions of contemporary industrial environmental issues must be attended to. This requires a willingness to interrogate the ways in which unconscious processes animate and inform our capacities for engaging with ecological threats. It also positions environmental engagement as a dynamic, often messy process of negotiating dilemmas, concerning how we constitute our everyday practices. In other words, engagement is not merely about how to get people excited about joining a green team or making ecologically friendly consumer choices. It is the character, texture and quality of how we choose to make contact with the awareness and implications of our industrial practices and how we negotiate our own deep investments in such practices. Engagement is about how we experience our own interrelationships in systems, including those we may not want to be a part of. I assert that inquiring into how such dilemmas are 'made sense of' is politically necessary, rather than a luxury reserved for the clinical consulting room or ecopsychology workshop. I would go so far as to say that separating psychological dimensions from environmental advocacy severely cripples our capacities for coherent and integrative environmental engagement and restorative practices (Searles, 1960, p. 4). To maintain such a separation is to participate in a fantasy that we can somehow evacuate the messy realms of human subjectivity from how we engage with ecological contexts. It also suggests a steadfast loyalty to the economic 'rational actor model' – long debunked – that presumes people change their behaviour based on facts, information and data.

The concept of *environmental melancholia* is inspired by Freud's work on unresolved mourning (1917). It explores engagement through the lens of melancholia, wherein one may be 'frozen' or otherwise arrested due to lack of acknowledgement or recognition of what has been lost. In contrast to losing a person, for example, environmental loss can be far more amorphous, particularly in a culture that does not recognize it as valid.[1] Further, environmental loss can be "anticipatory" (Randall, 2009), insofar as we are mourning for loss that is likely to come. In this state, we may not have as full access to our capacities to engage proactively to restore, protect or repair and may find ourselves in a form of perpetual, unresolved mourning.

This book is based on research, based on in-depth interviews, conducted in 2006–2007 on the affective dimensions of environmental degradation among people living in Green Bay, Wisconsin, in the Great Lakes region of the United States. My focus was on understanding how local environmental issues, specifically relating to the waters of Green Bay as a tributary to the Great lakes, are experienced by those who may appear apathetic based on their relative lack of engagement with environmental issues. I explored how people emotionally responded to these issues. Did they feel anxious and concerned, or did they actually not care? Why were they not more involved in local efforts to protect, restore and repair the lakes and rivers?

I explored these issues from a perspective different from the 'attitude-value gap' discourse that focuses on the so-called disconnect between what people say and what they do. I also moved away from the concept of 'barriers' so prevalent in environmental research and communities of practice. Rather than presuming a barrier or *lack* of something intrinsic, I instead to pursued an investigation into what is *present* or even in surplus (Lertzman, 2008a; Lertzman, 2012a). This inquiry was based on my own long-standing fascination with psychoanalytic theory, my commitment to qualitative psychosocial research and the sense that environmental studies and psychoanalysis are not as disparate as one may presume. As I shall discuss, from a psychoanalytic perspective, there are no 'gaps' between knowing and doing or between valuing and acting because we are conflicted beings with high capacity for contradiction. Rather, the focus is on how conflicts and dilemmas are negotiated, made sense of, socially supported and 'worked through' towards greater alignment and behavioural changes.

Psychoanalysis and environmental advocacy have some striking things in common; for example, both are keenly concerned with the concept and practice of *reparation* – that is, to repair, to heal, to fix. However, how reparation is taken up and engaged across these spheres is quite different. For example, whereas the psychoanalyst may be concerned with unconscious and often painful processes involved in capacities for reparation, an environmental advocate may be more concerned with the quickest and most effective way for finding solutions (see Lertzman, 2012b; Randall, 2009; Weintrobe, 2013; Dodds, 2011). While this assessment is a bit crude, how reparation is engaged across these disparate disciplines is contrasting – but also complementary. Activists' tendency for antagonism towards psychoanalytic modes of inquiry and reflection as a luxury *must* be tempered so that both modes can be seen as integral for a more effective environmental movement (Ward, 1993). I would go so far as to say that separating psychic dimensions from the environmental, and vice versa, severely cripples our capacities for coherent and integrative environmental response and restorative practices. To maintain such a separation inaccurately produces a partial psychoanalysis that historically ignores the biotic relations in which we are all embedded.

The concept of *environmental melancholia* presented in this book is premised upon the assertion that environmental threats involve a potential dissolution of traditionally held certainties, such as the availability of clean and fresh water, healthy soil and biodiversity. In this sense, environmental issues are situated as ontological issues that rupture our ground of being (Lifton, 1979; Nicholsen, 2009; Lertzman, 2008b). Depending upon the typology and context of the issue, environmental crises invoke ruptures in terms of who we are, what it means to be human beings in the context of nature and what we know as socially constructed rational and scientific beings. Although this is rarely referenced in environmental advocacy discourses, it is the proverbial elephant in the room we are manically in flight from (Mnguni, 2010). This situating directly references the material implications of psychic defence mechanisms, such as denial, apathy and distancing. Thus, the working concept of apathy as the primary 'barrier' (something to overcome and battle) to environmental action is directly challenged by a psychosocial orientation that presumes unconscious and often irrational processes informing actions in both intimate and political spheres. Thus, apathy and the related phenomena of denial and projection are engaged as a processes and defences against possibly distressing or overwhelming unconscious experiences, e.g. loss and anxiety. Harold Searles, one of the first psychoanalytic thinkers to address our ecological crises in the 1970s, also acknowledged how apathy is a signal of underlying currents and processes which demand our attention:

> The current state of ecological deterioration is such as to evoke in us largely unconscious anxieties of different varieties that are of a piece with those characteristic of various levels of an individual's ego-development history. Thus the general apathy . . . is based upon largely unconscious ego defences against these anxieties.
>
> (1972, p. 363)

Apathy – lack of public concern or care – is a powerful rhetoric in environmental and political sectors, as a viable explanatory trope for public inaction and lack of response to chronic and evident environmental threats. In setting out to explore the unconscious processes of environmental issues and relations with apathy, I found myself drawn to how concern, care and creativity (Winnicott, 1963) are expressed in response to collective and personal ecological contexts. While recent scholarship has referred to a kind of ecological loss in various terms – solastagia (Albrecht, 2005), requiem for a species (Hamilton, 2010) and climate suffering (Wapner, 2014) – the psychoanalytic concept of *melancholia* that I employ most accurately reflects a kind of collective and personal condition that appears as paralysis but may in fact obscure genuine, powerful capacities for actions.

By shifting the discourse from a *lack* of something to a *presence* of something perhaps not well understood, we then must also shift in how we practice environmental communications and strategy. It fundamentally changes how we position ourselves in relationship to the communities in which we work from one of motivating to one based on listening and collaborating (Randall, 2009; Lertzman, 2012b).

Going beyond the gap

The common puzzlement and perpetual surprise about how people are contradictory, inconsistent and irrational is most clearly illustrated through the concepts of the 'gap' between values and actions and 'barriers to engagement' that keep people from engaging with environmental issues. The basic idea is that whilst people report in surveys and polls strong values regarding nature, they continue to drive, fly, shop and otherwise participate in damaging practices. Thus, there is a 'gap' between what people say and what they do, and the discourse of 'barriers' tends to focus on variables, such as a poor understanding of the issues, particular partisan ideological and political orientations, that may keep people from more fully engaging with issues. The public as such are pathologized and patronized as uncaring, selfish, cognitively limited or in denial. Such assumptions rehearse ingrained ideas about the "Western subject" as rational, selfish and greedy (see Ross, 1994; and in particular, Arendt, 1958).

The concept of apathy falls neatly into these discourses. Apathy also signals a focus on the individual, which arguably blinds us to complex social and cultural systems (Shove, 2009). This is not surprising since the construct of 'public apathy' came into being in relation to public information campaigns and the emergence of market research (Fritz, 1937; Hyman & Sheatsley, 1947) which has historically focused on a transactional model of communication. Apathy continues to be widely circulating in political arenas, and the concept of *environmental apathy* is highly prevalent (cf. Cafaro, 2005; M2 Presswire, 2008; Bunting, 2000). An example of a contemporary environmental perception of apathy as a 'vice' and a form of laziness in spirit") According to Cafaro (2005):

> Over the course of the Middle Ages, the two vices of *tristitia* (pessimism, despair) and *accidia* (apathy, 'dryness of spirit') merged and morphed into the cardinal sin of sloth. Calling apathy and sloth vices, or sins, emphasizes the active nature of a good human life.
>
> Apathy is a key environmental vice, for several reasons. Our default procedures typically harm the environment, whereas doing better takes work, especially initially: bicycling to work rather than driving a car, setting up recycling bins rather than just tossing our garbage. One pop philosopher connects *all* our moral failures to laziness, and if this perhaps goes too far, it is true that doing right requires effort. Often, we need to *think* our way toward better environmental solutions, and apathy shows itself in lazy thinking as well as in halfhearted action or inaction. Sluggish thinking tends to be selfish, short-term, and unimaginative. It reinforces passivity, as when my students' inability to imagine any way forward beyond American car culture, combined with their understanding of its environmental harms, leaves them feeling defeated and hopeless.
>
> (p. 150)

To view a public as apathetic (without pathos) is to suggest that people do not care and as such are somehow immune to the highly distressing issues, so viscerally felt by those with more 'environmental concern', who then feel morally, personally and socially responsible for the broader wellbeing of our ecological contexts and fellow species. The idea of apathy therefore constructs a 'two cultures' paradigm, not dissimilar to C.P. Snow's (1959) notion of the arts and sciences as constituting two cultures. In this case, however, the two cultures are those who care and those who do not, or those who are morally responsible and those who are lacking in civic morals. From an environmental perspective, this appears accurate. However, it perpetuates damaging and ultimately counterproductive assumptions that undermine environmental communications strategy. And, moreover, it is also quite entirely inaccurate.

The field site: Green Bay, Wisconsin

In 2006, I became a fellow with the Biodiversity Project, an environmental communications organization based in Madison, Wisconsin, specializing in outreach concerning the Great Lakes. As a significant environmental site and resource in the United States, the Great Lakes have been receiving increased attention as water becomes higher on the policy and public radar as a future scarce resource (see Figure 1.1). The Great Lakes have long been portrayed in the American public imagination alternately as fragile, threatened, valuable, degraded, industrial, polluted, pristine and restored, depending on the historical moment and specific site. Like most significant bodies of water, the lakes hold an important place in relation to industry and American industrial development. The region has endured industrial processes such as contaminants, pollutant dumping and introduction of invasive species through ballast waters (Hickey, Batterman &

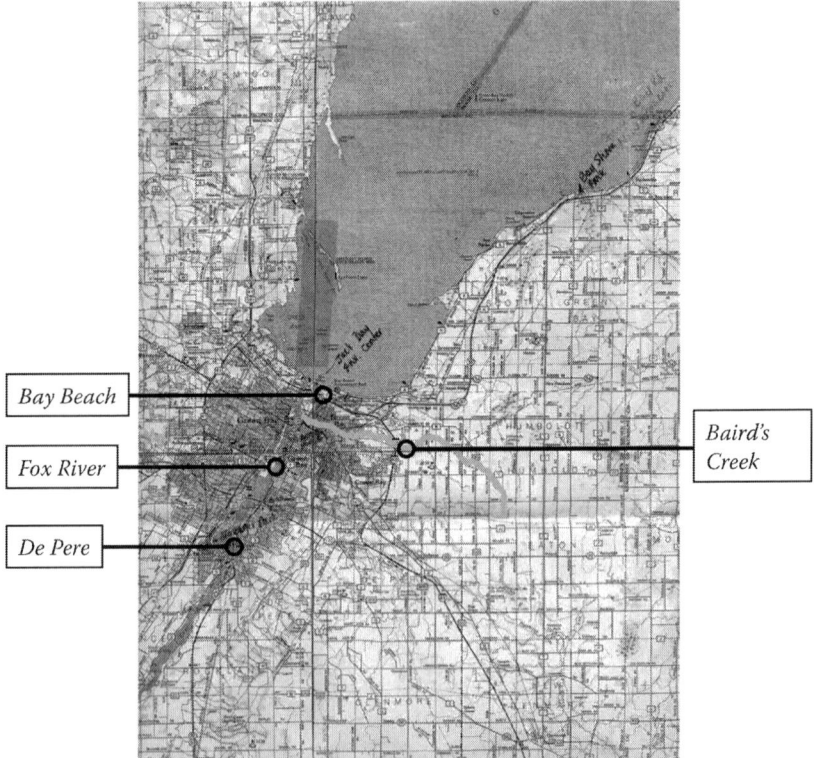

Figure 1.1 This map was offered during my first field site visit, and the notations indicate points of relevance (Voyager Park on the Fox River where PCB clean-up has been underway); see also locations of Bay Beach, Fox River, De Pere and Baird's Creek. (Map of Green Bay, © 2007 DeLorme (www.delorme.com) | Wisconsin Atlas and Gazetteer. Courtesy Kendra Axness.)

Chernyak, 2006). Due to the geographic scope, the lakes are identifiable both as an entity ('The Great Lakes') and as a plurality comprised of communities, states and nations. For this reason, collaboration and coalition building are essential, illustrated by the creation of the Great Lakes Coalition that brought together stakeholders and partners in an unprecedented alliance and network (Wege Foundation, 2004), later referred to as Healing Our Waters Coalition.

The lakes extend 575 miles from the north shore of Lake Superior to the south shore of Lake Erie, a spread of eight degrees in latitude. From west to east, they stretch nearly 80 miles. Their drainage basin encompasses 200,000 square miles in which 34 million people live, "each of them affected in ways large and small by the lakes" (Dennis, 2004). As there has been considerable media and advocacy activity in the past few decades surrounding the health and well-being of this particular vast natural resource, my interest is in exploring the ways particular communities have been "affected in ways large and small by the lakes". There is a particular interest in groups and individuals who may not self-identify as environmentalists or even as concerned citizens but who nevertheless are profoundly touched and impacted by the myriad ecological, industrial and social threats facing the Great Lakes.

Given the enormous scale of the Great Lakes, I decided to conduct research in a particular community of significance for the Great Lakes system at the confluence of the Fox River and Green Bay, tributaries of the Great Lakes basin. Green Bay is an ecologically beleaguered place. It attracted national attention as a proposed Environmental Protection Agency Superfund clean-up site due to the PCB-enriched sediments in the Fox River. With its high concentration of paper pulp mills lining the estuaries, Green Bay is an emblem of industrialisation and its ecological consequences.[2] Between 1850 and 1950, Wisconsin's Fox River Valley, where Green Bay is situated, experienced relatively stable patterns of social, political and economic development. The economy remained tightly bound to agricultural and industrial production, its politicians were mostly conservative, and its racial and ethnic make-up was nearly homogeneous, with largely German, Italian, Polish and Swedish Americans (Summers, 2006, p. 9). For decades, there was no environmental regulation for the industries, and as a result the rivers and bay, which flow into the Great Lakes basin, have withstood enormous levels of industrial degradation. Like many industrial cities in the United States, Green Bay is also a place of contradictions. The University of Wisconsin Green Bay (UWGB) was nicknamed 'Eco-U' and is said to have offered the first course in environmental studies in the United States in 1970. It also possesses a history of local environmentalism, as outlined by local historian Paul Wozniak (1996) and more recently recounted in Greg Summer's *Consuming Nature: Environmentalism in the Fox River Valley, 1850–1950* (2006). Green Bay remains home to a small but strong environmental community that includes the University of Wisconsin Sea Grant Institute, the Corfrin Center for Biodiversity, several environmental charity organizations and numerous environmental scientists and historians keen to help restore, protect and conserve Green Bay's ecological resources.[3] Efforts to reach out and mobilize communities in the Lower Fox River Valley to enact environmentally friendly practices, such as reducing phosphorous use, as well as instating regulations regarding the TMDL (Total Maximum Daily Load) entering the Lower Fox River are active. Such efforts are also constrained by what is perceived as resistance and inertia with regard to environmental protection (see Figure 1.2).

Figure 1.2 Healing Our Waters print advert campaign, 2008 campaign, summer 2007, "Girl on the Beach". (Reprinted with permission.)

This confluence of attributes – a small but dedicated environmental community, national recognition of Green Bay as a notoriously polluted region, its significant role as a heavily industrial tributary of the ecologically beleaguered Great Lakes and the association of the Midwest with American industrial development and disrepair – presented a rich site for exploring the topic of environmental anxiety, concern and apathy.[4] This work has direct implications for the cultivation of a politics of environmental advocacy attuned to issues of despair, paralysis, anxiety and related emotions. Such a politics is one that does not deny or gloss over difficult emotions and experiences but rather finds *creative* means of allowing a full range to be present. Rather than a politics of guilt or 'feel good' steps to save the planet, it is possible for an environmental advocacy to avoid simplifications and honour the difficult dilemmas contemporary environmental degradations pose for us as individuals, communities, institutions and political bodies. This ideally can translate to bring greater insight, skill and sensitivity to practices of environmental advocacy and outreach. Its relevance also lies in the capacity to initiate and establish meaningful dialogues across disciplines of cognitive psychology, psychoanalytic research and psychosocial studies, whose respective areas of expertise can enhance and complement one another (see Figures 1.3 and 1.4).

Figure 1.3 Exercising on the Health Trail, Fox River Trail, Green Bay, November 2007. (Photo: J. Galt.)

Figure 1.4 Fox River Trail, Green Bay, October 2007. (Photo: R. Lertzman.)

Notes

1 See Darian Leader's *The New Black* (2009), on how mourning is a social practice, as well as my interview with Leader (2010).
2 The Comprehensive Environmental Response, Compensation, and Liability Act (CER-CLA), enacted in 1980, is nicknamed Superfund; Superfund sites receive national attention namely concerning their toxic contamination. This law provides the authority through which the federal government can compel people or companies responsible for creating hazardous waste sites to clean them up. It also created a public trust fund, known as the Superfund, to assist with the cleanup of inactive and abandoned hazardous waste sites or accidentally spilled or illegally dumped hazardous materials. In 2001, the Environmental Protection Agency and the Wisconsin Department of Natural Resources announced the plan to conduct a clean-up effort of the Lower Fox River and Green Bay. In 2007, dredging commenced of a portion of the Lower Fox River (Little Lake Butte des Morts). Clean-up of Little Lake Butte des Morts was completed in June. Approximately 370,000 cubic yards of contaminated sediment were removed. To accomplish this, two dredges operated mostly in the southern half of the lake. After PCB-contaminated sediment was dredged from the lake, it was put into large plastic tubes nearby. Once the water was squeezed out, it was cleaned on-site and returned to the river. Contaminated sediment was taken to a nearby landfill for proper disposal. Remaining areas with lower levels of PCBs were covered with gravel and sand caps. This occurred mostly in the northern portion of the lake. This was the first of five regions to be addressed in the Fox River.

Clean-up of highly contaminated sediment in the area of the Lower Fox River just below the DePere Dam was completed in 2008. The area, or 'hotspot', near the dam had PCBs as high as 3,000 parts per million. Although this area contained the highest levels of PCBs in the river, it represented only about 2% of all of the contaminated sediment that needs to be cleaned up but nearly 10% of the total PCB "mass" (Environmental Protection Agency, 2009).

3   In 2006, the Lower Fox River Basin TMDL Outreach Committee was formed to guide communication and education efforts. The committee was chaired by Victoria Harris, UW-Sea Grant Institute Water Quality Specialist, and includes representatives from UW-Extension, Green Bay Metropolitan Sewerage District, Brown County, UW-Green Bay, Oneida Tribe of Indians, and Wisconsin Department of Natural Resources (WDNR). I was invited to and attended a meeting of the Lower Fox River Stakeholders group during my field site visit in 2007.

4   Environmental groups and programs in the Green Bay region include Wisconsin League of Conservation Voters, Baird Creek Preservation Foundation, Northeast Wisconsin Land Trust, Gathering Waters Conservancy, Fox River Watch, Lower Fox River Watershed Monitoring Program, Fox Wolf Watershed Alliance, Lake Michigan Forum and Rivers Alliance of Wisconsin, in addition to the Department of Natural Resources (DNR), who maintain an active presence in the region. It is worth noting the presence of these groups in light of the interview data, which did not reference these groups, with the exception of the DNR and the Wisconsin League of Conservation Voters.

References

Albrecht, G., 2005. Solastalgia, a new concept in human health and identity, *Philosophy Activism Nature* 3, pp. 41–44.

Arendt, H. 1958. *The Human Condition*. Chicago: University of Chicago Press.

Billig, M., 2002. Henri Tajfel's 'Cognitive aspects of prejudice' and the psychology of bigotry, *British Journal of Psychology* 41 (2), pp. 171–188.

Bunting, M., 2000. Let it rain: Apathetic about climate change and out of touch with the environment, Britain needs a short sharp shock, *The Guardian*, 16 October, Available at: http://www.guardian.co.uk/environment/2000/oct/16/comment.sweather.

Cafaro, P., 2005. Gluttony, arrogance, greed and apathy: An exploration of environmental vice. In Sandler, R., & Cafalo, P. (eds.), *Environmental Virtue Ethics*. Boston: Rowman & Littlefield, pp. 135–158.

Dennis, J., 2004. *The Living Great Lakes: Searching for the Heart in the Inland Seas.* New York: St. Martin's Griffin.

Dodds, J., 2011. *Psychoanalysis and Ecology at the Edge of Chaos.* New York: Routledge.

Freud, S., 1917. Mourning and melancholia. In Strachey, J., et al. (ed.), *Standard Edition* 14. London: Hogarth Press.

Fritz, E., 1937. Redwood forestry program jeopardized by public apathy toward fire, *Journal of Forestry* 35 (8), pp. 755–758.

Hamilton, C., 2010. *Requiem for a Species: Why We Resist the Truth About Climate Change.* London: Earthscan.

Heath, C., & Heath, D., 2010. *Switch.* New York: Crown Publishing.

Hickey, J. P., Batterman, S. A., & Chernyak, S. M., 2006. Trends of chlorinated organic contaminants in Great Lakes trout and walleye from 1970 to 1998, *Arch. Environ. Contam. Toxicol* 50, pp. 97–110.

Hyman, H., & Sheatsley, P., 1947. Some reasons why information campaigns fail, *Public Opinion Quarterly* 11, pp. 412–423.

Kahan, D. M., Hoffman, D., & Braman, D., 2009. Whose eyes are you going to believe? *Scott v. Harris* and the perils of cognitive illiberalism, *Harvard Law Review* 122.

Kahneman, D., 2011. *Thinking, Fast and Slow*. New York: Farrar, Straus & Giroux.

Leader, D., 2009. *The New Black: Mourning, Melancholia and Depression*. London: Penguin.

Leopold, A. 1949. *A Sand County Almanac and Sketches Here and There*. Oxford: Oxford University Press.

Lertzman, R., 2008a. The myth of apathy, *The Ecologist* 34 (4).

Lertzman, R., 2008b. Love, guilt and reparation: Rethinking the affective dimensions of the locus of the irreparable. In Willard, B., & Green, C. (eds.), *Communication at the Intersection of Nature and Culture: Proceedings of the Ninth Biennial Conference on Communication and the Environment*. Chicago: College of Communication, DePaul University.

Lertzman, R., 2012a. The myth of apathy: Psychoanalytic explorations of environmental degradation. In Weintrobe, S. (ed.), *Engaging with Climate Change: Psychoanalytic and Interdisciplinary Perspectives*. London: Routledge, pp. 117–133.

Lertzman, R., 2012b. Researching psychic dimensions of ecological degradation: Notes from the field. *Psychoanalysis, Culture & Society*, 17 (1), pp. 92–101.

Lifton, R. J., 1979. *The Broken Connection: On Death and the Continuity of Life*. New York: Simon & Schuster.

M2 Presswire, 2008. Public bored by green talk; ahead of climate change budget, environmental groups face public apathy, survey shows green groups tackling climate change and carbon emissions are facing yet another challenge – public apathy. M2 Presswire [accessed 10 December 2009].

Mnguni, P. P., 2010. Anxiety and defense in sustainability, *Psychoanalysis, Culture & Society* 15 (2), pp. 117–135.

Nicholsen, S. W., 2009. The Ecopsychology interview, *Ecopsychology* 1 (3), pp. 110–117.

Norgaard, K., 2011. *Living in Denial*. Cambridge, MA: MIT Press.

Pink, D., 2011. *Drive: The Surprising Truth About What Motivates Us*. New York: Riverhead Books.

Randall, R., 2009. Loss and climate change: The cost of parallel narratives, *Ecopsychology* 3 (1), pp. 118–129.

Ross, A., 1994. *The Chicago Gangster Theory of Life: Nature's Debt to Society*. New York: Verso.

Searles, H., 1960. *The Nonhuman Environment in Normal Development and in Schizophrenia*. New York: International Universities Press.

Searles, H., 1972. Unconscious processes in relation to the environmental crisis, *The Psychoanalytic Review* 59 (3), pp. 361–374.

Shove, E., 2009. *Time, Consumption and Everyday Life: Practice, Materiality and Culture*. New York: Berg.

Shove, E., 2010. Beyond the ABC: Climate change policy and theories of social change, *Environment and Planning A* 42 (6), pp. 1273–1285.

Snow, C. P., 1959. *The Two Cultures*. Cambridge: Cambridge University Press.

Summers, G., 2006. *Consuming Nature: Environmentalism in the Fox River Valley, 1850–1950*. Lawrence: University Press of Kansas.

Wapner, P., 2014. Climate suffering. *Global Environment Politics* 14 (2), pp. 1–6.

Ward, I., 1993. Ecological madness, a Freud Museum conference: Introductory thoughts, *British Journal of Psychotherapy 10* (2), pp. 178–187.

Weintrobe, S., 2013. *Engaging with Climate Change: Psychoanalytic Interdisciplinary Perspectives.* New York: Routledge.

Winnicott, D. W., 1965 [1963]. Morals and education. In Winnicott, D. W., *The Maturational Processes and the Facilitating Environment: Studies in the Theory of Emotional Development.* Reprint, London: Hogarth Press and Institute for Psycho-Analysis, pp. 93–105.

Wozniak, P. A., 1996. They thought we were dreamers: Early anti-pollution efforts on the Lower Fox and East Rivers of northeast Wisconsin, 1927–1949, *Transactions of the Wisconsin Academy of Sciences, Arts and Letters* 84, pp. 161–175.

Fox River, Green Bay, October 2007. (Photo: R. Lertzman.)

I think because of my upbringing, and maybe because of friends or family, I always respected nature. I think I evolved into it, just by education, and reading and exposure to so many different things in my life. I just became more and more aware of it. And perhaps, perhaps whomever [sic] is responsible for, for telling people, via television, or newspaper or magazine articles, about some of the problems, I tend to pick those kinds of things up, to read, or to watch, because, because I have an interest in it. I am not necessarily an activist. I don't go to meetings of environmental groups that are trying to do something about it. I haven't reached that plateau and probably never will. But what I do try to do is to continue to modify my life as best I can. To provide what I think is the ideal as far as respecting nature. And I have tried very much to make my children aware of their surroundings, and to become as, at least conscious of what's happening as I am. Again trying to set an example to them, of how I would like them to live their lives. I'm not the type of person that would become tremendously active as far as speaking to people, or trying to lead a group of people, or even joining a group for that matter. It's just a very private matter as far as I'm concerned, about what I feel about, about nature and, and the environment that we live in. So, it's pretty close to my own person.

– Donald, Interview 3

Chapter 2

Beyond behavior change

The myth of apathy – the presumption that people are not taking action to protect and restore our environment due to a lack of concern – and its counterpart for how to then mobilize action and trigger behavioral change underlie most environmental campaigns and outreach efforts. Action may take the form of signing a petition, composing a letter to an elected official, writing a cheque or showing support bodily through collective action. As discussed in the previous chapter, the concept of public apathy is a particular explanatory discourse that arises when a certain target population does not respond in preferred or anticipated ways on behalf of political, social and environmental well-being (e.g. see Hyman & Sheatsley, 1947). As such, public apathy as a concept and discourse is intractably tied to the practice of communications and stems from particular conceptualizations of subjectivity, agency and behaviour. As a discourse, behaviour change can be profoundly undermining as it perpetuates unhelpful narratives for why people are not being constituted as 'agents' and often positions environmental educators and advocates as agents battling a fight against public inertia, apathy and disinterest.

As suggested in Chapter 1, the focus on the gap between people's values and actions reifies problematic assumptions with regard to subjectivity and the complex dilemmas involved with the encounter with chronic ecological problems. Further, discourse on the 'gap' (between attitudes and behaviors or between values and actions and so on) paves the way for the concept of 'barriers' as a way of thinking about what keeps people from being more actively involved with environmental practices. The discourse of 'barriers' is one of the more prevalent in environmental advocacy today and contains blinkers and taken-for-granted assumptions about agency, subjectivity and lived social practice (Shove, 2010). At the linguistic level, a 'barrier' suggests an obstacle that must be overcome, transgressed, moved around or surpassed. As such, it constructs a more tangible and material entity than is warranted and, arguably, reifies a mechanistic view of what informs practices (see Shove, 2010, for a related analysis of how a focus on the "ABC" blinds us to the nature of social practices). What are commonly referred to as barriers often include complex processes such as costs, low self-efficacy and overwhelm, all of which are arguably psychosocial phenomena creating complications, not barriers at all. And, as suggested in this book, much of what presents as barriers may be viewed alternately as expressions of profoundly complex affective-laden and unconscious dilemmas that impede more coherent forms of alignment between what we value and what we practice. It is only through attending to these complicated aspects of living in and making sense of an ecologically threatened and degraded industrialized world that we can begin to design more integrative and deep-reaching forms of engagement.

Constructing the gap: Explanations for lack of action

One of the most dominant themes in psychological research into environmental issues is the aforementioned problem of the "disconnect" and "perception-action gap" (Lorenzoni & Pigeon, 2006) or the "American Paradox" (Jamieson, 2006), referring to Americans' perception of themselves as concerned about the environment yet not expressing these concerns in practice (Jamieson, 2006, p. 98). Generally speaking, this gap refers to the disparities between what people profess in terms of levels of awareness, concern and values and their subsequent actions and practices. It can also be seen as a gap between avowed concerns about environmental problems and choices made in the voting booth or supermarket. There continues to be a focus on "the gap between high-minded words and low-down behavior" (Jamieson, 2006), the persistent disconnect between scientific consensus and public perceptions of climate change threats and the puzzling way in which people note their concern but do not act on it (O'Neill & Nicholson-Cole, 2009, Weber, 2006; Leiserowitz, 2007). It is arguably the fastest growing body of research concerning human dimensions of environmental threats. Increasing studies are devoted to communication campaign strategies and analysis of fear-based appeals – now widely viewed as largely ineffectual, although for varying reasons – in motivating public responsiveness to environmental issues and climate (e.g. Marshall, 2014; Klein, 2014; Marx et al., 2007; Moser & Dilling, 2004; Weber, 2006; O'Neill & Nicholson-Cole, 2009). Social practice theory has more recently emerged as a compelling and vibrant theoretical framework, in response to the clear limitations of behavioral and cognitive orientations, and " reconceptualizes behavior as . . . a social phenomenon, guided by shared norms and embedded in specific contexts", including personal life histories (Hards, 2012, p. 761).

With the rise of behavior change thinking in popular circles, drawing strongly on behavioral economics, most of which leads with single-word verbs (cf. *switch*, Heath & Heath, 2010; *drive*, Pink, 2011; *nudge*, Thaler & Sunstein, 2009), there is often a tacit equation of a psychological approach to environmental issues with the need for *changing the behavior of people and society*. The range of psychological theories employed towards the facilitation of environmentally friendly behavior is vast, ranging from planned behavior (Ajzen, 1991) to research in implicit associations (Karpinsky & Hilton, 2001), social marketing (Kotler & Zaltman, 1971; Maibach, 1993), community-based social marketing (McKenzie-Mohr, 2011) and place identity theories (Proshansky, Fabian & Karminoff, 1983). What runs through these approaches is the focus on changing behavior and engineering certain outcomes by facilitating some practices over others. This includes identifying barriers that prevent people from changing their behavior (Lorenzoni, Nicholson-Cole & Whitmarsh, 2007). This orientation informs how environmental groups can communicate what needs to be done in response to certain issues and what tangible factors can enable different forms of practices (such as providing wheelie bins for recycling, applying congestion taxes or free passes for public transport) (Weber, 2006; Moser & Dilling, 2004). Critiques of behavior change models are on the rise due to the rise of competing approaches to social change, namely more participatory orientations. There is also a focus on cultivating an 'ecological identity' which can imply that if one can develop an ecological identity or experience a consciousness transformation, which inexorably leads in a straight line to a suite of pro-environmental actions and choices (cf. Thomashow, 1996; Leiserowitz, 2007; Speth, 2007; O'Sullivan & Taylor, 2004).

The question that often arises is how significantly information and awareness can influence behavior (i.e. Crompton, 2010; deGroot & Steg, 2007; Leiserowitz, 2006; Pike, Doppelt & Herr, 2010; Stern, 2000). The risk of conceptualizing a gap between awareness and subsequent practices as a failure in translating information effectively is that it can blind us to the embedded assumptions regarding social and cultural influences and subjectivity – that is, as if we can advance beyond basic awareness and knowledge to action. These assumptions relate to the role rationality plays in our practices, behaviours, and actions. In other words, research focuses either on information-based approaches that investigate how to make information more tangible, compelling and urgent or on values-based approaches that gauge whether people will act if they can see how issues map onto their existing value system. It is necessary to interrogate what exactly can be illuminated through this particular epistemic and ontological orientation to the subject as unitary, rational and self-aware and what may be obscured. For example, it is possible that affect can influence and inform how people process information, clouding cognitive capacities. Claiming a lack of awareness or information about specific issues may be related, therefore, to the tendency to refuse the integration of new and challenging data.

Significantly, as thinking about behavior change gradually becomes more nuanced, studies find the use of fear-based appeals in communication strategies as ineffective. Communication studies and social sciences, spurred by the intense focus on climate change–related messaging, is starting to look more broadly at emotional dimensions of response, such as Susanne Moser's work on "getting real" on emotional levels about climate change threats (2012), suggesting a capacity to incorporate emotion and experience into how we work with people around climate change messaging. Researchers, however, are coming up against certain methodological limits in terms of measuring the complicated emotional nature of environmental issues. The complex ways people negotiate awareness and recognition of serious ecological threats may be referred to as strategies or defence mechanisms (e.g. Stoll-Kleemann, O'Riordan & Jaeger, 2001) or more commonly as "barriers" (Lorenzoni, Nicholson-Cole & Whitmarsh, 2007). These studies are informing a new direction for environmental communication practices that accounts for affect. In the study conducted by O'Neill & Nicholson-Cole (2009), messaging about climate change using visual data was analyzed for emotional impact, specifically looking at the use of fear-based appeals to mobilize public response as being largely counterproductive, unless tied explicitly with both local avenues for engaging and a sense of overall potential for redress. As they argue, "climate change images can evoke powerful feelings of issue salience, but these do not necessarily make participants feel able to do anything about it; in fact, it may do the reverse" (O'Neill & Nicholson-Cole, 2009, p. 373). The recommendations are for the use of fear-based appeals to be used carefully "and in combination with other kinds of representations in order to avoid causing denial, apathy, avoidance, and negative associations that may come as a result of coping with any unpleasant feelings evoked" (p. 376).

This analysis, while coherent and insightful, overlooks the psychodynamics of defence mechanisms, of which denial, apathy and avoidance are expressions. It falls short of examining how people may experience visceral double-binds when it comes to ecological awareness and risks the presumption that making the issues more real, concrete or actionable are simply not the only answers. In other words, when we analyse emotional responses on their own, without a psychosocial context, it can lead to reductive thinking that we only need to make issues more real, tangible and actionable – ignoring the very real emotional responses to reconciling our own complicity in the very threats that undermine our collective futures. Such fraught conscious simply cannot be accounted for by studying discrete associations or emotions with specific message frames.

As an alternative, psychoanalytic and psychosocial approaches positions defence mechanisms as central for understanding the affective and experiential nature of environmental threats and our responses to them. While defence mechanisms as conceived by Freud (1915) were seen as defences against incompatible desires, experiences or thoughts and could relate to social or cultural norms, contemporary social psychologists have applied this understanding to threats to self-esteem and identity (Fenichel, 1945; see Crompton and Kasser, 2009 in relation to climate change). As Stoll-Kleemann, O'Riordan and Jaeger (2001) suggest, defences can also arise in response to broader sociocultural threats and anxieties; they need not be limited to individual psychologies but can also be collective forms of defence such as denial or disavowal. Drawing on focus group data, the research team conducted an empirical study of denial[1] as it relates to climate change. The authors discuss how denial – as a function of discursive, personal, social and psychological influences – does not shift with more information or exhortations to change, as found in most mainstream campaigns for behavioral change:

> Denial over the necessity to adjust behavior and lifestyle patterns is a function of discourse as it is of more fundamental personal, social and psychological

influences that are not readily shifted around by language or by exhortation unless the process of awareness raising is prolonged and set in constructive engagement with a wider array of socially sanctioned moral norms.

(p. 108)

According to Stoll-Kleemann and her colleagues, denial acts powerfully to create inconsistencies between professed attitudes and behaviors with regard to climate change norms. In order to explore these dynamics, the research was designed to analyse patterns of consistency and disjunction between "personal preference for a particular lifestyle, consumption habit, or behavioral choice and the need to respond electively to climate change mitigation strategies" (Stoll-Kleeman, O'Riordan & Jaeger, 2001, p. 112). The study found that "people may profess anxiety over climate change, but be faced with internal resentment or even denial over what they cannot accept as a justifiable change in behavior (e.g. to travel by public transport, ride a bike in the rain, or invest in high-cost domestic insulation)" (ibid.). Hence we see highlighted here the identification of inner conflicts, which can give rise to particular practices and behaviors, even if they are counterproductive both for the individual and for the broader issues at stake.

Psychoanalytic considerations

While the focus on 'barriers' and 'gaps' between what people profess to value and their actions may appear as intuitive – after all, people *do* say one thing and do another – psychoanalytic practitioners and scholars may be more inclined to view these phenomena as outward expressions of ambivalence, anxiety, potentially unresolved mourning and unconscious defence mechanisms such as denial and projection. This marks one of the key distinctions between a psychoanalytic and psychosocial orientation and behavior change thinking. This emphasis on unconscious processes signals one of the more critical reasons for taking a psychosocial and psychoanalytic approach to environmental engagement. Recognizing how unconscious processes inform and shape individual and collective responses to chronic environmental degradation has its origins in clinical psychoanalytic research and theory. This view is predicated on a concept of subjectivity that is not necessarily unitary, rational or self-aware. Since Freud's writings on the topic, the ability to investigate the powerful role of unconscious dimensions in everyday life has grown increasingly sophisticated through clinical practice and the evolution of psychoanalysis and psychosocial research methods (see Symington, 1996; Bateman & Holmes, 1995; Kohon, 1986). The psychoanalytic enquiry is one toolkit amongst many for investigating broader social, political and economic issues such as how we live and engage with our environment. The distinction between it and others is the emphasis on and acknowledgement of inner worlds expressed through the often inchoate but provocative media of dream, language, sensation, free association, desire, fears, pleasures and phantasies, as a viable site for study and as bearing powerfully on the world of practice, action and behaviour. Neville Symington (1996) states:

> Psychoanalysis is a method of investigating the unconscious mind, and its particular focus is on the inner world. There are other ways of understanding the individual's manifest or external behavior. A sociologist would account for it in terms of the social system of which the individual is a part. An economist would understand it in terms of the economic structure in which the person is situated. A theologian would stress the person's values, ideals and so on. The psychoanalyst attempts to understand manifest behavior and communications, too, but in terms of the individual's inner conflicts and phantasies. Yet psychoanalysis does not have possession of the whole truth.
>
> (pp. 16–17)

So while psychoanalysis does not have possession of the 'whole truth', the focus on understanding inner conflicts and 'phantasies' – how unconscious conflicts drive the behaviors we seek to 'change' though behavioural economics and social marketing – arguably constitutes a powerful and largely overlooked praxis for social change.

Taking a psychoanalytic approach to subjectivity in the context of a psycho-social research study presumes contradictions, ambivalence, internal conflicts and the ongoing work of constructing meaning and coherence out of our past and present experiences. Such a conceptualization of subjectivity allows for anxiety as a central human experience and attends to the ways in which anxiety is negotiated. For a more positivist point of view that equates the real with what we can sense, such an orientation may present difficulties: "[m]ost psychological realities do not have the property of extension or tangibility: a dream, a hallucination, a belief, a thought, a relationship, love, hatred or desire. But it is not true that these realities exist in some non-material sphere only. They are inextricably linked with the physical – this is so even of a thought" (Symington, 1996, p. 17). Certainly the role of imagination, thoughts and dreams inform how we shape our lives, from the formation of policy to whether or not we recycle, contribute-to a local environmental group or decide to cut down on long-haul flights. Arguably, how we respond to increased news of ecological threats is often fraught with issues that invoke conflicting desires and anxieties and that pull on particular biographical contexts and socially situated forces and behavioral constraints. As Paul Maiteny notes, "Environmental policy and social research tends to neglect the inner, experiential dimensions of human life" (2000, p. 339). While there is an abundance of social and psychological research on the problems of public engagement with environmental problems, there is a surprising lack of attention to these inner, experiential dimensions of human life.

The very issues environmental advocacy groups and initiatives spend enormous time focusing on – the human dimensions of environmental problems, which include denial, lack of engagement and so-called attitudes – are the focus of entire fields of practice and research in clinical and applied psychology. Clinical psychoanalytic work offers a nuanced conception of subjectivity that may prove to be highly productive for those working in the area of subjectivity and responses to chronic ecological threats. Psychoanalytic scholarship has been slow to come to the topic of environmentalism and ecological threats, with the exception of a few notable scholars: Harold Searles, Hanna Segal, Robert J. Lifton and more recent debates in the psychoanalytic community (Ward, 1993; Weintrobe, 2013). As psychoanalytic work tends to focus on the intra- and inter-psychic dimensions of subjective experience, I turn to psychoanalytically inspired social scientific qualitative research. Psychoanalytic psychosocial studies offers productive means for thinking through the interrelations between 'psychic', affective or interiority dimensions of the encounter with degraded ecologies and the social and cultural dimensions of post-industrial, capitalist ideologies that may produce profound epistemic and ontological dilemmas. It is in psychosocial studies that dimensions of the social and political contexts can be joined up, in some capacity, with the largely unconscious processes that play such powerful roles in how we respond to serious environmental threats. Psychology tends to bracket social and political ideological contexts – and sociological studies typically bracket issues of subjectivity and affect. Psychosocial studies recognize the complex dialectical relationships and inseparability of these domains. As with psychoanalytic work, psychosocial studies are slow to respond to ecological challenges and remain primarily concerned with intra- and inter-personal relationships and social issues, such as class, race, gender etc.

There has been a move in recent years – in both therapeutic and academic circles – to bring psychoanalysis into the social (Ward, 1993; Minsky, 1998; Samuels, 2001; Cargill, 2006; Clarke, Hahn, Hoggett & Sideris, 2006; Segal, 1997; Hillman & Ventura, 1993; Searles 1960).[2] From Searles's assertion that psychoanalysis ignores the environment at its peril (1960, 1972), to the development of community psychoanalysis (Clarke, Hahn, Hoggett & Sideris, 2006), the field appears to be taking account of what is outside the consultation room.[3] The one area where psychoanalysis, as well as psychosocial studies – in terms of clinical practice and research applications – has yet to fully engage is how humans interact with our nonhuman environment and, in particular, how we live with and relate with our natural, often vulnerable and threatened world.

Most salient, and arguably tragic, about the muteness around environmental issues in psychoanalytic circles is the potential contributions psychoanalysts can make to support environmental advocates who are struggling with fears and anxieties regarding behavior change and mobilizing reparative energies. Such day-to-day concerns in advocacy and educational sectors include the ways in which people cope with difficult and painful information (e.g. the ice caps melting, the toxics in the nearby lake, an incident such as a fish kill or accident), the perception of public apathy (inability or unwillingness to act or engage), the issue of loss and mourning (in the face of ecological degradation) and what it means, quite simply, to live in a world presented as continually under threat. In other words, many of the concerns expressed in environmental policy and advocacy circles, around what is seen as a profound and frightening 'disconnect' between action and values or between knowledge and action, are the focus of much attention and application in psychoanalytic theories and practice, but with a different emphasis and context.

There have been attempts in recent years to open up a dialogue across these domains. It tends to be an uneasy, tense relationship, however. Often analysts are perceived by activists as hopelessly out of touch with the 'real world' and overly fixated on the individual; activists and advocates can be viewed as manic and lacking introspection. The Ecological Madness conference at the Freud Museum in London brought together a group of psychoanalysts and members of the Green Party (Ward, 1993) and more recently, the event convened at the Institute of Psychoanalysis in 2010, resulting in the collection *Engaging with Climate Change* (Weintrobe, 2013). In both cases, psychoanalysts were in conversation with environmental professionals, activists, social scientists and scientists. Despite these activities, there has been little evidence of a psychoanalytic sensibility or 'analytic attitude' as legitimized in environmental activism and advocacy sectors. Ward explains how a psychoanalytic approach – contrary to accusations of not being pragmatic or practical enough – is not antithetical to a political orientation. Indeed, the ability to inquire into motivations, desires and (often) unconscious forces is needed for an effective political movement (Ward, 1993, p. 179). Ward provides the distinction that unique to an analytic perspective is the focus on the relation between what is *conscious* and *unconscious*, rather than between the *individual* and *social*.

With this move, Ward manages to override the tendency to reify a binary between the individual and the social that has plagued psychoanalytic thought for decades, alienating political and advocacy circles from taking it seriously as a praxis or having relevance for social issues. Throughout all domains of human experience, we arguably need to attend to how potentially unconscious processes are at work and the political relevance of bringing such processes into consciousness.[4]

Several themes emerge in psychoanalytically oriented work offering potent theoretical, conceptual and analytic resources for engaging with ecological degradation. Generally, psychoanalytic and affect studies concern unconscious processes: notably strategies mobilized and engaged psychically and socially for managing anxieties and distressing experiences. Depending on the analytic orientation, this includes a concern with our capacities for splitting (e.g. Segal, 1973), both in terms of internal splitting (dissociation with parts of ourselves too threatening or overwhelming) and compartmentalizing our dependence on earth systems (Mishan, 1996). Much of what chagrins and worries those working for environmental repair and health is the human capacity to dissociate from our embedded, interrelatedness with the earth's biotic systems, even if not referred to explicitly as 'dissociation' – a widely recognized forgetting, wilful ignorance, disconnection between ourselves and our biotic relations throughout environmental advocacy (Lertzman, 2010). Psychoanalytically, this capacity for dissociation is related to issues of vulnerability and anxiety, evoked in dependency contexts, and exemplified by our relationship with nature and ecological systems for survival (Searle's, 1960). How this relationship is negotiated can be seen in terms of fantasies of omnipotence, patterns of consumption as "spurious satisfactions" (Mishan, 1996, p. 62) or substitutes (Randall, 2005) and compulsive forms of activism (Zizek, 1992). There has been work addressing 'psychic numbing' as strategies to avoid trauma, specifically large-scale events such as the bombing in Hiroshima or 9/11 (Lifton, 1968; Lifton, 2003); however, this has been applied rarely to the topic of ecological crises, though this is starting to change (Dodds, 2011).

Several observers have noted the relative silence from psychoanalytic circles on the nonhuman and natural environment and speculate on the causes for this omission (Fisher, 2013; Kidner, 1994; Hillman & Ventura, 1993). One of the first individuals to draw attention to this dissociation in the psychoanalytic community was the American psychiatrist Harold F. Searles.[5] In 1960, Searles published a monograph, *The Nonhuman Environment: In Normal Development and in Schizophrenia*. The book was addressed to an audience of practicing psychoanalysts and practitioners who work with schizophrenics and severely neurotic and psychotic patients. It was presented as an intervention to invoke analysts to incorporate the role of the nonhuman environment in the experience of troubled patients. Searles also acknowledged the value and benefit of such work for normal psychologies as well and presented the work as applicable in a broader sense. The timing and content of this particular monograph are important for understanding the way in which the role of the nonhuman environment was introduced to a psychoanalytic community, the cultural and social context in which Searles was writing and the way in which his early theorizations paved the way for subsequent work in 'ecopsychology', 'ecotherapy' and environmental psychology.[6] The central hypothesis of *The Nonhuman Environment* (1960) is expressed by Searles:

> The nonhuman environment, far from being of little or no account to human personality development, constitutes one of the most basically important ingredients of human psychological existence. It is my conviction that there is within the human individual a sense, whether at a conscious or unconscious level, of relatedness to his nonhuman environment, that this relatedness is one of the transcendentally important facts of human living, that – as with other very important circumstances in human existence – it is a source of ambivalent feelings to him and that, finally, if he tries to ignore its importance to himself, he does so at peril to his psychological well-being.
> (p. 6).

Essentially, Searles' kinship hypothesis is that humans are, by their very nature, part of the larger, nonhuman (natural) environment. Following the kinship thesis is the complex nature of relatedness that humans have with their environment as both carriers of meaning, as well as intersubjective and on its own terms (e.g. Plumwood, 1994). Object relations theory is one of the platforms on which Searles builds his argument about why we ignore and disparage the importance of the environment in our lives. As in this book, Searles finds object relations a viable lens for understanding how humans relate with our 'environment', and how specific objects are far from discrete but are imbued with often unconscious meanings and material.

Searles does speculate on the lack of acknowledgement of the nonhuman environment in the field:

> Here we are beginning to get some hint of the anxiety which, I believe, is aroused in one who attempts to investigate the subject at hand. To my mind, much of the delay in our coming, in the psychoanalytic profession, to a realization of the importance of the nonhuman environment, is attributable to the circumstance that any determined effort to penetrate this area brings up in us the kind of the kind of anxiety which, I surmise, we knew all too much of as infants, when the world around us seemed, oftentimes, comprised largely or even wholly of chaotically uncontrollable nonhuman elements.
>
> (p. 37)

More significant is his proposition for the source of anxiety that impedes our exploration of this subject: the anxiety that in large part is tied to defending against the primitive loss of self and the trauma of differentiating ego from world. That is, Searles claims that, at our core, we are dependent on and related to the nonhuman environment and, stemming from this sense of oneness with the world prior to our individuation, we actively defend and deny our relation to it. He writes, "Not only do we have unconscious memory traces of infantile experiences in which we were surrounded by a chaotically uncontrollable nonhuman environment that was sensed as being a part of us; in addition, we presumably have unconscious memory traces of our experience with losing a nonhuman environment which had been our sensed, heretofore, as a harmonious extension of our world-embracing self"[7] (1960, p. 39). Thus the exploration of this whole subject, no matter on how scientific a plane we attempt to pursue it, impinges upon a deeply rooted anxiety of a doubled-edged sort: the anxiety of subjective oneness with a chaotic world and the anxiety over the loss of a cherished, omnipotent world-self.[8]

Environmental anxiety

Searles asserts that psychology's engagement with this vital aspect of human experience and existence – the environment – is hampered not only by ignorance but by anxiety concerning our relatedness with the nonhuman environment.

He presents a series of arguments for what causes this anxiety that stem directly from Freudian and neo-Freudian concepts of psychic defences and object relations theory. He applies his Freudian orientation to his thesis regarding our inseparability in Nature and the ways in which the human struggle to differentiate itself as distinctly human (while having desire to become nonhuman, e.g. the death drive) arouses deep anxieties. In this sense, it is an existential psychoanalysis, placing in the frame the individual struggle to become more fully human and the complicated relationship we have by necessity with the nonhuman environment. Namely, as humans we are embedded in and part of nature. The human goes through the evolutionary process beginning at conception, and this memory trace remains with us. To access our deep relation with nature – the nonhuman – is therefore to stimulate and spark anxiety and ambivalence regarding our origins and what it means to be human. Thus we begin to approach a context for the intense defences that can arise when affective relations with nature or nonhuman environment are felt and threatened.

The second aspect of this argument draws on the research of object-relations theorists. It suggests that the postnatal infant experience of the environment was chaotic and overwhelming and as adults we carry this association with us. Searles is articulating his sense of acute resistance and denial demonstrated by modern humans to what he feels to be an in-built kinship and relatedness with the nonhuman world. (He indicates that this seems too obvious to state; I agree.) He is trying to understand what leads people to overcompensate this relatedness by creating an artificial separation that enables destructive practices and insulates our consciousness with denial regarding the degradation of the environment. In observing how his psychotic patients relate with the environment – and indeed how profoundly important a role it plays in their development and their subsequent healing – he suggests that this holds important insight for our society as a whole. He recounts patients who clearly have strong relations with animals (a patient who grew up with horses or with a beloved pet) and how it was often the nonhuman environment that helped troubled individuals cope with highly fraught upbringings.

Apathy as defensive mechanism

A later paper, and arguably his treatise on the topic, "Unconscious Processes in Relation to the Environmental Crisis" (Searles, 1972), uses both Freudian and Kleinian theoretical frameworks to illuminate the complicated dynamics of living in and contributing-to a polluted and ecologically imperilled world. Here he names what is rarely spoken about apathy – that it is to be understand in the context of defence mechanisms and not taken at face value:

> My hypothesis is that man is hampered in his meeting of this environmental crisis by a severe and pervasive apathy which is based largely upon feelings and attitudes of which he is unconscious. That lack of analytic literature

about this subject suggests to me that we analysts are in the grip of this common apathy.

(1972, p. 362)

Searles' work (1972) relates to environmental communications in his analysis of unconscious meanings in environmental discourses. This includes the moralistic spirit that most environmental communications are imbued with and the role of ecologists in stimulating intense Oedipal guilt that calls on us to relinquish our hard-won achievements of

> genital primacy, symbolized by our proudly cherished but ecologically offensive automobile, and return to a state of childhood, when genital mastery was something longed for but not achieved; our apathy includes an unconscious defiant refusal to do this.
>
> (p. 364)

He positions future generations and progeny as unconsciously hated Oedipal rivals which compete with our desire to repair and protect the earth's finite and precious resources. He describes the depressive and paranoid positions as theoretically robust frameworks for understanding the contradictory and irrational ways in which we currently respond to the threat of serious ecological pollution and threat. This includes the symbolization of pollution and its threat to the future:

> Pollution serves not only to foreclose the future upon a progeny we unconsciously hate and envy, but also to obscure a past which we unconsciously resist remembering with poignant clarity. We equate the idealized world of our irretrievable lost childhood with a non-polluted environment. We tend to erroneously assume that nothing can be done about the pollution of the present-day environment because of our deeper-lying despair at knowing that we cannot recapture the world of our childhood and at sensing, moreover, that we are retrospectively idealizing the deprived and otherwise painful aspects of it . . . In this sense, pollutants unconsciously represent remnants of the past to which we are clinging, transference-distortions which permeate our present environment.
>
> (Searles, 1972, p. 366)[9]

This idealized world of childhood is observed throughout my interview data as participants recall playing in the sparkling water and white sand dunes, swinging under a blue sky, without a care in the world. It became harder to be able to parse out, throughout the interviews, a profound sense of nostalgia and longing for an innocence lost and the association of the natural world, prior to the more recent despoliation (i.e. algae, invasive species, toxics, and so on).

Per Searles' arguments, the ecologically deteriorating world in which we live is arguably fostering in us, at a largely unconscious level, an intense fear of being contaminated by everything. The way in which pollutants can be felt or seen as pervasive and invisible can paralyze us into 'terrorized inactivity'. In this deeply regressed mode, we are not well enough differentiated from the environment and hence have no clearly separate self with which to wage a struggle with an 'outer' threat.

This is a sophisticated theorization and attempt to explain the outwardly irrational lack of political action in the face of evidence about an ecologically precarious world. It is a bracing counter to a strictly political or scientific analysis of public engagement with contemporary issues (in Western, developed countries in particular), as well as an alternative to cognitive and behavioural schema employed to explain public engagement in terms of rational choice and decision making. His urgent call for psychoanalysts to draw on their own resources and theoretical tools is cogent, yet it seemingly fell on deaf ears. It is not entirely clear why this was the case. I suspect it was because his vivid psychoanalytic interpretation of contemporary ecological problems was not based on clear empirical evidence. This book seeks to remedy this, in part, through exploring some of these ideas in an empirical research investigation based on in-depth interviews and acute attention to what is being communicated by people otherwise considered 'apathetic'.

Psychoanalysis of contemporary threats

During the past decade, a few psychoanalytic thinkers have continued where Searles left off articulating possible unconscious psychic processes involved with ecological crises. This work includes Shierry Weber Nicholsen's *The Love of Nature and the End of the World* (2002), Joseph Mishan's paper "Psychoanalysis and Environmentalism: First Thoughts" (1996), Ivan Ward's "Introductory Thoughts" on *Ecological Madness: A Freud Museum Conference, December 1992* (1993) and the proceedings (Samuels, 1993; Orbach, 1993; Hinshelwood, 1993; Richards, 1993), Mary-Jayne Rust's presentation "Climate on the Couch" and related publications (Rust, 2007; Rust, 2006); Rosemary Randall's two papers, "A New Climate for Psychotherapy?" (2005) and "Loss and Climate Change" (2009); Sally Weintrobe's work on anxiety and green and climate change (2009; 2013), and Joseph Dodd's tour de force, *Psychoanalysis and Ecology at the Edge of Chaos* (2011). More philosophically theoretical writings include Zizek on the ecological crisis (in *Looking Awry*, 1992), van Wyck's work on nuclear waste burial site signage (2004; see Lertzman, 2006), and Guatarri's *The Three Ecologies* (2000).[10] Common to all authors, despite variations and theoretical frameworks, is the central role of unconscious processes, specifically guilt, anxiety, loss and related defence mechanisms in how we relate with our ecological threats. This work contributes-to the growing argument, made fervently in these various quarters, for the important role psychoanalysis has to play towards helping people respond more effectively to serious ecological threats and understanding our current predicament.

Randall (2005) also provides a lucid analysis of our predicament, focusing squarely on unconscious defences against the problems we face and the complex relations between ecological anxiety, compulsive consumption and shopping and the rise of therapeutic culture to help individuals manage their 'personal distress' more effectively. All facets create a constellation of avoidance and denial of what is taking place, and Randall provides a much needed analysis of the role psychotherapy has to play in the problems we currently face. For Randall, it is the process of loss and mourning which has particular salience for the ways in which people – often unconsciously – negotiate the awareness and prospects of climate change and mitigation practices. She argues persuasively for more nuanced language and models for mourning by looking to Worden's work on mourning (2008). Based on her work as a psychotherapist and designing so-called Carbon Conversation" as part of Cambridge Carbon Footprint, she claims that it is in the recognition of loss and support for mourning that the behavioral changes so desperately desired by environmental advocates may be enabled. In this sense, we see again the recognition of the psychic power of acknowledging and naming emotional truths.[11] Randall (2009) writes:

> Building on the work of Bowlby and Parkes, Worden suggests that the work of grief is a series of tasks that can be embraced or refused, tackled or abandoned. He sees the work as always in progress, never complete. Life will never be the same again, but meaning may be restored and it may become possible to flourish once more. The work may falter or stall, the bereaved person may return to an earlier stage, sink into depression, abandon their attempt at recovery, take heart again, move forward and so on. In each of the stages Worden suggests that either the task, or what he calls its negative, may be embraced.
>
> (p. 121)

Shierry Nicholsen, a psychotherapist and critical theory scholar, published a book of reflections on environmental crises (2002) in which she weaves analytic theory (Winnicott [1965] on concern, Bion [1961] on binocular perception) with aesthetics, art theory and ecopsychological literature (see Lertzman, 2004). Her writings are personal, interdisciplinary and poetic, as well as infused with a psychoanalytic sensibility, e.g. attention to unconscious processes. Indeed, she acknowledges Searles as one of the first and few voices and a major influence (Nicholsen, 2002, p. 1). Nicholsen discusses apathy by citing Harry Stack Sullivan, who wrote, "Apathy seems to me to be a miracle of protection by which personality in utter fiasco rests until it can do something else" (1970, pp. 174–175) and, describing herself as having a way of adopting and defending oneself in a situation:

> that is utterly overwhelming and where there is no end in sight. We all need this kind of protection in our current environmental situation, certainly, in

which there is so much destruction of so many kinds, in so many places, affecting so many people and so many other creatures, and with no end in sight. No wonder environmental activists complain about the widespread apathy that meets their efforts to arouse concern.

(Nicholsen, 2002, p. 147)

For Nicholsen and colleagues in the psychoanalytic field, the task of reparation includes the ability to tolerate discomfort and uncertainty. As Segal notes, the schizoid flight into manic defences is a flight from anxiety, an inability to tolerate ambiguity, ambivalence and uncertainty (Segal, 1997). The analytic attitude, then, as Ward expresses it and also reflected in Nicholson's writings, is one of *curiosity* and *investigation*. In fact, this is widely recognized in much psychoanalytic work: to 'work through' one's own resistance, defences, compulsions and neuroses requires the ability to be aware; this requires the capacity to be curious without the constant recrimination of the superego (inner critic) attacking us. The capacity to be disturbed is linked with the capacity to be curious, and both require certain levels of containment and safety to help tolerate such experiences. As she writes, "It is clear that the capacity to be curious is very useful. Since the environmental situation is a part of current reality, albeit a disturbing part, and since it is something we do not yet understand or know how to deal with, it is useful to be able to turn our attention to it, to notice how disturbing it is, and yet to be interested in it and inquire into it" (p. 156). This aspect of the work – the implications for environmental practice, specifically for communications and outreach – remains undeveloped yet poses enormous potential.

The fields of environmental psychology and ecopsychology have been largely dominated by two broad psychological paradigms: social psychology and humanistic/therapeutic psychology. As a result, much of the research investigating how people respond to environmental problems and perceive chronic ecological risks is interpreted in terms of cognitive processes based on observable behavioral practices or self-reporting of particular beliefs and opinions. Alternately, the same issues are rendered as deeply emotional and falling on humanistic ideological underpinnings concerning the human rift from a dynamic and life-giving Earth, with a focus on how to mend this rift or 'disconnection'. Underpinning these two broad paradigms are epistemic and ontological assumptions that do not, and perhaps cannot, account for the complicated psychic and social processes of managing anxieties, fears, threats and desires. Nor can they account for the importance of psychic resistance to such distress and the ways in which perceptions of reality are often distorted to conform to certain affective requirements, e.g. safety, security, stability or continuity. These epistemic and ontological underpinnings – either rigidly positivist that do not allow for the invisible, inchoate, or messy aspects of psychic and social phenomena or a romantic alienation from nature as cause of all our ills – leave out accounting for how humans respond often irrationally to anxiety, loss and perceived threats.

Notes

1 It's important to emphasize that how 'denial' is conceptualized commonly in climate change circles is not the same as how denial is understood in a clinical, psychodynamic context. While denial is often viewed simplistically as 'ignoring' or willful ignorance, denial as a clinical phenomenon is a complex defence mechanism, designed to avoid intolerable levels of anxiety, stress and conflict. It is both unconscious and socially produced, as Norgaard has astutely pointed out (2011).

2 It is important not to overlook the work on psychoanalysis and the nuclear threat; e.g. Levine, Jacobs and Rubin (1988). Hanna Segal, along with Vamik Volcan, Robert J. Lifton and Daniel Jacobs, are part of a small but dedicated group of psychoanalytic thinkers who addressed nuclear threats; however, as nuclear issues are distinct from ecological threats in several specific ways (e.g. intentionality and consequences), I do not include this literature in this chapter.

3 For example, the large body of work devoted to the treatment and analysis of survivors of political trauma and violence constitutes a significant focus in psychoanalytic studies (Felman & Laub, 1992) and since 9/11 more psychoanalysts have been speaking to themes of terrorism, fear and political anxiety (Wirth, 2004; Coates, Rosenthal & Schechter, 2003).

4 Certainly, (primarily) British psychosocial research, the Tavistock Institute and its formidable legacy and publications as *Psychoanalysis, Culture and Society* have been attempting to forge these links between the psychic and the social. Notable is Ward's explicit exhortations for the environmental community of activists, educators and analysts to appreciate these relations.

5 It must be mentioned that Carl Jung was also a forerunner in articulating psyche with nature and environment; for the purposes of this study in highlighting contributions from object-relational psychoanalytic thinking, I chose to bracket Jung's contributions for now.

6 The work appears to not have been picked up in the psychoanalytic community, a point I will discuss; however, his work is now appearing more recently as psychoanalysts are increasingly forced to contend with environmental concerns as a feature of social and cultural life.

7 He cites Stärcke: "It is this separation in the primitive ego, the formation of the external world, which, properly speaking, is the primitive castration" (Searles, 1960, p. 9).

8 Of course, there is also the relation with nature as a retreat from the chaos of everyday life, and the move towards greater connection with nature as a reflection of our inherent interconnectivity (cf. the North American nature-connect project Weaving Earth, inspired by the work of Jon Young, founder of the 8 Shields (cf. Young, 2010). This connection of nature with anxiety/chaos refers to the unpredictability and argument that humans manage the chaos of nature through means of control, domination and order.

9 On a related point regarding bring born into specific environmental conditions and the role of memory, see Peter Kahn's work on 'generational amnesia' (1999, pp. 110–111).

10 Emerging work by Cameron and Forrester are also making links between Freud, psychoanalysis and the founder of ecology, Tansley (see Cameron & Forrester, 2000).

11 As Moser points out, Roosevelt's famous statement, "Let me assert my firm belief that the only thing we have to fear is fear itself – nameless, unreasoning, unjustified terror which paralyzes needed efforts to convert retreat into advance" was so effective because in "acknowledging people's fears, he went on to say, 'only a foolish optimist can deny the dark realities of the moment' and then called for a renewed vision and concrete action plan" (Moser, 2007, p. 70). Randall's emphasis on naming the fear and anxiety, as well as our sense of loss, resonates with Moser's observations.

References

Ajzen, I., 1991. The theory of planned behavior, *Organizational Behavior and Human Decision Processes* 50, pp. 179–211.

Bateman, A., & Holmes, J., 1995. *Introduction to Psychoanalysis: Contemporary Theory and Practice.* London: Routledge.

Bion, W., 1961. *Experiences in Groups.* London: Tavistock.

Cameron, L., & Forrester, J., 2000. Tansley's psychoanalytic network: An episode out of the early history of psychoanalysis in England, *Psychoanalysis and History* 2 (2), pp. 189–256.

Cargill, K., 2006. Off the couch and onto the streets: Toward an ethnographic psychoanalysis, *Psychoanalysis, Culture & Society* 11 (1), pp. 99–105.

Clarke, S., Hahn, H., Hoggett, P., & Sideris, T., 2006. Psychoanalysis and community, *Psychoanalysis, Culture & Society* 11, pp. 199–216.

Coates, S. W., Rosenthal, J. L., & Schechter, D. S., 2003. *September 11: Trauma and Human Bonds.* Hillsdale, NJ: Analytic Press.

Crompton, T., 2010. *Common Cause: The Case for Working with Our Cultural Values.* London: WWF-UK.

Crompton, T., & Kasser, T., 2009. *Meeting Environmental Challenges: The Role of Human Identity.* London: WWF-UK.

De Groot, J.I.M., & Steg, L., 2007. General beliefs and the theory of planned behavior: The role of environmental concerns in the TPB. *Journal of Applied Social Psychology*, 37, pp. 1817–1836.

Dodds, J., 2011. *Psychoanalysis and Ecology at the Edge of Chaos.* New York: Routledge.

Felman, S., & Laub, D., 1992. *Testimony: Crises of Witnessing in Literature, Psychoanalysis and History.* New York: Routledge, Chapman and Hall.

Fenichel, O., 1945. *The Psychoanalytic Theory of Neurosis.* New York: W. W. Norton.

Fisher, A., 2013. *Radical Ecopsychology: Psychology in the Service of Life*, 2nd ed. New York: SUNY Press.

Freud, S., 1915. The unconscious. In Strachey, J. et al., (ed.), *Standard Edition* 14. London: Hogarth, pp. 166–204.

Guatarri, F., 2000. *The Three Ecologies.* London & New Brunswick, NJ: Athlone Press.

Hards, S., 2012. Tales of transformation: The potential of a narrative approach to pro-environmental practices. *Geoforum* 43 (4), pp. 760–771.

Heath, C., & Heath, D., 2010. *Switch.* New York: Crown Publishing.

Hillman, J., & Ventura, M., 1993. *We've Had a Hundred Years of Psychotherapy, and the World's Getting Worse.* San Francisco: Harper.

Hinshelwood, R. D., 1993. The countryside, *British Journal of Psychotherapy* 10 (2), pp. 202–210.

Hyman, H., & Sheatsley, P., 1947. Some reasons why information campaigns fail, *Public Opinion Quarterly* 11, pp. 412–423.

Jamieson, D., 2006. An American paradox, *Climatic Change* 77, p. 98.

Kahn, P., 1999. *The Human Relationship with Nature: Development and Culture.* Cambridge, MA: MIT Press, pp. 110–111.

Karpinsky, A., & Hilton, J. L., 2001. Attitudes and the implicit association test, *Journal of Personality and Social Psychology* 81 (5), pp. 774–788.

Kidner, D., 1994. Why Psychology Is Mute About the Environmental Crisis, *Environmental Ethics* 16 (4).

Klein, M., 2014. *This Changes Everything: Capitalism Vs. the Climate.* New York: Simon & Schuster.

Kohon, G., 1986. *The British School of Psychoanalysis: The Independent Tradition.* London: Free Association Books.

Kotler, P., & Zaltman, G., 1971. Social marketing: An approach to planned social change, *Journal of Marketing* 35, pp. 3–12.

Leiserowitz, A., 2006. Climate change risk perception and policy preferences: The role of affect, imagery, and values. *Climatic Change* 77, pp. 45–72.

Leiserowitz, A., 2007. Communicating the risks of global warming: American risk perceptions, affective images and interpretive communities. In Moser, S., & Dilling, L. (eds.), *Creating a Climate for Change: Communicating Climate Change – Facilitating Social Change.* Cambridge: Cambridge University Press.

Lertzman, R., 2004. Ecopsychological theory and critical intervention, *Organization & Environment* 17 (3), pp. 396–402.

Lertzman, R., 2006. Book review: *Signs of danger: Waste, trauma and nuclear threat,* van Wyck, P., *Organization & Environment* 19 (4), pp. 542–545.

Lertzman, R., 2010. Psychoanalysis, culture, society and our biotic relations: Introducing an ongoing theme on environment and sustainability, *Psychoanalysis, Culture & Society* 15, pp. 113–116.

Levine, H., Jacobs, D., & Rubin, L., eds., 1988. *Psychoanalysis and the Nuclear Threat, Clinical and Theoretical Studies.* Hilldale, NJ: Analytic Press.

Lifton, R. J., 1968. *Death in Life: Survivors of Hiroshima.* New York: Random House.

Lifton, R. J., 2003. *Superpower Syndrome: America's Apocalyptic Confrontation with the World.* New York: Nation Books.

Lorenzoni, I., Nicholson-Cole, S., & Whitmarsh, L., 2007. Barriers perceived to engaging with climate change among the UK public and their policy implications, *Global Environmental Change: Human and Policy Dimensions* 17 (3–4), pp. 445–459.

Lorenzoni, I., & Pigeon, N., 2006. Public views on climate change: European and USA perspectives, *Climatic Change* 77 (1/2), pp. 73–95.

Maibach, E., 1993. Social marketing for the environment: Using information campaigns to promote environmental awareness and behavior change, *Health Promotion International* 8 (3), pp. 209–224.

Maiteny, P., 2000. The psychodynamics of meaning and action for a sustainable future, *Futures* 32 (3), p. 339.

Marshall, G., 2014. *Don't Even Think About It: Why Our Brains Are Wired to Ignore Climate Change.* New York: Bloomsbury USA.

McKenzie-Mohr, D., 2011. *Fostering Sustainable Behavior: An Introduction to Community-Based Social Marketing.* Gabriola, BC: New Society.

Marx, S. M., Weber, E. U., Orlove, B. S., Leiserowitz, A., Krantz, D. H., Roncoli, C,, & Phillips, J. 2007. Communication and mental processes: Experiential and analytic processing of uncertain climate information, *Global Environmental Change* 17 (1), pp. 47–58.

Minsky, R., 1998. *Psychoanalysis and Culture: Contemporary States of Mind.* Cambridge, MA: Polity.

Mishan, J., 1996. Psychoanalysis and environmentalism: First thoughts, *Psychoanalytic Psychotherapy* 10 (1), pp. 59–70.

Moser, S. C., & Dilling, L., 2004. Making climate hot: Communicating the urgency and challenge of global climate change, *Environment* 46 (10), pp. 32–46.

Moser, S. C., 2007. More bad news: The risk of neglecting emotional responses to climate change information.In Moser, S., & Dilling, L. (eds.), *Creating a Climate for Change: Communicating Climate Change and Facilitating Social Change.* Cambridge: Cambridge University Press, pp. 64–80.

Moser, S. C., 2012. Getting real about it: Navigating the psychological and social demands of a world in distress. In Rigling Gallagher, D., Andrews, R. N. L., & Christensen, N. L. (eds.), *Sage Handbook on Environmental Leadership,* London: Sage, pp. 432–440.

Nicholsen, S. W., 2002. *The Love of Nature and the End of the World: The Unspoken Dimensions of Environmental Concern.* Cambridge, MA: MIT Press.

Norgaard, K., 2011. *Living in Denial: Climate Change, Emotions and Everyday Life.* Cambridge: MIT Press.

O'Neill, S., & Nicholson-Cole, S., 2009. Fear won't do it: Promoting positive engagement with climate change through visual and iconic representations, *Science Communication* 30 (3), pp. 355–379.

Orbach, S., 1993. Psychological processes of consuming, *British Journal of Psychotherapy* 10 (2), pp. 196–201.

O'Sullivan, E., & Taylor, M., eds., 2004. *Ecological Consciousness: Selected Transformative Practices.* New York: Palgrave.

Pike, C., Doppelt, B., & Herr, M. 2010. *Climate Communications and Behavior Change: A Guide for Practitioners.* Eugene: University of Oregon, Climate Leadership Initiative.

Pink, D., 2011. *Drive: The Surprising Truth About What Motivates Us.* New York: Riverhead Books.

Plumwood, V., 1994. *Feminism and the Mastery of Nature.* New York: Routledge.

Proshansky, H. M., Fabian, A. K., & Karminoff, R., 1983. Place-identity: Physical world socialization of the self, *Journal of Environmental Psychology* 3, pp. 57–83.

Randall, R., 2005. A new climate for psychotherapy? *Psychotherapy and Politics International* 3 (3), pp. 165–179.

Randall, R., 2009. Loss and climate change: The cost of parallel narratives, *Ecopsychology* 3 (1), pp. 118–129.

Richards, B., 1993. Technophobia and technophilia, *British Journal of Psychotherapy* 10 (2), pp. 188–195.

Rust, M., 2006. Ecolimia nervosa, *Therapy Today* 16 (10), pp. 11–15.

Rust, M., 2007. Climate on the couch: Unconscious processes in relation to our environmental crisis. Guild of Psychotherapists Annual Lecture, London. November 17th 2007. *Psychotherapy and Politics International* 6 (3): 157–170.

Samuels, A., 1993. 'I am a place': Depth psychology and environmentalism, *British Journal of Psychotherapy* 10 (2), pp. 211–218.

Samuels, A., 2001. *Politics on the Couch: Citizenship and the Internal Life.* London: Profile Books.

Searles, H., 1960. *The Nonhuman Environment in Normal Development and in Schizophrenia.* New York: International Universities Press.

Searles, H., 1972. Unconscious processes in relation to the environmental crisis, *The Psychoanalytic Review* 59 (3), pp. 361–374.

Segal, H., 1973. *Introduction to the Work of Melanie Klein.* London: Institute of Psychoanalysis, Karnac.

Segal, H., 1997 [1995]. From Hiroshima to the Gulf War and after: Socio-political expressions of ambivalence. In Segal, H., & Steiner, J. (eds.), *Psychoanalysis, Literature and War: Papers 1972–1995.* Reprint: London: Routledge and Institute of Psycho-Analysis, pp. 157–169.

Shove, E., 2010. Beyond the ABC: Climate change policy and theories of social change, *Environment and Planning A 42*, pp. 1273–1285.

Speth, J., 2007. All for one: The immediacy of fighting climate change, *Conservation Biology* 21 (4), p. 914.

Stern, D., 2000. *The Interpersonal World of the Infant: A View from Psychoanalysis & Developmental Psychology.* New York: Basic Books.

Stoll-Kleemann, S., O'Riordan, T., & Jaeger, C. C., 2001. The psychology of denial concerning climate mitigation measures: Evidence from Swiss focus groups, *Global Environmental Change* 11, pp. 107–117.

Sullivan, H. S., 1970. *The Psychiatric Interview.* New York: Norton, pp. 174–175.

Symington, N., 1996. *The Analytic Experience: Lectures from the Tavistock.* London: Free Association Books, pp. 16–17.

Thaler, R., & Sunstein, C., 2009. *Nudge: Improving Decisions About Health, Wealth, and Happiness.* New York: Penguin.

Thomashow, M., 1996. *Ecological Identity: Becoming a Reflective Environmentalist.* Cambridge, MA: MIT Press.

van Wyck, P., 2004. *Signs of Danger: Waste, Trauma, and Nuclear Threat.* Minneapolis: University of Minnesota Press.

Ward, I., 1993. Ecological madness, a Freud Museum conference: Introductory thoughts, *British Journal of Psychotherapy* 10 (2), pp. 178–187.

Weber, E., 2006. Experience-based and description-based perceptions of long-term risk: Why global warming does not scare us (yet), *Climatic Change* 77, pp. 103–120.

Weintrobe, S., 2009. On runaway greed and climate change denial: A psychoanalytic perspective. In *Lecture Series, Psychotherapy in the 21st Century, 25 April 2009.* London: Lincoln Clinic & Centre for Psychotherapy.

Weintrobe, S., 2013. *Engaging with Climate Change: Psychoanalytic Interdisciplinary Perspectives.* New York: Routledge.

Winnicott, D. W., 1965. *The Maturational Processes and the Facilitating Environment: Studies in the Theory of Emotional Development.* London: Hogarth Press & Institute of Psycho-Analysis.

Wirth, H. J., 2004. Psychoanalytic thoughts on 9/11, *Journal of Psycho-Social Studies* 3 (1). Available at: http://www.uwe.ac.uk/hlss/research/cpss/Journal_Psycho-Social_Studies/v3-1/WirthH.shtml [accessed 15 October 2009].

Worden, J., 2008. *Grief Counseling and Grief Therapy*, 4th ed. New York: Springer.

Young, J., McGown, E., & Haas, E., 2010. *Coyote's Guide to Connecting with Nature.* Santa Cruz, CA: OWLink Media Corporation.

Zizek, S., 1992. *Looking Awry: An Introduction to Jacques Lacan Through Popular Culture.* Boston: MIT Press.

Fox River and Fort Howard, November 2007. (Photo: R. Lertzman.)

It's calming you know, water is, ah, for me you know and cause yeah, I love one of the things I love watching about when we go to the river and stuff, I love watching the birds that gather around the water. And there's been um, a couple of bald eagles that in the last couple of years have been, in the area down here in Green Bay that have been by the Fox River. And watching that and, it, it's just that's just neat, I just get a sense of joy and you know, seeing you know, birds, big birds of prey like that you know. And the sand cranes, and the pelicans that have been coming back too, to the area, the water quality must be getting better. Otherwise animals wouldn't be coming back. But you know, there's a ways to go . . . You know cos, probably before when I was younger, then I was like, "hey look, neat, water, you know, you drink water, you know". You know the bay is water, you drink water, you cook with water and all that, and then realizing that water could be dirty.

– Scott, Interview 2

Chapter 3

Why methods matter

Innovating methodology for environmental concern

The methodologies we use in our research investigations are expressions of underlying epistemic and ontological assumptions, that is, what constitutes as knowledge, data and how we frame our investigations into human experience. This much seems obvious. Yet when it comes to investigating how environmental issues are perceived, experienced and made sense of, research design is rarely critically interrogated. Given what we know about 'top of mind' perceptions and self-reporting – that we are rarely completely transparent to ourselves – why do we continue to use surveys, polls and direct Q&A format interviews to explore perceptions of environmental issues? What if we are capable of simultaneously being concerned, alarmed, sceptical, cautious and outraged? What if these states are highly contextual and sometimes buried below our consciousness, until we have the opportunity to express through interaction the array of experiences and feelings? How well designed are our methodologies to help access both conscious and unconscious dimensions, affective and emotional? It is time to innovate and revise our methodologies to allow for understanding the complex, actual motivators for engaging in new practices, even if inclusive of psychic and social, cognitive and emotional variables. I argue that environmental research in the social sciences – particularly focusing on behavior, engagement and perceptions – requires and demands research methodological innovations to account for unconscious processes. Namely, anxieties, ambivalences, loss and meaning-making are often well below the surface of our conscious, rational minds. Our research methodologies need to 'get underneath' and uncover the often contradictory, inconsistent, irrational, affective and complicated ways in which people engage with our most pressing environmental challenges. It is only then that we are able to design and inform our engagement, messaging and campaigning strategies with relevant insight.

I designed a methodology – the Dialogic, Relational Interview (DRI) approach – that focuses on the use of in-depth, free associative open-ended interviews with 10 participants in Green Bay (Lertzman, 2012a, 2012b) and the use of object-relational, psychoanalytic data analysis. The approach, informed by several psychosocial and psychoanalytic research methodologies as will be discussed, utilizes dialogic, successive, iterative interviews per participant, each building on the previous. While the number of interviews can vary with DRI, in this project each participant was interviewed three times, each for about one hour, over a period of about three to four weeks. Participants were selected based on survey and short-answer responses to an online survey disseminated through a local market research firm in Green Bay. I chose to interview participants who reported in the survey to think about environmental issues in the "middle range" of the spectrum (from "never" to "frequently") and to have no environmental organizational involvement and appear to know a bit about local environmental issues (see Appendix A). The interviews used an opening 'prompt' (Single Question to Induce Narrative, to be discussed) and were unstructured and intentionally free associative, becoming progressively focused during the second and third interviews as I presented questions, clarifications, feedback and occasional interpretations. Towards the end of the third and final interview, I presented a campaign advertisement that had run in local media from the Healing Our Waters campaign ("Girl on the Beach", 2007; see Figure 1.2) with the following prompt: "Please tell me whatever comes to mind for you." I then allowed people to respond at length and without interruption. Final interviews concluded with a brief debriefing session during which participants could ask any questions about the study, the process or whatever came to mind. Each participant was given the option to receive copies of the transcripts and/or the final write-up. Interviews took place in participants' homes with the exception of one who wished to meet in her office. The data analysis was conducted using principles from qualitative social scientific research, psychoanalytic work and psychosocial studies, in addition to environmental contextual factors. Field notes were incorporated, and countertransference was viewed as part of the research methodology. In what follows, I discuss some of the decisions and processes by which I came to design the methodology as I did and to illustrate how psychosocially inspired methods have a great deal to offer environmental social science research.

Context matters

Context has been increasingly recognized as salient for psychosocial and psychoanalytically oriented work in clinical and research settings, as relevant for making accurate interpretations (Cartwright, 2004; Schafer, 1985; Spence, 1982). In fact, it can be argued that attention to context is one of the most significant differentiating attributes of psychosocial research methods, where "context refers broadly to the host of factors, internal and external, that come to bear on the way an individual communicates and how the communication is understood" (Cartwright, 2004, p. 220).

My initial inquiry into psychosocial dimensions of environmental issues stemmed from observations about anxiety and distress in relation to environmental issues, first as a student taking environmental studies courses and later while working in the environmental communications sector for 20 years. I have often reflected about my own ways of negotiating my concerns and lack of 'action' in recognizable forms of activism and protest and what informed the choices I made.[1] These personal experiences and reflections inform my desire for researching affective, unconscious processes in relation to environmental issues, as forms of social and cultural trauma (Lifton, 1979). I was interested in exploring the more painful and perhaps less conscious expressions of the dilemmas of negotiating chronic ecological issues, some of which touch our lives in profoundly direct ways (as reflected in one participant's story of contaminated drinking water or that of another who contracted hepatitis probably from swimming in the Fox River; see Figure 3.1). These dimensions, I knew, would not be readily available through more 'frontal' or easily observable forms of research, and I was in sympathy with the concept of the 'defended subject' (Hollway & Jefferson, 2000) to help bring psychoanalytic concepts of unconscious defence mechanisms into research context (e.g. the 'subject' is 'defended' and therefore the story told is not necessarily straightforward or 'reliable'). I also knew that issues of anxiety, loss or other potential psychic complications which may constitute environmental subjectivities and forms of agency were potentially elusive and, if 'defended', then potentially out of view. As an environmental scholar, I was also cautious about making certain claims regarding environmental subjectivity or agency, whilst being mindful of the enormously

Figure 3.1 Fox River View. (Photo: R. Lertzman.)

relevant and complex material, social, economic, cultural and political contexts involved with contemporary environmental degradation.

The task was to design a research methodology that could effectively explore unconscious processes and dynamics, attend to (environmental) object relations and contexts, provide the space and depth required to meet the needs of a psychosocial investigation. The mandate of a particular environmental region (as opposed to issue area, e.g. climate change or a topic such as environmental media, e.g. the BBC *Planet Earth* series) – even one as vast as the Great Lakes, spanning six states and two countries – necessarily informed how I approached the interrelated 'registers' of ecology, sociality and subjectivity,[2] rendering the study not only psychosocial but *place based*, a hitherto uncharted territory for psychoanalytic psychosocial qualitative research.

Negotiating these tensions between exploring unconscious processes and the mandates of conducting reliable, empirical qualitative research is what constitutes the methodological design of DRI. As this was an environmentally contextual project, I will also speak to the way in which the place and the site-specific context were incorporated into the research design as a vital dimension of an environmentally sensitive psychosocial research project.

Psychosocial Orientations

The tendency in social sciences is to presume a rational subject who is in control of his or her actions and behaviours, or at least conscious of them, and thus whose values, attitudes and opinions can be measured and presented as 'fact'. This orientation presumably is what informs the heavy and extensive use of surveys, polls, focus groups and interviews in which participants are asked point-blank about their values, preferences, attitudes and beliefs about environmental topics.

In contrast, I was starting with the premise that environmental engagement is largely unconscious and highly contingent on contextual factors both psychic and social. Further, I was working with the assertion that these issues arguably arouse anxieties, which can inform and cloud perceptions, cognitive function and accurate assessment of reality. In other words, as discussed in the previous chapter, I began with recognizing the presence of defence mechanisms – activated by anxieties – as central to establishing a new form of environmental social science research approach. I was tasked with designing research that therefore presumes "a subject whose actions, behaviors and biographies are not solely determined by conscious will, agency or intent (or indeed the lack of these things)" (Walkerdine, Lucey & Melody, 2001, p. 84). Psychic and social processes are seen as existing in complex dialectical relations that disrupt the notion of a private 'interior' and the outer, social and public sphere, that is, "to get beyond conscious, rational explanations to a greater understanding of the influences and behavior of our subjects, both the psychic and the social processes of how they have come about need to be investigated" (Walkerdine, Lucey & Melody, 2001, p. 87).

In addition to presuming a less conscious subject or participant is extending this as well to the researcher as partial, involved and subjective. Taken together, the methodology is concerned with *unconscious relational processes* between participants and researchers, such as countertransference, to help make sense of the researcher's own involvement with the material and as co-producer of data generated through interviews (cf. Stopford, 2004). Therefore, the methodology must both account for the unconscious nature of environmental subjectivity, as well as the researcher's own subjectivity.

It follows that the methods employed for exploring perceptions of and relations with ecological degradation cannot rely on self-reporting such as polls, surveys and focus groups (e.g. see Baumieister, Smart & Boden, 1996 for discussion of self-reports and defence mechanisms). To counter prevailing approaches to the study of environmental communications and engagement as focusing on attitudes and behavior, I needed to design into the methodology elements afforded through a qualitative psychosocial study: depth (e.g. smaller sample and higher levels of contact), immersive experience (*in situ* and familiar with local ecological discourses and histories) and an emphasis on providing 'space' and 'context' for as much narrative scope as possible. In other words, what was needed was a carefully considered contextualization within which to approach and explore the complexities of how local and global ecological issues were made sense of, experienced and narrated.

Designing environmental, object-relational approach

Thus one of the central methodological issues concerns the aforementioned "transparent self problem" (Hollway & Jefferson, 2000) that claims we cannot assume people are 'telling it like it is' or that we even know what makes our own selves tick and thus cannot self-report in the context of an interview, poll or survey. Further, integration of defence mechanisms into research is predicated on the theory that anxiety precipitates defences against the threats it poses to the self and that these operate at a largely unconscious level (Hollway & Jefferson, 2000). The consideration of how to conduct research into subjectivities informed by psychoanalytic and poststructuralist thought has been underway in recent years. In formulating my approach, I turned to several studies as resources, notably the Biographical Narrative Interpretive Method (BNIM) (Wengraf, 2001), Free-Associative Narrative Interviews (FANI) (Hollway & Jefferson, 2000) and the Psychoanalytic Research Interview (PRI) (Cartwright, 2002).

BNIM, as a narrative-based approach, is centrally focused on the richness of stories and 'particular incident narratives' as conveying meanings which may not be elicited using more straightforward, linearly conducted interviews using direct questions. I was able to utilize two techniques from BNIM that helped constitute aspects of DRI. The first was a carefully selected and considered opening question and its importance in the setting up and conducting of a genuinely free associative interview. The opening question is what BNIM practitioners refer to as the "Single Question aimed at Inducing Narrative(s)" (SQUIN) (Wengraf, 2001). Given BNIM's primary interest in the 'lived experience' and biographical material, a typical SQUIN would be, "Can you please tell me your life story . . .," followed by a carefully worded preamble about how the interview will be conducted (e.g. the interviewer will not interrupt while the participants speak as long as they wish). The role of the SQUIN in the BNIM interview sequence is crucial, and I found this to be the case in my interviews as well. The spirit of the SQUIN is an *invitation* to speak, encourages free association and backgrounds the interviewer, and yet it provides containment and structure. This must be viewed in contrast with the conventional design of interviews that begin with asking participants their direct views, perceptions or beliefs about certain issues. I used the carefully chosen opening question in the first interview as a prompt for free association, not only in relation to the question but with all elements of the encounter, e.g. the online survey, ethical consent form and any other associations or projections potentially stimulated by my presence, words, appearance and so on.

I therefore developed an opening question for the first interview of the three interviews, after extensive consideration: "Tell me about where you grew up. Please start wherever you wish and say whatever comes to mind." This question was designed to be both encompassing and broad and to deliberately unconsciously reference the topic of the study. While BNIM uses a script for the opening statement or 'preamble' in which the participant is instructed on how the interview will be conducted, that they will not be interrupted, I did not always adhere to this *exact* wording, but the question was always more or less the same, and it *followed* from a preamble very similar to the one used in BNIM, particularly regarding the fact they will not be interrupted and are encouraged to speak at length about whatever comes to mind; I discuss this later in the chapter. Therefore, using this broad question provided a context in the interview to perceive what sorts of (unconscious) associations are formed to start with the topic of water, nature, environment or Green Bay. The use of a SQUIN in my work became integral to how I encountered all three in relation to one another (discussed in Part II).

In addition to the use of the SQUIN, I obtained from BNIM the practice of following the *gestalt* of the narratives and topics of interest in each interview session, as well as the importance of noting down topics, ideas, thoughts that arise in the interview which seem particularly charged or significant. In the subsequent interview session, the interviewer can then pick up these topics, but only in the *same sequence in which they appear in the participant's narrative*. For example, if a story such as a fishing trip on the Fox River appears early in Interview 1 and then another story later in the interview, in the second interview I would inquire about these in the order they appeared. If a participant recalled an incident in Interview 2, I would revisit that in the third interview in the order it appeared. In other words, I would respect the way in which certain associations emerged for the participants in the context of their psychic process. The metaphor used, which I found myself returning to often, was that of tracing footsteps in the snow. The intention is to acknowledge a flow of associations as reflected in the sequence of stories, topics or themes that have an integrity and significance ('deep structure'). There is nothing random about the ordering and ways in which certain associations are invoked, similar to the clinical psychoanalytic session. To disrupt this sequence is to 'trample' on the way in which the psyche orders and makes meaningful certain stories or topics of relevance.

As with BNIM, there were aspects of Free-Associative Narrative Interviews (FANI) that I found useful, and others less so. The central technique of FANI is the production of a semi-structured interview, attention to biographical material and the way in which the participants (or 'subjects' as they refer to them) provide often complex, indirect and meandering narratives. Hollway and Jefferson's approach informed how I considered my own approach to interviews, particularly with reference to biographical and psychic nuances in relation to charged topics (e.g. fear of crime). The most valuable aspect of their work of 'doing qualitative research differently' was introducing defensive mechanisms such as splitting, denial and projection into the context of qualitative research practice.

Inspired by psychosocial research methodologies, I was tasked with bringing psychoanalytic theoretical frameworks to bear on the way research is conducted. I looked to Cartwright's Psychoanalytic Research Interviews, as they were also an example of this application, described as "part of an ongoing project aimed at developing research methods that focus on the specific needs of psychoanalytic enquiry" (Cartwright, 2004). The method centers on conducting in-depth, psychoanalytic interviews that incorporate free association, countertransference and transference, and the recognition of unconscious dynamics in the research interview context. As with BNIM and FANI, the PRI is a narrative-based qualitative methodology. I worked to integrate Cartwright's psychoanalytic theoretical principles, namely object relations, transference and countertransference, an appreciation for meaning in narrative and psychodynamic 'core' themes. Cartwright's method is based around the conducting of three in-depth, open-ended (unstructured) interviews that utilize the practice of free association in a way I found more productive than FANI and BNIM, in that the interviews were conducted as more spontaneous and dynamic (e.g. genuinely open and exploratory in the absence of set questions and the commitment to following up with clarifications and feedback in the second and third interviews). The researcher is encouraged to be attuned to her sensations, reflections and responses and to maintain a sense of 'presence' and dialog with the participant. It was in terms of data analysis that Cartwright informed my work most strongly. Cartwright suggests an innovative technique for data analysis in attending to themes, dynamics and object relations as they surface in the material: careful attention to feeling states and corresponding thoughts or perceptions both before and during interviews, the search for core narratives, and the exploration of identifications and object relations in the data (within each interview and across the set of three interviews). He also advises the use of triangulation as a sort of measure against the threat of 'wild analysis' – similar to the 'panel' used by BNIM to create a sense of validity or checking one's potentially unconscious projections and interpretations onto the data – in the analysis process.[3] I felt his rationale was more coherent than BNIM's panels in accounting for countertransference impressions.

Designing data collection

In light of my research questions and interest in unconscious processes, how ecological issues were experienced and negotiated and what may inform the appearance of 'apathy' (e.g. a flatness or absence of caring or concern), I conducted three in-depth interviews with 10 participants, using interviews of approximately one hour each. The interviews would be conducted in their homes, ideally, and digitally recorded. In addition to the interviewing process, I would reside in Green Bay for two months and 'immerse' myself as much as possible in the local community; I arranged to stay with the owner's mother of a local and popular coffeehouse, who had a room for rent, and followed up on the contacts I had made during my field site visit. I now present the specific components of the fieldwork, data collection and how I went about designing and conducting the data collection.[4]

Participants: Survey, selection and logistics

I designed a basic online (web-based) survey to use for the initial screening of prospective participants (see Appendix C), to be emailed to people within 20 miles of Green Bay. The database included Internet and phone participants, so it was sent to *Internet participants only*, a total of 1067 receiving the survey. We received 163 responses for a response rate of 15.3%. A 'drawing' of three prizes, valued at $20 each, provided incentive for completing the survey (a standard practice with market research firms) and potentially increase the response rate. The survey was designed with 'screening questions' to screen suitable participants and fulfilled multiple functions: in introducing a survey instrument, I was able to generate a valuable second set of data to correspond with the interview material as I saw fit. Further, the data set generated by the survey tool provided a useful screening for selecting suitable participants for the interviews (the 'target population'), the 'quota' or sample size from the target population. The survey was designed with three basic types of questions: multiple-choice, numeric open-end and text open-end ('verbatims') and included an opening letter that included consent to be contacted for interviews in completing the survey. Included in the multiple-choice questions, I used rating scales and agreement scales (see Appendix C). The survey was designed with the primary intention of gauging levels of environmental concern, engagement, literacy (knowledge of issues) and verbal acuity (provided through the use of text open-end, or verbatim, questions).

From the 163 survey respondents, I reviewed the responses in light of both of how they rated their own level of concern regarding environmental issues and, in particular, the rating scale used to measure how *frequently* they thought about environmental issues, also referred to as the frequency scale (see Appendix E). My goal was to select participants who might be perceived by active environmentalists or public opinion researchers as apathetic or not caring; the group I interviewed is not a 'sample' in the sense of being representative of a larger group. Priorities were depth as opposed to 'breadth' and microanalysis as opposed to generalizations regarding a particular demographic. I wanted to talk with people who may be easily overlooked as being either too preoccupied with personal concerns for environmental matters or who may literally not care as much about nature or the environment as those who were actively occupying positions of 'agency' in recognizably 'good' ways (e.g. part of a local nature group, involved with environmental protection campaigns and the like.) I was drawn to those in working-class or 'labour' categories, as likely subjects to be constructed as lacking concern or as being 'apathetic' based low levels of environmental engagement and tended to rule out professionals or higher-educated individuals (who tend to be more liberal and progressive; this is supported in the analysis of 'frequency' responses in Appendix E). As such, the criteria included eliminating any participants who were actively involved in any environmental groups, activities, educational efforts or activism. I wanted to go into the 'eye of the storm' and meet with those who either expressed a moderate to low level of conscious thought regarding environmental issues or, in the case of two participants, expressed 'frequent' thought of environmental issues but not engaged in any recognizable activities, e.g. restoration or local environmental groups (see Appendix E).

How we interview matters

As Hendin, Gaylin and Carr (1966) note:

> The information elicited by the usual interviewing procedures, even when conducted by trained observers, is of limited value and can be misleading. The answers to questions usually reflect what the subject wants to feel, thinks he feels, or thinks he is expected to feel. As psychoanalysis has demonstrated, individuals are not consciously aware of most of the significant attitudes and dynamic patterns shaping their thinking and behavior.
>
> (p. 1)

When considering the increasing relevance of studies concerning public engagement with chronic ecological issues, including climate change, for policy decisions and public marketing campaigns, using an approach informed by psychoanalytic practice – based on free associations, unconscious reactions, dreams, fantasies, attention to object relations, desires and defences – arguably widens the spectrum of knowledge production, even given its limits and cautionary aspects (as discussed later in this chapter).

There are two key points of overlap between the therapeutic and research contexts to signal, before discussing the research interviews and the specific issues and considerations involved. First, much is made of the fact that in treatment contexts, the 'patient' or client has sought out the encounter, as opposed to being recruited by the psychotherapist or analyst (as in the research context) (e.g. see Cartwright, 2002, pp. 215–216). The context for psychoanalytic treatment is marked by the mutual objectives of facilitating a process of healing, development and support, regardless of the analytic persuasion (e.g. relational, Lacanian, etc.) The production of case studies for publication is a dimension of therapeutic work that is often not mentioned, suggesting a potential valorization of the therapeutic encounter as entirely focused on the well-being of the patient; in fact, much psychoanalytic theory is based largely on the presentation of detailed case studies, in which the therapist is often constructed as wise, effective and innovative (e.g. see Frosh, 1997; Miller & Rose, 1994). Thus the boundaries between how the material generated through the encounters is perhaps more blurred than we tend to assume. Secondly, while there is a frequent emphasis on the fact that in treatment patients are choosing to see the therapist, there is an oft overlooked aspect of unconscious motivations on the part of the participants for choosing to engage in the interviews. I was aware of this factor in the production of the survey, consideration of who would elect to complete the survey (investing the time and energy) and the level of thoughtfulness reflected in some of the responses; the willingness to participate in three one-hour interviews was a level of commitment that reflected perhaps the presence of certain motivations or desires evoked by an invitation to participate (of which the survey was the first step).

The interviews were conducted very specifically according to the psychoanalytic and qualitative principles previously discussed. In conducting three interviews, I was creating a context through which much terrain could be covered in a very open, unstructured way. This would facilitate both free associations, which felt important for me in terms of tracking unconscious material and affect, as well as rapport, trust and a sense of safety or containment (to be discussed). As I will describe, each interview was conducted with these principles in mind: a sense of spaciousness and enquiry, mutual engagement in particular topics (a sense of mutual exploration and dialogue), containment in terms of safety and rapport, and active, attentive listening. Each interview, however, progressively narrowed in scope; whilst the first interview was conceived as casting the 'big net' with the opening SQUIN, the second interview would follow up the 'footsteps in the snow' with both feeding back ('what I heard') and requests for elaboration or clarification, and the final interview inevitably became the most focused on the topic – the environment and water, generally – as I presented both gentle interpretations or confrontations, and the incorporation of the advert at the end bringing together many of the disparate themes we may have touched on throughout the three interviews. Therefore, each interview was viewed as having a specific function in relation to the whole set, and the use of the advert at the end was deliberately employed as a 'focusing device' and prompt, the most specific acknowledgement of the topic thus far in the three interviews. In this sense I was able to 'push' the topic forward whilst using an advert to carry this function. This is important relationally and dialogically in that the participants were then responding *to the advert* and not to me if I had asked a rather frontal or direct question regarding their feelings about ecological threats facing the Great Lakes.

Trust, rapport and containment

As noted, the context of the research interview is significant and raises several issues with regard to the issue of emotional safety, trust and disclosure. As in the analytic setting, where the fixed frame and the formation of a constant long-term relationship minimize the extent to which extraneous factors impinge on the relationship, it is a relatively stable context and makes it easier to isolate the context around which associations are organized (Cartwright, 2002, p. 220). Thus the onus is on the researcher to provide as much stability and containment as possible in the conduct of psychoanalytically informed, in-depth interviews. I was acutely sensitive to this as both a research and ethical concern. The initiation of the relationship in my view was in participating electively in the online survey. Therefore, I was conscious of both the language used in the opening 'blurb' and the way the questions were framed in the survey itself, as inviting and non-confrontational. The consent form, used in accordance with the Cardiff School of Social Sciences Research Ethics Committee, initiated the trust and rapport building. In making the research topic known enough to inform the participant of the general area of research but without providing too much detail as to skew their responses, I aimed to cultivate respect and trust.

There were three central practices for creating a relative sense of containment, in the sense of providing a space to 'hold' the participant and whatever material or emotions were to arise. The first was my initial preamble, in which I let the participant know of the 'style' of the interview, the comment that they were encouraged to speak on whatever comes to mind and to let me know if at any point they wished to stop or ask a question. In orienting the participants to the unusual style of the interview (most were anticipating a set series of questions, i.e. a structured interview), I began to help set them at ease by talking through how the interviews would be conducted and how this process may be different from what they have encountered previously. I also asked if they had any questions or concerns before we got started. I found it very important to let the participant know I was interested in her or his own thoughts about the topic (of environment, water, etc.). I would also make it very clear I was interested in also hearing about anything participants might want to tell me about their life or background, even if it may appear as 'off topic' – I often used the analogy of there being no 'trail' to depart from, but rather the whole 'field' was valuable. I did this to ensure that the participant felt relatively at ease to speak freely, and, most important, I would encourage participants to start wherever they felt like. If this was with specific literal memories of their childhood home, excursions into nature, or direct references to the river or the lakes, it was all encouraged as valuable and relevant.

The second technique for cultivating safety and rapport was the practice of active listening and feeding back (as previously discussed). In the activity of 'feeding back' what I had heard, I was letting the participants know they were being listened to. This in itself I found had profound implications, and participants seemed quite encouraged once they realized I was paying attention to material they may have felt would be either irrelevant or mundane. Specifically, prior to each interview subsequent to the first, I would listen to the digital recording right before the next interview and recount certain topics or details that had struck me as particularly interesting or relevant. This practice, which I had consciously initiated help *me* with recall and with following up on the most pertinent points, ended up performing a dual function of fostering trust and rapport. I could almost visibly see participants relax as they comprehended their words had been recalled and considered. As part of this practice, I would always ask participants if anything had arisen since our last meeting that they wished to speak about or that raised concerns, or if they had any questions about any aspects of the process. Third, if any material was evoked that seemed to pose potentially painful emotions, I would ensure they were comfortable with the interview and with continuing; I would then follow up in the next interview meeting with enquiring how they were doing (in light of what had transpired).

For example, in my first interview with Victoria (where I was 'trying out' the FANI approach, using six questions modelled after Hollway and Jefferson's study [2000]), she spoke about topics of great pain, particularly her anxieties about divorce in her family and community. She spoke of the breakdown of her relationship with her father, who had started a new relationship soon after her mother died (which she related to being "like a divorce"). She ended up bursting into tears, and I 'held the space' and let her cry; when we met for the second interview, the first thing I asked was if she was okay with what had happened (she seemed, frankly, quite relieved to have gotten it off her chest and surprisingly unself-conscious). In addition to responding with empathy when possible, I approached the activity of providing 'containment' (Bion, 1962) as existing on a spectrum depending on the dynamic with the participant, from active engagement to listening, e.g. listening so that the participant felt understood as a form of 'containment', to being attuned to the affective mood in the room and how best I could respond in the moment-to-moment interaction. Interpretations in the context of the interview were used cautiously, often supporting the mood of 'containment', e.g. the participants either confirming ("That's very perceptive of you") or correcting but in the spirit of intersubjective meaning ("Yes and no, let me tell you what I am feeling or thinking"). How I approached the practice of containment was centrally about cultivating a mood of receptivity, so that I could 'take in' and create a mental space for the participant's experiences, including any anxieties they may have regarding the research interview.

As discussed, one of the assumptions underlying the project and the approach to methodology concerns subjectivity – the construction of meaning, what constitutes psychoanalytic knowledge and how this may have informed the way we approach the issue of environmental concern, engagement and 'apathy'. This relates to how the interviewer and participant, or interviewee, co-construct a narrative around a particular focus in the interview. In this sense, the interview is not about uncovering an essential truth or mining for 'stories' as reflected in the BNIM approach, but about facilitating the construction of a story or narrative (Cartwright, 2002, p. 217). This point concerns how narrative is engaged and approached; Cartwright cites Spence (1982), who holds that historical truth is impossible to access after the fact, as it is subject to numerous interpretations and revisions. This view is in alignment with a psychoanalytic *and* psychosocial theoretical purview, informed by poststructural thought, that challenges the quest for essential 'structures of meaning' and that presumes a filtering or lens through which we engage with the world from our particular subject positions. This recognition does not preclude the conduct of meaningful empirical research and insights but requires considerations of *how* the self reconstructs a particular happening, more than a concern regarding factuality, as well as the role of the researcher's own subjectivity, influence on the data and interpretation. Further, how the researcher best facilitates the process in the interview encounter becomes an important part of the interview technique (Spence, 1982). In the following discussion, I highlight four characteristics of the interview approach in light of these epistemic assumptions: taking a dialogic approach (in recognition of the co-construction of meaning and narratives); facilitating trust, rapport and containment (in relation to the capacity for participants to free-associate and feel 'held'); the recognition of 'objects', both internal and external, as arising in the interviews (engaging object relations as central expressions of unconscious processes and psychosocial dynamics); and the importance of attending to my own inchoate transference and countertransference impressions.

Balancing dialogic and free-associative dynamics in the interviews

There appears to be a tension with regard to preserving elements of free association, as engaged in psychoanalytic practice (in which the patient or client is enabled, through the 'abstinence' of the analyst and the sense of containment, to free-associate) and a dialogic, relational approach in the research interview method. While I wish the participants to free-associate openly, so that I may be more able to trace and track core narratives that help provide certain threads of meanings (to be discussed), I also want them to be able to address the topic at hand. The balance I strove for was between active, dialogic interviewing and providing the participants space to free-associate in response either to my questions, reflections or prompts or to perhaps another variable, such as the experience completing the survey and any associations that may have been stirred, the language in the consent form (to be discussed), my presence as an academic or researcher or any number of projections that may have been elicited. Free association where the analyst (researcher) sits back, remains primarily silent and allows the patient (participant) to say whatever comes to mind is clearly not possible or desired in the research interview: the encounter is already framed and contextualized by the research focus, topic and whatever the participant may know of the study. Cartwright (2004) notes:

> Making it very clear to the interviewees what the specific subject of the interview is serves not only to inform them about why they were selected; it also provides the central context around which they are urged to associate (consciously and unconsciously). From this point I am interested in how the interviewee chooses to start and where this eventually leads. In other words, we are interested in the emergent structure or 'shape' of the narrative here. I see my role at this point as simply being a facilitator of the process, making mental notes of evoked feeling states and any difficulties in accessing some degree of empathy toward the interviewee.
>
> (p. 224)

The emphasis in using free-association style and dialogic interviewing is on the *way* in which meanings are produced and constructed, with particular attention to affective themes, repetitions of certain topics or themes, and on the way in which the participant moves between topics or ideas as conveying unconscious processes or motivations. As will be discussed, the attention to object relations, both internal and external, shifts the emphasis and focus of the discourse, to be less precious perhaps regarding the nature of what is said, in what form.[5] Attention is given to broad core themes, object relations, evidence of conflict, ambivalence, or contradiction, affect and countertransference in the encounter. Therefore, the emphasis was not on capturing concrete moments (particular incident narratives) as crystallizations of psychic and social life but on the way the self constructs meaning or organizes associations to create narratives (e.g. Schafer, 1967). This view contrasts with the more positivist tendency in qualitative research that presume an existence of a 'fixed deep structure' that the interviewer sets out to excavate from the material. For these reasons, as discussed, I used the opening prompt, "Tell me about where you grew up. You can start anywhere, and say whatever comes to mind."

The question was broad and expansive enough to allow participants to 'roam' – e.g. answering the question literally, going straight to environmental issues and so on – and worked dialectically with the *consent form* (to be discussed). The ethical consent form both fulfilled the mandates of the ethical consent process and also constituted part of the interview process as an important object and discourse from which free association could take place, as Cartwright noted at the beginning of this section. I did not want to ask explicitly and straight-forwardly about environmental problems: a decision based on the theoretical assumption regarding unconscious defences (asking frontal questions would not necessarily elicit fruitful responses) and the underpinning *ethos* of the project that assumes how people engage with environmental issues must be seen in the widest context of both intrapsychic and interpsychic dynamics, social and psyche, internal and external object relations, and affective investments which may have no apparent 'rhyme or reason'.

While I endeavoured to give the participant as much space as possible for free associating (at times more successfully than at others), I would openly engage in questions, clarifications and occasionally steer the discussion further into a par-ticular theme or topic. What I did do was to note, very carefully and with great detail, what themes and topics arose in the interview and in what order; follow-ing the interview, I would listen to the digital recording and partially transcribe and note the pattern, if any, of themes that emerged through the interview. Prior to the second interview, I would listen again to the interview to 'refresh' my recollection and to enter with great recall of many detailed accounts from our previous session. This practice fulfilled a vital function: it allowed me to pay close attention to "repetitive narrative structures" as mirroring more consistent and prominent factors contributing–to the intrapsychic life of the individual (Cartwright, 2002, p. 218). In not disturbing the 'footprints in the snow' of the ordering of narrative content and themes, I could preserve a semblance of the free associations and their possible meanings. As Cartwright notes:

> Psychoanalysis is particularly interested in implicit forms of association. Here the idea that thoughts are associated with one another through unconscious forms of psychic determinism holds great importance for understanding the interview dialogue. The way the interviewee begins to tell me about him- or herself and then changes to another subject at a specific point, how the interviewer's tone of voice alters in association with particular subjects, and how things are described in different ways – all of these suggest possible ways in which elements of the dialogue are unconsciously associated. This in term yields an underlying structure that can be used to understand the intrapsyshic processes most apparent in the interview material related to the topic being discussed.
>
> (p. 219)

Therefore, I used prompts (observations) and questions for facilitating free association in the interviews. In returning to the subsequent interviews, I would raise points only in the order in which they arose (e.g. tracing the *gestalt* of the participants' associations). I also took a more actively dialogic approach than practised in BNIM and FANI, as discussed above. I practised this in the fol-lowing ways: first, at the start of the second and third interviews, I would 'feed back' to the participant what I had 'heard' in the previous session, based on my reviews of the material and my own note taking. I would be as detailed as possible both to freshen the participant's recollection of what had transpired as well as to communicate implicitly the level of my attention and listening (this relates to the point to come regarding trust, rapport and containment). I would then share what aspects of points struck me as particularly interesting, moving, provocative or unclear and ask the participant to expand on these points (in the order in which they had arisen in the previous session). Second, I would share with the participant my own impressions in the context of the interview, such as "That sounds painful to me", to elicit further expansion but also to 'check' my impressions with the participant's version of events or reality. Third, I would occasionally make 'interventions' in the psychoanalytic sense of confronting the participant, as gently as possible, with possible contradictions or incoherence that arose in the interviews; I practised this with great care and with some trepidation and only in the final interview session. As indicated by relational researchers and analysts Stopford (2004) and Jiminez and Walkerdine (2011), the practice of conducting this sort of intervention is central to both leveraging the opportunity for exploring previously unconscious processes and, out of respect for the participants; to not assume that the researcher 'knows best' and can be trusted to have an accurate understanding or account of what is being communicated. This aspect of a dialogic approach is arguably quite central to a *relational* approach of conducting qualitative research interviews. While I adhere to the notion of the defended subject (Hollway & Jefferson, 2000) (as well as of the 'defended researcher') and assume how people respond to such interventions or feeding back may not be taken at face value, I maintained that whatever response *did* arise (even if 'defended') was valuable and informative. Again, this is due to the epistemic assumption regarding the construction of meanings in narrative and less of a concern for uncovering a form of 'essential' truth, as if there is a fixed 'truth' to be accessed through the research process.

I felt able to do this largely because I was not seeking to capture some sort of essential version of the participant's reality and had a fundamentally relational view of the research encounter – that all research is an expression of both the investigators desires, intentions and unconscious processes and that what evolves in the research encounter is co-produced and mutually constitutive. In other words, my subjectivity, intentions, desires and phantasies were *already present* in both the initial phone calls to set up the interviews, the survey, the consent form and the way I conducted myself in the interviews. There was no point in maintaining an illusion, in my view, that I was somehow absent from the interaction.

Dialogic approach: Interviewer as active participant

I now provide two examples from the data of this dialogic approach: an interaction with Sally on the topic of 'save the whales' (see Appendix B) and another with Donald on the topic of his father's accident and dismissal from the paper mill. The vignettes illustrate in various forms the 'active' role I took in my interviewer capacity. First, in my interviews with Sally, the topic of her earlier involvement with the whales arose in the second interview. Sensing possible complex affective relations with this topic and her foray into environmental activism, I enquired explicitly, in the third and final interview, as to what emotions may arise for her in considering this. Provocatively, I raise the topic of 'loss'; this reflects the practice of sharing my own reflections (and countertransference) with the participant, as well as making quite transparent my own possible projections. (An ellipsis within brackets, [. . .], indicates a pause, not an elision.)

S: [Laughing] After you left, I was rather, um, I thought about it a lot after you left the last time.

R: About what?

S: All the different things I talked about. I hadn't thought about Save the Whales in years and I still, like I said I still have three of those cards that you can, and you know, it's just really nice cards with envelopes you can mail out, I think I may even still have the T-shirt, and all the different environmental issues that came up, that I remembered, it was [. . .] interesting to remember them all. And just, be that animated about it because, when you can't do anything about it, a lot of times, after a while, it's just, yeah, okay. Well there's nothing I can do. And, like for example, with the water 30 years later they are saying get going, there's nothing I can do in that 30 years. You know. So, sometimes you can just watch and see how things happen and what, what happens. So it was kind of, um . . . fun to touch back on that, how [. . .] intense I was at one point with the Save the Whales thing. And all the environmental stuff. And over the years you just kind of realize there's nothing you can do and you just go on, so it was, kind of um,

R: What does it mean to you that you were once passionate about those issues?

S: Hmm! Somebody once said when you're young you need to have a heart, and when you're older, you need to be able to you know, have heart, be passionate over those things when you're young because when you're older your priorities change a bit, and as you're, in your 50s to 60s you start thinking more about retirement, and how you're going to live out your final years, things like that, and if you can help out you do. But on the whole, your priorities change. So. Um. It was [. . .] actually, I was glad. I mean everybody knew about the Save the Whales thing, I mean, my family thought it was hilarious that I would just, [laughing] get into that. But, it um, I don't know. It brought back good memories. I don't know if that's answering your question or not.

R: Yeah. Well, I guess I'm wondering, how, what it means to look back and to see that you were once really engaged with those things. And, um, I mean I hear you saying that you kind of have to move on, at a certain point. And realize –

S: – yes.

R: What you can and can't do. But that's kind of like, um, that's, that's analyzing it, um, from your perspective now. Whereas, um, I guess when I ask what does it mean for you, when you look at yourself as a younger person –

S: Hmm hmm

R: Really passionate and, really um, yeah I guess, I guess I'm wondering what feelings come up around that. Um, if you feel maybe, like it, do you feel you lost something, or –

S: Yes and no. Because, [. . .] when you're young and you're not exactly sure which direction your life is going to go, how you're going to go, what your calling is in life, I guess calling, I don't know if calling is the right word, but what your abilities [. . .] are, and where you can make the difference. Um. You look, you know when you're young you're just kind of looking at everything trying to figure out where do I fit into this whole, where's my path, where's my [. . .] thing and that was it for a little bit, but as I got more into the music that consumed more of my time. So priorities changed, because of, with music there's practice, and there's rehearsals, you know there's performance, things like that. So priorities [. . .] Knowing that I have the ability to do different musical things, I can play guitar, I can play viola, I can sing, and [. . .] having those abilities, not using those and focusing on total environment things, is not a good use of the talents and the abilities that I have. And there are other people who, [. . .] don't have those talents or not willing, it's not their passion. Music is my passion. So I think over the years, it just, it was a matter of, the music taking over more and more of my time.

R: Hmm hmm. [. . .] And did you find you thought about environmental things less? As you became more focused on other things?

S: Not so much less, but you pay attention, you read it like I would have read the article and I would have looked at it and saying, I hope they start it soon. I hope they really don't let them out of it. I hope you know, that they will follow through and really make them do it this time. And that's about as far as this time, and otherwise it would go. Because there's nothing I can do.

In this exchange, my questioning and reflections prompts Sally to free-associate in her attempt to 'meet me' and communicate her experiences and reflections. She both corrects me – "Yes and no" – and uses the questioning as a springboard into a series of associations I never could have anticipated. What matters here is not so much if I am 'correct' or 'incorrect' in my perceptions – e.g. "Um, if you feel maybe, like it, do you feel you lost something", whether Sally feels she lost something – but in the way in which she responds to the prompt. The vignette is also an example of a subtle form of 'intervention' and confrontation, in that Sally begins the topic laughing, with a sort of jovial quality, which I then sought to 'confront' by asking her about loss. I was resisting her tendency to present material in a light and joking manner, suspecting this was in fact a form of defence against potentially distressing emotions (I address this sensitive aspect of intervention in the ethics discussion to follow). What is also observed is the repetition of a 'core theme' (an element of the analysis, to be discussed) concerning her sense of agency; "there's nothing I can do" appears throughout the three interviews, in varying contexts, but largely in relation to ecological problems. The ability to observe these repetitions would not be possible through conducting a structured or even semi-structured interview, as the researcher may entirely miss areas of potential importance for the participant. In a dialogic, free-associative style interview, there is enough structure to facilitate a meaningful exchange but also enough spaciousness to enable tangents, memories, flashbacks, joking and so on.

In the example with Donald, during the first interview I present him with my response to a story about his father's accident and dismissal from his job at midlife (discussed in the case study, Appendix B). I observed a contrast with the content of the story and the affective tenor with which he relayed it. I sought to both 'test' my perceptions and 'prompt' him potentially to disclose more of his experiences of these events as part of the larger picture regarding his relations with Green Bay, industry and environmental degradation, via the accident his father had in the paper mill. The excerpt picks up while Donald is recounting his own career trajectory and a close brush with working for the paper mill.

D: So thank god, they had that policy at the paper company, I probably would have ended up like my father, working in a job, in a paper mill [. . .]

R: What would that mean for you?

D: That would mean just mean that I would, I would have a . . . middle income job, probably wouldn't have been feeling as fulfilled as I do today after spending an entire life in more of a management position, and um, who knows, if I would have been [. . .] I may have been so frustrated, just working in menial labour jobs, I would have . . . Lord knows what would have happened [laughs] I have no ideal. So having the opportunity number one to get the education that I did, to get me into more a white collar job, and then secondarily having the opportunity to learn a business, in a small company, thoroughly learn a business, gave me just a great opportunity to move into other areas of food processing business, where I fit, and enjoy my career and . . . uh did OK financially. And so . . . was able to provide my family and myself with a comfortable living, and I provided all of my children with an opportunity for education. So. [. . .]

R: I am kind of interested in what happened [. . .] to your dad [. . .] Because it sounds, uh, quite traumatic actually. And, I'm just curious, how that affected [. . .] maybe, some of the choices you made, as well as how you experienced that industry, and it seemed to affect him, and I am surprised to hear that he went back to work in paper [. . .]

D: Well, uh, you're very perceptive, that was a very, very traumatic time. The man put in, he started with the paper company right out of high school, and that was [. . .] his entire education, high school diploma. And he [. . .] Fort

Howard Paper Company was one of the very good companies to work for in Green Bay, it was a non-union operation, and was up until the day they stopped being Fort Howard. But they, they did that, or kept themselves non-union by paying good wages, and keeping their people reasonably happy, so they didn't have anybody upset, and trying to push a union into the operation. By the same token, they had no protection, the workers had no protection from some of the decisions, some of the things that management did. So when dad was hurt, I can, I can remember, again I was just a young man at that time, I was in high school, and after he had gotten out of the hospital, he was confined to his bed for a number of months, and a couple of times executives from the mill would come and talk to him, and say don't worry about a thing, we will take care of everything, and I think financially they paid for his medical bills, for workman's compensation for his injuries and I don't know what kind of deal they gave him for his salary, I never paid any attention to that, but nevertheless he went back to work for them [. . .] and [. . .] I don't think any of us know what happened, including my dad [. . .] they just fired him. They just told him, he no longer had a job. And it was so soon after he came back, that it was just, just a weird, way for professionals to treat somebody, that was injured while he was doing his job. And you know, when I look back on that, I don't think that could happen today, they couldn't get away with pushing somebody out the door just because he had been injured. [Umm hmmm] So you know, it, it just . . . practically destroyed the man. Because that was the only thing that he did in his life, and then he had to go and try to find work [. . .] and it was almost like he was black-balled, as I tried to explain, if you were fired from Fort Howard, you must really be a problem guy, and no other paper company would hire him. He had applied to all of the paper companies up and down the valley and simply couldn't find anything. So [. . .] he had to take [. . .] after [. . .] he went to vocational school to try to get some other training for himself, but needed a job, so he went down to Kanosha, and my mother and his family, his family, this is right when I was married, and moved out of the house, but he had three daughters at home, they all stayed back in Green Bay, and he was down in Kenosha, and commuting once and a while to see his family [. . .] you know, it was a tough, three years I think he worked down there, and then he, he moved back into upper Northeast Wisconsin, and that's when he found this job at a paper mill in Nina Wisconsin. And he moved his family down to Nina then. So it was a tough time, it was a real tough time for [. . .] he and his marriage, and his family, and everything, just because of the separation, and uh, his inability to find a job that was meaningful and fulfilling for him. And uh, it was a very difficult, very difficult time.

In this vignette, we can see how the question posed to Donald is also a form of free association on my part; I share my impression of the story as "quite traumatic" but then continue to free-associate, perhaps reflecting my collusion with

Donald to skirt around the traumatic nature of the story. He responds primarily to my comment regarding the traumatic aspect of the events and his detailing of *how* traumatic and "very difficult" it actually was for his father and the family. He does not address the comment regarding career decisions, although he does return to this a bit later in acknowledging the events may have had a "subconscious" effect on his decisions.

The balance between free association and dialogic interviewing is held in place through the understanding and location of the context, internal or interactional, around which associations are organized (Cartwright, 2002, p. 219). In approaching how free associations constitute certain forms of narrative and 'core themes', it is not enough to pay attention to the ordering of certain topics or memories; rather, naturally the ordering and language used in my questions and reflections help shape what is shared. In this sense, the interviews are viewed as mutually produced and context specific. As Benjamin (2004) has noted in her work on the intersubjective space produced through the interaction between two individuals, addressing the conceptual division between the 'doer' and the 'done to', I occupied my role in the interviews quite actively. I was both the 'doer' and the 'done to'. In order to accomplish this successfully, I had to attend fully to issues of trust, rapport and containment, so that both participant and myself felt adequately safe to come together and share rather intimate discussions over the course of three hours.

The "Girl on the Beach" Healing Our Waters advert

Given the context of the research support through Biodiversity Project and in connection with the Wege Foundation, sponsors of the *Healing Our Waters* (HOW) initiative, I wanted to incorporate an element of HOW into the research. I introduced the advert, "Girl on the Beach", a magazine print ad that had run in Wisconsin magazines a few months prior in the summer, as a prompt for free association, at the end of the final interview (see Figure 1.3). The decision to bring in the advert at the end of the three sessions was the sense that enough trust and rapport may have developed to foster a frank and candid discussion; I hoped more affective disclosure may be possible as a result. The image also served a dual purpose of providing a highly effective prompt for the topic of environmental action, identity and concern, without my needing to enquire directly or 'frontally' about it. In many cases, the advert was a spur to expand on themes or topics that had arisen in the course of the three interviews, pertinent to environmental issues. The advert was an effective tool for introducing the topic of the Great Lakes. I was careful to present the image with a disclosure to indicate that I was not involved in the production or use of the advert, so they could speak as openly as they wanted. Only in one case, did one participant (Sally) take interest in the advert and request to record the details.[6] Finally, as I had viewed focus group video footage of groups discussing this advert, as part of Biodiversity Project's work for HOW in 2006, incorporating the advert at the end of three in-depth interviews provided a useful contrast to the quality of discourse prompted in the context of a highly structured, facilitated focus group and a more free-form style dialogic interview.

Scones, brownies and cats: Objects in the room

The incorporation of material and psychic objects into the data translates into a methodological practice of maintaining curiosity for how certain objects carry and hold meanings, are repositories but also agents that can act upon our subjectivity as well (an attitude of mutuality and recognition of the agency of objects – and particularly how they arise, and how we use them – in our world) (Bollas, 1992). While not a central focus in the data and interview process, I took note of how certain objects were engaged in the interviews by the participants and myself. As I discuss in Chapter 5, certain object relations provide indications of *reparation* that may fall under the radar for 'agency'. Such objects included animals, food, drinks and various artefacts presented (maps, photographs, artwork, books etc). For a few participants, pets were a continual presence in the home and the interview space. I would often interact with the animals to pet, talk to or otherwise alleviate my own anxieties, particularly at the beginning of conducting the interviews. Sally, for example, had two cats, and often we would break into a discussion of them; I noticed at certain opportune moments, Sally would suddenly break off topic and start addressing the cats. (I regarded this as a moment of 'changing the subject' and noteworthy in terms of what it suggested about the topic and possible issues raised.) The cats also served as a common language between us, as fellow 'cat lovers', and they helped put me at ease. During my first interview with Jeff, his dog Rudy kept poking his head in my lap, which caused much amusement. With Kerry, I had a strong sense of how her animals – a cat and a dog – were functioning in relation to the core narratives presenting in the interviews, particularly around loss of a sense of home and hearth, a childhood place on the farm where animals were a part of life. So the animals in this sense seemed transformational objects, connecting her to particular affective relations and investments, and coloured how I engaged with the material.

Various artefacts surfaced in the interviews, contributing to the research encounter. Jeff, for example, pulled out maps of the region and his hometown of Sheboygan in our first interview; later, he brought down from the attic copies of a university report and exams from an environmental studies course in 1972, and he subsequently gave me copies. This object clearly had significance for Jeff (as I discuss in Chapter 6, regarding expressions of creativity and concern). Howard brought out family photograph albums and black-and-white photographs he had taken of the Fox River decades ago. (Howard has since, over a year after the interviews took place, emailed me several black-and-white aerial photographs taken of his childhood home on the Fox River.) The ways in which objects were employed to communicate or convey specific meanings, affects or associations was profoundly important for a holistic, more 'environmental' approach to the data, going 'beyond the text' and discourse to appreciate the materiality of the topic and how affect circulates through things (as relations), as well as language, bodily sensation and metaphor.

An additional dimension regarding objects and their significance relationally was through the use of food or refreshments. I noticed when participants offered me tea, coffee or something to eat and when they did not.[7] I also found myself wanting to bring an offering of some kind, perhaps out of my desire to say 'thank you' for their time and energy but also undoubtedly out of an impulse to share something of myself with them, to introduce a sense of reciprocity within the constraints of the interview encounter. During my first interviews with Jeff, I brought scones from the local bakery, which his wife served with great pleasure with a special kind of tea (which they seemed to take great pleasure in doing). The scones and tea became a 'ritual' even though we met only three times; after the three interviews were completed, they invited me to their home for 'afternoon tea' before I left Green Bay, to which I brought the scones and they served the tea. The desire to share food became even more pronounced when I brought a bag of pastries from a Greek bakery to Howard, one of the participants I felt most moved and affected by through our interactions. I brought Howard *rugelach*, a Middle Eastern pastry that is also popular in Jewish culture. I also brought him a brownie, a specialty of the bakery, along with a scone or two. In this sheer abundance of pastries for Howard, I could witness quite clearly something *I* was trying to communicate or share through the use of food. My encounters with him and the material generated had seemed to evoke a maternal instinct to 'care' for him, through the use of food (nourishment). I also desired to share something of 'me' through pastries from a bakery he would never normally visit and pastries from my culture. We also had them together, so there was the additional sense of 'breaking bread' in a ritualistic way. In feeling touched by Howard's narratives, energy and presence, I was moved to share something of myself and to 'gift' him. The integration of objects also extended to the method of analysis, in attending to material objects in the context of the interviews – the interiors of homes, how they were decorated, if they had views of the water, their proximity to the water – that contributed to the data analysis as constituting environments, both imagined and actual.

Relationships

Relationships within the interview process are an important consideration within ethical research practice (Lincoln & Guba, 1985). I positioned myself in Chapter 1 within an ethic of relatedness where attentiveness and reciprocity are important dynamics in any relationships. This was particularly evident as the study was 'shortitudinal' in design, collecting data over two months spent *in situ* in Green Bay. I found participants were often interested in my story, the nature of the study and remembered events between interviews. Often, as was discussed, people would share physical materials with me relating to the water,

Figure 3.2 A daily run on the Fox River Health Trail, Green Bay, November 2007. (Printed with permission by J. Galt.)

Great Lakes or region, such as family photograph albums, artwork, maps, university reports, childhood books and, in one case, the contents of her freezer (to show me her organic, locally sourced meat). (See Figure 3.2.) Setting up the interviews also elicited data; one participant was so eager to do the interviews, she rang me when I had neglected to follow up after a few days and chatted at length about her interest in the study and suggested her parents may want to participant too. Closures for interviews were important moments and at times quite difficult to negotiate as a connection and relationship had been formed. Some people encouraged me to look them up in my future visits (Jeff and his wife Jane), and others seemed content with wishing me and the research well. There is a reciprocity to in-depth interviewing; the relational dialogic approach only strengthened this (Holloway & Freshwater, 2007; Wenger, McDermott & Snyder, 2002).

Reflections on strengths and limitations of the methodology

As discussed, the activity of researching unconscious processes presents a formidable challenge for the qualitative, social science researcher. In contrast to attending to what can be easily observed and tracked, this process relies more on several complex and at times tenuous variables regarding how to design, conduct and analyse the research data. There are many 'choice points' along the way, regarding specific interviewing methodologies and theoretical frameworks, scope and focus of the data collection, ethical considerations and the thorny issue of interpretation and incorporating the subjectivity of the researcher.

In light of these challenges, the research design enabled the exploration of how to investigate unconscious processes, and engaging in a psychoanalytically informed epistemology. This epistemology embraces a complex view of subjectivity that presumes irrationality, conflict, ambivalence and contradiction; it is also a view that accepts anxiety as central to human experience and is concerned with how anxieties are managed in relation to political practices and actions. The data generated through such a study therefore has the potential to bridge the political and the social domains and can potentially introduce clinical concepts that may prove highly constructive to a more complicated and grounded view of environmental subjectivity. In conducting in-depth interviews over three meetings, what transpires is an interaction fostered by trust and rapport, which can bring dignity and restore integrity to the messy and complex ways we constitute our lives. Further, in attending to object relations, both internal and external, we can begin to appreciate the need to consider how our practices and use of objects are performative, affective and meaningful and can be 'read' akin to dream analysis.

There are aspects of the method that warrant caution and present limitations. There are certain questions regarding the conduct of psychoanalytically informed research that must be addressed, e.g. the issue of training – whether it is possible to conduct this research without some form of clinical training, supervision or background. I managed to resolve the issue somewhat through the engagement of occasional clinical supervision, in addition to academic supervision; I consistently had the nagging feeling that the work would have benefited from a clinical background and perhaps training in infant observation, particularly with regard to researching affect and the inchoate dimensions of experience which may exceed the limitations of representation through language (discourse). I felt capable of conducting this research by virtue of my years spent in various forms of psychotherapy and psychoanalytic therapy, in immersion in psychoanalytic literature and as a journalist conducting dozens of in-depth interviews for magazine publishing.

The second limitation, or issue, with regard to this methodology concerns the issue of team or group work in the process of analysing and interpreting the data. There are mixed views on this issue; Cartwright (2002), for example, advocates the use of a 'triangulation' to verify and check findings in order to protect against 'wild analysis'. Hollway and Jefferson (2000) worked together as a team, and many psychosocial studies seem to employ a team model for effective analysis (e.g. Walkerdine, Lucey & Melody, 2001; Hoggett, Beedell, Jimenez, Mayo & Miller, 2006). The intentions for using teams or group work for psychoanalytic psychosocial research are important. Working with others is not an attempt to mimic or emulate some form of 'objectivity' valorized in the sciences; it can be a recognition that, when engaging with such intimate material that is inevitably going to evoke certain projections, associations or feelings due to our particular subject positions, it is beneficial to have others to share ideas and observations with. This model has long been in practice in clinical training, and infant observation training uses the small-group seminar as a foundation for clinical development. A similar approach needs to be adapted in the production of psychosocial knowledge, and the role of teams and group work cannot be underestimated.

A third limitation to this method is the labour-intensiveness. As noted, conducting in-depth interviews across three sessions was extremely intensive in terms of time, as well as mental and emotional resources. In addition to conducting the interviews comes the task of writing up and then analysing the material, which all takes huge amounts of time. In contrast to software programs that help with coding or organizing the data analysis (e.g. Atlas.ti), this is all done by hard graft and 'by hand' as it were. I cannot imagine doing the data collection and analysis any differently. What would be required for longer-term application of this approach would be the sufficient resources to allow for teams to work collaboratively and to distribute the labour, which would also then afford a greater number of participant interviews.

In investigating the topic of environmental engagement and potential 'apathy' – what is often perceived as the biggest impediment to environmental advocacy and restoration – I found, in fact, through conceptualizing this particular methodology, I was able to perceive it as predicated on complex assumptions regarding what constitutes agency, guilt, shame and lack of recognition of innate human creativity and sources of concern.[8] Throughout the research, my own epistemic orientation shifted from viewing intra-psychic and inter-psychic (and often unconscious) dilemmas, contradictions, tensions and ambivalence as *barriers* (the common parlance, reflected in the literature on engagement, as discussed in Chapter 2), to apprehending expressions or forms of environmental subjectivity that *may* or *may not* facilitate, impede or foreclose particular practices. I endeavoured to observe these dilemmas with a compassionate curiosity and to take a holistic approach to psychosocial processes as conducive to creativity, concern and care – *including* aggression, guilt, destruction and reparation (Winnicott, 1986; Winnicott & Winnicott, 1986). In so doing, my own assumptions (and frustrations) regarding 'public apathy' became clearer, primarily through active attending to *countertransference* impressions during the research, tracking my various fears, anxieties and at times dread in conducting a study in the 'heartland' of industrial United States. Embodying a psychoanalytic epistemology in relation to the research project was to ultimately transform my conceptions of conducting qualitative psychosocial research, in terms of how knowledge is generated, experienced and the task of interpretation and analysis (as discussed below). The following Part II presents in three thematic chapters, the core affective dimensions surfaced through the data.

Notes

1 As Paul Hoggett has noted, there is 'good agency' and 'bad agency:' "radical social policy has only been able to conceive of human agency in terms of its positive and optimistic dimensions . . . other forms of agency that are destructive towards others and ultimately towards self cannot find a comfortable place in radical social policy" (2009, p. 69). My particular expressions of agency in relation to environmental issues have certainly spanned the spectrum, as I have wrestled with how to come to terms with both the magnitude and related issues of scope and personal efficacy.

2 What Guatarri (1989) calls "the three ecologies".

3 The use of research groups, panels or triangulations is a central issue and point of much debate and deliberation in the evolution of psychoanalytically informed psychosocial qualitative research; I will discuss this in more depth in the final chapter, in which I review lessons learned and the potential value (and possibly requirement) of research groups or teams for effective psychoanalytic, psychosocial work that takes on board issues of unconscious processes, both in the research data and on the part of the researcher.

4 The selection of Green Bay as a field site for the research is discussed in Chapter 1.

5 The approach I used diverges from a critical discourse analysis approach; see Wetherall (2003); Gough (2009); Frosh, Phoenix & Pattman (2003) on the relations (and tensions) between a CDA approach and a psychoanalytic data analysis methodology (and Midgley, 2006, on psychoanalytic and qualitative paradigms in research). In contrast to CDA, I did not feel it necessary to conduct microanalysis on the speech utterance but rather to attend to core themes, narratives and psychodynamics, in particular object relational. I found it essential to note when pauses, abrupt change of topics, repairs, jokes and humour occurred, as indicators of unconscious dynamics (e.g. Wetherell, 2003; Billig, 1997), but the focus in this study was centred on thematic analysis. I felt it possible to integrate attention to this level of discursive phenomenon with analysis of thematic, narrative material. I do feel a microanalysis of the discourses in the interviews would yield a fruitful investigation.

6 She told me in September 2009, in response to a communication regarding the delivery of the transcripts she had requested, that she had donated to the *Healing Our Waters* project on their website.

7 In one example, a participant, Victoria, in our third interview, offered me cookies she had baked for a church charity event; my sense was perhaps she was feeling the need to 'mother' me as we discussed my distance from family over the holidays and her own sense of bereavement over her two daughters leaving home.

8 This point regarding apathy being perceived as the greatest barrier and obstacle for environmental advocacy will be picked up in the final chapter. As I was to realize later, in fact from an 'engaged' environmental subjectivity, i.e. for those who are active in their environmental commitments and passions, the labelling of inaction as 'apathy' presents indications of projection and splitting, so that apathy itself becomes the Other and those who appear to constitute an apathetic subject position are therefore demonized and Othered quite unreflexively. The 'apathetic subject' is the repository for disavowed and self-hated aspects of an inactive, uncaring or aggressive self.

References

Baumeister, R. F., Smart, L., & Boden, J. M., 1996. Relation of threatened egotism to violence and aggression: The dark side of high self-esteem. *Psychological Review* 103, pp. 5–33.

Benjamin, J., 2004. Beyond doer and done to: An intersubjective view of thirdness, *Psychoanalytic Quarterly* LXXIII, pp. 5–46.

Billig, M., 1997. The dialogic unconscious: Psychoanalysis, discursive psychology and the nature of repression, *British Journal of Social Psychology* 36, pp. 139–159.

Bion, W., 1961. *Experiences in Groups.* London: Tavistock.

Bion, W., 1962. *Learning from Experience,* London: William Heinemann [reprinted London: Karnac; reprinted in *Seven Servants,* 1977].

Bollas, C., 1992. *Being a Character: Psychoanalysis and Self Experience.* London: Routledge [reprinted 1997].

Cartwright, D., 2002. *Psychoanalysis, Violence, and Rage-type Murder: Murdering Minds.* London: Routledge.

Cartwright, D., 2004. The psychoanalytic research interview: preliminary suggestions, *The Journal of the American Psychoanalytic Association* 52, pp. 209–242.

Frosh, S., 1997. *For and Against Psychoanalysis.* East Sussex, UK: Psychology Press.

Frosh, S., Phoenix, A., & Pattman, R., 2003. Taking a stand: Using psychoanalysis to explore the positioning of subjects in discourse, *British Journal of Social Psychology* 42, pp. 39–53.

Gough, B., 2009. A psycho-discursive approach to analysing qualitative interview data, with reference to a father–son relationship, *Qualitative Research in Psychology* 9 (5), pp. 527–545.

Guattari, F., 1989. *Les trois écologies.* Ian Pindar and Paul Sutton, trans. London and New York: Continuum. Paris: Editions Galilée [2000 translation, *The Three Ecologies*].

Hendin, H., Gaylin, W., & Carr, A., 1966. *Psychoanalysis and Social Research: The Psychoanalytic Study of the Non-Patient.* New York: Doubleday Anchor Books.

Hoggett, P., 2009. *Politics, Identity and Emotion.* Boulder, CO: Paradigm.

Hoggett, P., Beedell, P., Jimenez, L., Mayo, M., & Miller, C. 2006. Identity, life history and commitment to welfare, *Journal of Social Policy* 35 (4), pp. 689–704.

Holloway, I., & Freshwater, D., 2007. *Narrative Research in Nursing.* Hoboken, NJ: Wiley-Blackwell.

Hollway, W., & Jefferson, T., 2000. *Doing Qualitative Research Differently: Free Association, Narrative and the Interview Method.* London: Sage.

Jimenez, L., & Walkerdine, V., 2011. A psychosocial approach to shame, embarrassment and melancholia amongst unemployed young men and their fathers. *Gender and Education* 23 (2), pp. 185–199.

Lertzman, R., 2012a. The myth of apathy: Psychoanalytic explorations of environmental degradation. In Weintrobe, S. (ed.), *Engaging with Climate Change: Psychoanalytic and Interdisciplinary Perspectives.* London: Routledge, pp. 117–133.

Lertzman, R., 2012b. Researching psychic dimensions of ecological degradation: Notes from the field. *Psychoanalysis, Culture & Society* 17 (1), pp. 92–101.

Lifton, R. J., 1979. *The Broken Connection: On Death and the Continuity of Life.* New York: Simon & Schuster.

Lincoln, Y. S., & Guba, E. G., 1985. *Naturalistic Inquiry.* Beverly Hills, CA: Sage.

Midgley, N., 2006. Psychoanalysis and qualitative psychology: Complementary or contradictory paradigms, *Qualitative Research in Psychology* 3, pp. 213–231.

Miller, P., & Rose, N., 1994. On therapeutic authority: Psychoanalytical expertise under advanced liberalism, *History of the Human Sciences* 7 (3), pp. 29–64.

Schafer, R., 1967. How was this story told? In Schafer, R., *Projective Testing and Psychoanalysis.* New York City: International Universities Press, pp. 114–169.

Schafer, R., 1985. Wild analysis, *Journal of American Psychoanalytic Association* 33, pp. 275–299.

Spence, D. P., 1982. *Narrative Truth and Historical Truth: Meaning and Interpretation in Psychoanalysis.* New York City: W. W. Norton.

Stopford, A., 2004. Researching postcolonial subjectivities: The application of pelational (postclassical) psychoanalysis methodology, *International Journal of Critical Psychology* 10, pp. 13–35.

Walkerdine, V., Lucey, H., & Melody, J., 2001. *Growing Up Girl: Psycho-social Explorations of Gender and Class.* London: Palgrave.

Wenger, E., McDermott, R., & Snyder, W., 2002. *Cultivating Communities of Practice: A Guide to Managing Knowledge.* Boston: Harvard Business Review Press.

Wengraf, T., 2001. *Qualitative Research Interviewing: Biographic Narrative and Semi-structured Methods.* London: Sage.

Wetherell, M., 2003. Paranoia, ambivalence and discursive practices: Concepts of position and positioning in psychoanalysis and discursive psychology. In Harre, R., & Moghaddam, F. (eds.), *The Self and Others: Positioning Individuals and Groups in Personal, Political and Cultural Contexts.* New York: Praeger/Greenwood, pp. 99–120.

Winnicott, D. W., 1986. *Holding and Interpretation.* London: The Hogarth Press & Institute of PSA; New York: Grove Press, 1987; London: Institute of Psycho-Analysis & Karnac Books, 1989.

Winnicott, D. W., & Winnicott, C., eds., 1986. *Home Is Where We Start From. Essays by a Psychoanalyst.* New York & London: W.W. Norton; Harmondsworth, UK: Penguin.

Part II

Psychic dimensions

Snowy factory, Fox River, December 2007. (Photo: R. Lertzman.)

I have strong feelings, I don't think it, it goes anywhere, I mean I just, I live with it. It's ah, it's tolerable feelings, because it's more tolerable than the other way. I don't know, I think a lot of people might do that, that would be, "yeah I don't like it but I'm not going to do anything about it because, cos I just don't feel like it". Or something like that, they might get angry about but, but yeah, I don't see it manifesting itself into anything strong. Other than just, I'll do my, what I can in my, and what I can do is what I can do, you know what I mean. And what I can't do I can't. Um, doesn't stop me from having opinions. I mean it's, it's ah, the way to get things done is to be obsessive about it, I believe in that, so the people in the organizations trying to, to get the things done for the environment have to be that way, and I don't want to become that. That's why I don't think the feelings go anywhere. And I don't think not having that feeling satisfied, um, has any detriment to me. Now if I'm wrong then okay, there's something underlying that I'm not recognizing and [laughing] I should focus on that and give it a try.

– Howard, Interview 3

Chapter 4

Loss, mourning and melancholia

Hidden dimensions of environmental subjectivity

This project arose out of my sense of powerlessness as I contemplated my own complicity and inadequate response to our ecological crises. It was born out of my environmental subjectivity as anxious, sad and concerned. However, I was simultaneously experiencing an inchoate, mute sadness in the face of rampant industrial development. Inchoate because such losses exceed the language needed to express them and mute because of the lack of socially sanctioned forms for sharing emotional responses about ecological issues. Mourning is a social process, and in the absence of sharing it, we remain stuck and our mourning in stasis (Leader, 2009, p. 155).[1] Might the affective dimensions of anxiety, loss, mourning and melancholia inform the ways in which people respond to and make sense of serious and chronic ecological issues? How can an appreciation of these complex psychic processes, individually and socially, inform how we understand environmental public participation and issues of agency?

From anxiety to apathy

I approached the interviews anticipating expressions of anxiety. My working hypothesis was that anxiety is a central affective dimension of contemporary environmental threats. This is due to scope, scale, lack of clarity regarding redress and the imbricated nature of our practices with the very issues that threaten ecological well-being. However, rather than anxiety, I found narratives of loss dominating my interviews. Immediately following my opening prompt, "Tell me about where you grew up, whatever comes to mind," unexpected stories of loss unfolded. I was surprised and curious because participants had given little to no indication in their survey responses of their strong connections with local water activities, the Great Lakes, family and general associations of childhood innocence and freedom. Moreover, I had internalized the frustrations of the local ecologists who had been taking me on tours of the area and telling stories about their ongoing and often thwarted efforts to get citizens on-board to help protect and conserve the already damaged ecosystems in the region. The environmental community in Green Bay was relatively tiny and included the team of environmental scientists housed at the University. Its marginal position only supported the sense that people were unconcerned about their local ecosystems. The construction of apathy as a viable explanation for lack of engagement is so prevalent in environmental advocacy that I presumed people had more pressing things to worry about than their environment.[2] Therefore, participants' articulations of deep sadness regarding their local environment struck me. It made me curious about the nature of the loss. What precisely was being mourned?

In order to address this foundational question, I shifted my focus from anxiety as the affective response, to a constellation of psychic and social processes that might include anxiety. Specifically, I focus in my analysis on melancholia, ambivalence and reparation. As I developed the data analysis, the picture became kaleidoscopic as the dimensions of each moved imperceptibly into one another. The shifting nature of my object of evaluation raised important analytic and methodological questions (discussed later in this chapter) and presented unique challenges to presenting a linear account of the data. What the following three chapters explore in detail is what can be learned from narratives of loss, ambivalence and reparation, as well as how this new knowledge may inform a deeper understanding of human agency. In order to connect the analysis of environmental loss with broader, psychoanalytically informed theorizations, the following questions inform my analysis:

1   What is the nature of this loss? How does it appear, and in what form?
2   What has been lost, and what is being mourned?
3   What is the 'quality' of the loss; is it one of mourning, ambivalence, guilt?
4   How might loss relate to capacities for reparation and expression of concern?

Based on the data, I argue that much can be learned about public engagement with local ecological issues through an exploration of how loss is negotiated psychically and socially. I maintain that such negotiations are related with capacities to *take action* and experience a sense of agency in the face of what may seem to be overwhelming forces over issues that actually matter a great deal to people. It is also an honest account of the sense of insignificance that people feel in the face of genuinely huge, systemic issues.[3]

Applying psychoanalytic concepts of mourning and melancholia to social forces is not novel. Such concepts have been employed for decades in critical theory (e.g. Fromm, 1941), in the context of social memory and trauma (e.g. Santner, 1993; Caruth, 1996), and Holocaust psychoanalytic studies (e.g. Felman & Laub, 1992). More recently, there has been a 'discovery' in social theory of Kleinian psychoanalysis and object-relations, in particular the emphasis on 'modernist melancholia' (e.g. Sanchez-Pardo, 2003; Nussbaum, 2001) and engaging melancholia as a viable political philosophy (e.g. Kristeva, 1992). Literary theorist Alice Kunziar's (2006) work on melancholia and mourning as features of human–canine relations is a valuable addition to thinking through human–nature relations. However, a coherent focus on the role that loss, mourning and melancholic affect may play in making sense of the decline of species and eco-systems due to human industrial practices has yet to be done.[4]

What follows therefore is an exploration of some aspects and dimensions of loss from the interviews. I first focus on loss in the context of nature and show how memories and associations of nature and childhood often appear interwoven and inseparable. This is the 'narrative' part of the analysis to understand *what* has been lost, as articulated by the participants, and possible limits for expressing (discursively) what has been lost. The following section focuses on affective dimensions and environmental 'objects' that have been lost, focusing on the Fox River (as a vivid illustration of the objects arising in the data). This section presents the more process-oriented dimension of the analysis, which enables an interrogation of the 'quality' of the relationship to the losses. Is there a sense of mourning, retreat, ambivalence? When disappointment arises, what is the nature of the disappointment, and where is it directed? How might we understand the narratives of loss in the context of the biographical interviews? Finally, I conclude the chapter with consideration of ambivalence in relation to capacities for reparation, the focus for the subsequent chapter.

As discussed, I draw on object relations theory, in particular Bollas's understanding of the nonhuman object world as reflections of our unconscious lives, similar to dreams. As tempting as it has been to create a neat list of 'objects' as they arise, as practiced in my initial data analysis of the interviews, such as 'the Fox River' or 'sandbox' (see Appendix F), I resisted fragmentation of topics/objects in favour of addressing processes, dynamics and psychic and objective qualities of the object relations presented.[5] While codification was helpful in processing the material in terms of patterns or key objects, once I began to isolate an object from its context, whether narrative or the context of the three interviews, I began to lose the thread. This leads to my final introductory comment pertaining to data analysis.

It is tempting to provide a linear and tidy explanation, following from the research questions, as to 'why x equals y' or in this case, a progressive argument illuminating why it is that people are not acting on ecological issues that they may care very much about. Due to the aforementioned 'kaleidoscopic' quality of the data, it was not possible to present a clear-cut exposition of why x equals y, a declaration of why people who care deeply about their environments do not take publicly recognized forms of action, otherwise known as the 'values-action' gap (e.g. Lorenzoni, Nicholson-Cole & Whitmarsh, 2007). As much as I would like to present a tidy narrative summary of the data, in a sequenced progression, the material, research design and epistemology do not allow this. The strategy for approaching and presenting the analysis and the subsequent presentation, as informed by a psychoanalytic view, are among the exploring themes and concerns arising from the data material as a series of *constellations*. The themes are presented as part of a *constellation* of features that may help us gain a richer understanding of environmental subjectivities.

For example, themes of childhood, innocence and possibility arise in the material but do not necessarily get us closer to an object-relational approach. In a sense, a thematic organization is at cross-purposes with the object-relational view. I discovered this tension whilst struggling with the best way to present the data analysis write-up. I found it helpful to locate specific themes as a way of getting closer to the significance of certain object relations in the context of the interviews. In other words, I suspect that in speaking of the local environment and childhood experiences, the loss becomes quite vivid. It is also clear that the nature of this loss is not entirely straightforward, precisely because of the dynamic, psychic and material nature of external and internal objects; e.g. the water (as object) is both *internal* and *external*. The loss involves both the object (e.g. no swimming access, the water, sand etc.) and the introjected qualities associated with the water and swimming (e.g. goodness, purity, safety). I cannot reduce one or the other.

Additionally, while a thematic focus is productive for the exploration of certain object relations, focusing on *themes* makes it difficult to address the psychic processes involved. The psychic processes relate to the ambivalence felt around these objects, specifically industry and the paper mill. Therefore, the format for presenting narrative 'themes' is potentially at cross-purposes with the format for presenting psychical, analytic processes and dynamics. This is an aspect of qualitative, psychoanalytic data analysis that requires more research. For in this particular mode of analysis, both the demonstration and performance of the complexities underlying environmental relations are attended to and not reduced to what the relations *are* as a matter of fact. If I can help to complicate how we approach apathy as a viable environmental subjectivity, then I would feel some measure of success has been attained.

Melancholic narratives

Much psychoanalytic literature on loss, mourning and melancholia concerns bereavement: the loss of the mother or father in the infantile world, the loss of loved ones and family relations in childhood and adulthood. The losses I am concerned with here that surfaced in the interview material are of significant 'objects' in the participants' lives, notably environmental 'objects' such as water or a specific lake or river. I am also interested in associated self-states with environmental objects, such as innocence or purity. I am interested in how participants negotiate awareness of ecological problems, such as water contamination, loss of fish and other wildlife or the removal of a place via development. This inquiry is in contrast to a focus on values or attitudes – where people may have clarity or alignment – and instead where things may feel unclear or blurry. It became evident there was nothing straightforward about these objects, nor could they be separated from related associations with specific relationships, memories and aspects of the self.

To explore the loss of a wetland or a lake was also to explore the loss of potential associations and strong memories and how this constitutes an enduring sense of self and identity. At times, the loss of individuals and relationships did arise. For example, in my first interview with Victoria, discussed later in this chapter, her grief and sense of loss surrounding her father's remarrying and the sense of family disintegration broke through, and she expressed her grief through tears. More often, as people recounted their associations with specific places and their experiences over the years in the local waterways of Green Bay or nearby environs, there was an acute sense of longing and sadness, although it was not always clear *what* this loss was linked to. It was this sense of subjective distress and sorrow that I was most struck by: a quality of loss without clear origin or cause. The key difference between the work of mourning and melancholia is the (often) unclear nature of the original loss. It was not clear what exactly had been lost, albeit the object may be clear. This can be seen in the data when Sally is speaking of her time playing in the dunes. I am left wondering if it is the dunes she misses, the sense of connection and safety with her family, the open horizon of Lake Michigan or all of this and more?

I begin with loss in the context of childhood recollections and the associations suggested in relation to environmental sites and objects. I then shift to the more tangible and concrete dimensions of loss of specific places, water, and experience. In this sense, I examine the ways in which objects are real and constructed, essential and imaginary, and how we may understand certain objects as psychic keys expressing more unconscious content than narrative and language are able to (Bollas, 1987). In looking at the memories and significant internal and external object relations that surface in the material, the concept of "screen memory" is useful (Freud, 1917). A screen memory (like forgetting and amnesia) is a compromise between repressed elements and defence against them. Inasmuch as screen memories cover up that which is unacceptable to the ego, they may be considered essentially defensive in nature. In terms of qualitative research interviews, the screen memory – one in which an early event is 'screened' by a later memory – reflects the way in which illusion may inform remembering, rendering memories and recounted events as suspected of having a 'screen' function. This is significant in how the material is viewed as not necessarily 'the facts', but how a particular moment in time is connected with the present and what meanings may be contained therein. The notion tends to subvert the idea of historical reality and, in this case, how interview material is engaged by prompting the question of whether such a reality is the outcome of creative interpretation or genuine access to mnemonic traces—that is, devices to aid and anchor particular memories. Did she *really* swing on the swing for hours, feeling profoundly happy and free? Did he *actually* swim in the Fox River every day? What matters more is what is being conveyed, through the selection of the memory and how its potential associations function in the present.

A paradoxical feature of these types of recollection is that they are less childhood memories than they are memories *about childhood*. The latter are characterized by their singular clarity and the apparent insignificance of their content. Important facts are not retained; instead, their psychic significance is displaced onto closely associated but less important details, e.g. the blue sky or the sand under bare feet. Displacement is indeed the main mechanism here, as it is in the case of mnemic symbols or in the forgetting of a proper name, although to some degree condensation may also be present. Bollas expands on mnemic symbols in the dreamlike way we occupy our world. Not that life is dream-like itself but that we express unconscious material through our investments in particular object relations and aspects of the self projected into objects are re-experienced in our contact.[6] It is a phenomenological orientation to the self in the world that informs the analysis of the interviews. The objective is *not* to reduce environmental objects to 'mere' constructions or fantasy, but rather to appreciate how these relations are often inseparable with imbricated psychic and social meanings.

Childhood: Innocence, sanctuary, possibility, freedom

As previously noted, the opening prompt for the first of three interviews was, "Tell me about where you grew up, anything that comes to mind." In some cases, the narrative would start out very general, and I would gently press for more specifics. In other cases, as with the first interview with Dana, her response to my prompt was literal. She launched into an extended description of the house where she grew up with her six siblings, indicating psychic and emotional sig-nificance of the house and her room as objects in her early life. However, there are two key variables to note: all had reviewed the ethical consent form and were aware of the interest in the environment, specifically the water and Great Lakes, and all had completed the survey and consented to be interviewed. Thus the opening question allowed a level of free association beyond the question itself with the context and nature of the interviews and my expressed interest in water and the Great Lakes.

Innocence

One of the core themes running throughout several participant interviews was a palpable sense of having lost something intangible from childhood. These associations presented in the interviews were bound up with images of imagina-tive play and the enjoyment of water and nature. In recounting associations and memories of nature and childhood, the overwhelming affective qualities were of recalling a self-state of innocence or perception of the world as a safer place than it is now. The water, specifically, and nature, more generally, are experienced as sites of innocence prior to the 'fall' of adult knowledge and awareness. Related to the feelings of innocence are of feeling safe and contained.[7] This is not surpris-ing since the narratives were about childhood experiences, yet I was nonetheless struck by how water and playing outdoors featured so significantly. For example, when I ask Sally about her experiences with Lake Michigan, she recounts with reverie and enjoyment the thrill of running around on the dunes ("pure sand, back then they were all sand"), feeling "safe and at ease" and "being young and knowing, not knowing that there's anything wrong".

Innocence and freedom are possible only through the felt presence of boundaries and containment. While Sally recounts the joy of free play, "Building sand castles, and just having lunch and relaxing out there, playing in the water," she also acknowledges the presence of parental boundaries by "going swimming and going as far as we'd be allowed [laughs] and coming back in." Donald's story (Appendix F) about camping in Baird's Creek during a rainstorm and being rescued by a parent exemplifies this, as does Jeff's story of taking a raft down the Fox River during a snow melt and, after a harrowing adventure, washing up in town soaking wet as his parents drove by going home from church. Victoria, who grew up in a small town in Wisconsin, conveys a powerful sense of childhood idyll and specifically a sense of safety and protection, in her simple statement of her mother telling her to return home "when the streetlamps come on", invoking a simpler and more innocent era in the American Midwest. She describes a scene in our third and final interview that captures this sense of utter freedom, innocence and safety, whilst swinging:

> [Her eyes closed] I am thinking of our backyard, there used to be an apple tree, in our backyard and a sandbox. There was originally one swing in the apple tree. And my dad, um, extended a board from the tree, to the garage, so that he could add two more tr – two more swings. Because I had one brother and one sister and we each would have one swing. And I remember spending so much time swinging, on the swings. And you would swing as high as you could, and um, I guess I would describe it as free. Carefree . . . a time when you were just alone with yourself . . . And, secure and safe. Not a care in the world.

I continue while Victoria is in her reverie to ask her to imagine where she is and how old she is at the time. She says she is about 6 or 7 or 8. I then follow with how she sees herself. Victoria rarely mentions her siblings in the interviews and the psychic space she seems to inhabit is one of herself and father with an anxious mother in the background.

R: In your mind, are you with – are you on your own, or are your brother and sister there with you?

V: I am by myself. And in my mind, the sky is real blue, and the clouds are, um, real white and puffy. And it was so innocent, and so, um, uninhibited. I mean I remember swinging, and singing! At the top of my lungs! [Laughs quite a bit] Oh dear! Seemed like a simpler time.

R: Do you have any other associations with being outside when you were younger?

V: Well we played in the sandbox . . . with an old tractor tire, and we sat on the edge because it was black and when the sun beat down on it, it was really warm. Um. S-s-so. Being outside, was comforting when the sun was beating on you, and, and I played with more kids in the sandbox, um, my brothers and sisters and we each had friends, on one side of the street or in back of us, we'd play in the sandbox. Um. And physical things like riding our tricycles, we had a long driveway, we'd make believe they were streets and we were going different places . . . hooking together the tricycle with the wagon and hauling our dolls around. [Laughs] Oh dear! What was the question about feelings again?

R: Hmm! How it felt to be outside, and doing these various things you are telling me about.

V: Some – you know I look back and see it as so innocent and so simple. So carefree.

In this example, the swing as object is infused with the sensations of freedom and being alone in the world. No siblings to compete with, just the sun, sky and movement through space. In a sense, the swing is a condensation of memory, a screen memory. Although she is laughing, there is an enormous sense of wistfulness in her recollections through the discourse of looking back on something prior that has since been lost. Back then, playing house was with wagons, dolls and leaves. Now as an adult she is faced with chores, upkeep, work and unfulfilled expectations. Victoria describes the bright blue sky and big white, puffy clouds and singing at the top of her lungs, and there is a visceral sense of freedom and possibility, as she recalls her 7- or 8-year-old self on the swing (notably no sense of siblings around). When asked about playing outside, her associations are largely of domesticated play: dolls, wagons, playing house. She recalls the sandbox as warm, pleasurable, the heat of the rubber tire on summer days, poking around for ants. This is in sharp contrast to the sense of the water and the local river as being dangerous, risky and unsafe, discussed in the following section.

What emerges is the positioning of childhood and certain experiences in nature with an innocence and sense of safety, which is to become lost at some point later. The sense of loss articulated around the water and its degradation is therefore affectively connected with the loss of something inchoate and prior to adult knowledge: a time of blissful innocence. In speaking about her hometown, she is also speaking of loss, as the city has fallen into economic decline, the buildings once restored and maintained have been left to become derelict, and it is no longer seen as a desirable place to live.

Sanctuary

To appreciate the sense of inchoate loss, we need to understand what has been lost in the first place. Nature and experiences outdoors conveyed both a sense of innocence and purity, as well as containment and sanctuary. Britton (1992) discusses *sanctuary* as "a sense of being in a safe place, which itself expresses an idea of being inside something good" (p. 103). This is related to Winnicott's concept of the "sense of being held" (1960), and Bick describes this ontological containment as a sense of envelopment like a skin around oneself, which protects and enfolds (Britton, 1992, p. 103; Bick, 1968). The containment and sanctuary provided for by nature and the local waterways was expressed most vividly in Heather's narratives about her experiences on her extended family's farm in Menominee.

Heather, a single woman in her early forties, who works as a state administrator, grew up a rural area in Menominee. However, her parents moved the family about 20 miles away to Green Bay when she was about 10. Heather continued to spend as much time as possible with her larger extended family on the farmlands, once even cycling the 20 miles to visit. The land with its woodlands, farmland, animals and the network of close familial relations – outside of her own nuclear family, which is portrayed as chaotic, noisy and abrasive – is constructed as a site of nourishment, connection and sanctuary. When asking Heather about specific memories of her time on the farm, she describes a visceral scene of taking naps in a swing, being fed and having her needs anticipated and met.

> I guess the most times that I was, or a lot of times just our family gatherings at the farm, the picnics you know and everybody there, all the cousins and their kids . . . my Aunt T. had a closed porch, kinda L-shaped on the front of the house, and it was all screened in, we had a table out there so, you know, kids nearly always got fed out there you know, she always made lemonade and stuff, and she had a swing too and that was one of my favorite things and when we were little she used to put a blanket a pillow and put me in and one of my cousins on there we'd nap on there and fall asleep, so . . . playing games, you know, she always brought out games for us you know . . . and turn the sprinklers on and run around and a big yard she had big lilac bushes and we used to play inside those until the bees would get us [laughter].

The sense of sanctuary, containment and envelopment all refer to a visceral and material sense of being *inside* something, protected. This quality comes through in the narratives of being in and around water. For Heather, being on the farm was an experience of being enveloped by loving relatives and cousins and having the woods, hills and waters to roam and explore. I contrast the affective qualities of her experiences on the farm, as well as her discussion of the summer she spent living outdoors working in Door County – during which time she felt completely at home and relaxed in nature – with the following narrative relating to her more contemporary experiences with water and the environment in Green Bay:

H: Um, when I first moved to Green Bay there in 1991, um, I would say it probably must have been about '92, um, when I was with my ex-fiancé, um, he had a boat or his dad actually had a boat and we would go out on the bay, sometimes fishing and sometimes get in the water, but that was probably the most, and that was only 3–4 times maybe, out of almost four years, so you know, unlike in Menominee when I at least when I was younger, um, and living at home and stuff we were probably there in summer two to five times a week, you know and we'd spend half a day you know.

R: What was it like, the water and the beach there?

H: Um, it used to be really good, it's, it's not good any more, just in the last few years have been really bad, but you know, before I had you know gone to college and that it was, was clear, it was nice, I don't know, I said sometimes the water would be so shallow it would be so far out so it would never get really deep or you know, but, um it was always just you know really nice swimming, I don't remember ever there being signs up saying you know, 'the beach is closed' you know.

Heather relates the dramatic drop in her access and contact with the water from two to five times a week – to three to four times *over four years*. The water quality years ago, she recalls, was always good for swimming. She then recounts more recent experiences with the water, this time with her dog.

H: You know my dog likes to swim and probably about two summers ago I'm like 'let's go up the bay a little bit out of town' and there's some small little like, um, I don't even know if they're actually, well one's Airport Beach I think it's called, and I don't know if it's owned by the county or what it's kind of like a wayside off, a few picnic tables and that's about it, um . . . there was like . . . um, I don't know what to call it, but the weedy grass stuff was so tall and so close to the top I was like 'oh my gosh it's so overgrown', it was as tall as us but you could see there was a track where people were going through it to get to the water and so we started heading and then it was just like, really, the smell was just horrendous, and it was like 'oh my gosh, what is that' and . . . it was just green muck, really.

R: Algae?

H: Algae, and oh it was horrible, and of course they're still ashore so we were filthy and so we were like oh man, then no clean water to hose 'em off, and we had towels I believe but, um, yeah, so that was really disappointing, and so we drove further north along M35 and um, to where someone we know lives, um has a house there and then the other side of the highway she owns the land along the bay, we thought well maybe, you know, it's better there, and no it was the same

H: And so, you know, we just went home and then we were talking to my dad and he was like 'oh yeah you can't go in there it's so polluted and so algae and stuff is going on', so for me that was really disappointing because only probably, you know, two years before that it seemed just fine, we were going to there all the time and so.

There are degrees of loss in Heather's narratives, from the move away from family in Menominee to her life in Green Bay and the change in lifestyle with far less contact with nature. Later in life, she had settled in another midsized Wisconsin city, but she then had to relocate to Green Bay, reluctantly, for work. Here we see another level of adjustment. She is not able to take her dog swimming. (It becomes the *dog* that likes to swim, not herself, although she admits earlier in the interview she has spent almost entire childhood summers in the water.)

It is in the interviews with participants who grew up outside of Green Bay who appear to find the water unwelcoming. It does not call to them due to its industrialized context and history of ecological problems. As Heather notes, she had heard about water problems, as does Victoria, as something in the background, and foregrounded were other 'features' of Green Bay life, notably shopping and town-related benefits. Jeff, who moved to Green Bay from Sheboygan, as Sally did, spent summers in the water and boating had been a huge recreational activity for him. Having moved to Green Bay, Jeff declared he and his wife found the water "shockingly polluted." This sentiment is reflected by those who came to Green Bay from elsewhere, in this case from communities in the Great Lakes region: Victoria, Jeff, Sally, Heather and Ray. In these cases, individuals, with the exception of Victoria, grew up close to the water and have strong associations with playing, family, recreation, fishing and boating. There is a sharp drop in water-related activities, and the water is either tolerated or enjoyed only in a superficial way, e.g. Sally angling herself when sitting by the Bay away from the view of industry or Heather walking along the Fox River Trail as a peaceful and relaxing reference to her times walking in the country, trying not to notice the rubbish collecting under the bridge.

After moving to Green Bay from Sheboygan, Jeff kept his boat parked in the driveway. He lives directly on the Fox River, although rarely takes his boat out on the water. A form of loss has taken place in the relocation, and the sanctuary the water brought previously is no longer available. Rather than find new places to enjoy the water, such as Door County, the activity itself is curtailed. This is the case even with those who relocated within the Green Bay region, such as Howard who moved from rural De Pere to town – a short distance but a huge expanse, psychically and topographically.

Water symbolically evokes strong sensations of containment, being held; it is sensory, experiential and immersive. For many participants, this sense of immersion in place via the water has been lost in varying degrees. Donald (discussed in Appendix F) describes the sensation of wading out in the water at Bay Beach to the raft, where he first learned to swim, and describes the sensation of the sand under his feet and the water supporting him. This is lost when the beach is closed and the only swimming available is in small "concrete" pools where one has to "pretend" to swim by scooting along the shallow bottom and holding onto the sides. Sally recounts swimming in the freezing waters of Lake Michigan, and, although, her visits to the Lake declined as she got older, she pines for the wild waters with its open and endless horizon once the family is uprooted and moved to Green Bay. The water then becomes frozen for Sally as a powerful association with something that has been lost, and although she rarely visits, she places a poster of waves above her bed to remind her of the rough waters and what it felt like to be held in those waters (see Figure B.1 in Appendix B). Her lack of 'action' in relation to protecting the Great Lakes is not reflective of her connection or even affective investment in the water but arguably related to the sense that it's already lost – the relationship is marked by melancholia. For her, it has been both literally and symbolically lost.

For Victoria, sanctuary and containment are centered on the domestic space. Play is domestic imaginary play, such as dress-up and 'library' in the attic, creating an imaginary house with her neighbour out of leaves and carrying dolls around in wagons. Affectively, the home is an object of safety and protection, and the outside and water are perceived as risky and dangerous. This perception of water and weather as risky appears to be mediated through her experience of her mother's fear of the water and fear of storms, which can cause serious damage in that part of the country. They are forces beyond human control. In considering how strongly home is a sanctuary for Victoria, any perceived threat to home is what is acutely felt. Issues pertaining to the local environment such as the Fox River (which flows behind their home) do not seem to register other than in a dim sense. She mentions taking a boat down the Fox River with a church group and how fun it was, but by the third interview, she laughs at this, "Did I really say that?" and now comments that the area was "ratty." (Note the 'movement' between initial idealization and subsequent reality, something difficult to observe in traditional interviews and surveys measuring perceptions.) In contrast to the other participants, Victoria's sense of refuge and sanctuary was bound up in the domestic domain. Her hometown was containing, and she speaks of it as a "very safe place for children" the way everyone knew everyone else. In the interviews, we see therefore a demarcation in how she experiences certain environments; specifically, nature is seen as risky, and town and home are experienced as safer. The river as it appears in her life becomes more prominent as she begins dating, suggesting an association of sexuality, adulthood, risk and danger.

In my interviews with Victoria, several significant environmental issues are discussed. When I ask her to describe any emotions she has in relation to the environmental issues, e.g. air quality, leading to frequent sinus infections in family members, the smells from the large-scale farms nearby or the "ratty" and polluted river, she cites "disappointment." She relays the story of how when they moved to Green Bay, her infant daughter immediately began to have sinus infections and, laughing, recounts how people would say ironically, "Welcome to Green Bay!" This was as close as Victoria came to asserting a clear connection between the health concerns and the local environment (related to ambivalence, discussed in the following chapter). She also conveys the loss of a sense of containment and security in her acknowledgement of how, when she goes out into the garden, all she sees is 'work to be done' and endless chores. Gone are the carefree days of swinging and singing up at the blue skies and white clouds. More importantly, however, is the way in which Victoria felt her home to be a refuge and sanctuary as a child – even though she recounts their poverty and huddling around a small coal stove to keep warm in winter – and how nature itself became a threat, which sent her hiding with any hint of an approaching storm or hurricane. "I was always afraid of thunderstorms and tornados, so at the first sound of thunder, I started to worry." Despite the fact that she and her husband finally went to Door County after years of living in Green Bay (the resort area on the shores of Lake Michigan) for their anniversary, her descriptions of the nature and water are removed, and she focuses on the culture, shops and restaurants. The omission of nature is clarified in our final interview when she mentions that, in fact, she has both positive and negative associations with Door County. It reminds her of her youth (parts of the park resembling her childhood terrain) and her discomfort with large bodies of water. She describes developing a phobia of water after being with her mother during a picnic alongside a riverbank and her mother's palpable fear of the children falling in and drowning:

> There was one park where we had a picnic with my family, and my dad's baseball team, and I can't remember the name of it, but it was a very dangerous place. The land was level and then it was a drop-off to the river. And I remember, being a small child and my mom, I could feel, a sense, the fear my mom had for her children. The urgency with which she spoke to us, about not getting near the edge, I don't know if that, at that point as a kid, um, made me have some fears of large bodies of water.

The revelation about the fear of large bodies of water placed Victoria's narratives about water into context. It also reflects that how people respond to ecological issues may involve unconscious associations that defy discourses focusing exclusively on 'values' and behaviour. Victoria's internalized fear of water relates with what Bollas (1987) calls the "unknown thought" as an embodied experience of her mother's anxiety around water becoming her own; the image of the picnic by the water also suggests its potential function as a screen memory in its quality of a condensed memory, a snapshot conveying her mother's parental fears around wild nature and the risks associated with water.

As with Donald's tooth accident (described later in the chapter), these images are condensations of affect and memory that convey more than the simple representation of the story. They convey complex meanings as well, which likely operate on a dreamlike level of consciousness. As an adult, Victoria could engage with nature and the water only in terms familiar for her – through the domesticated space of her marital relationship and family – although there are signs she can also connect as well with nature as a positive object from her childhood. As she recounts, in our final meeting, the experience of being in nature and by the water in Door County was comforting to her because it made her feel young again; however, it remained mediated by loss. When she is driving with her husband through a winding road in Door County, she is reminded of the council grounds in her hometown where she spent much time. I asked her what feelings are associated with that.

> Oh [sighs], I suppose, more, more youthful. You feel [laughing] a bit bit younger, remembering things you did, um places you were when you were younger . . . that everything in childhood hasn't gone away. And I even said to my husband, I wish I would have brought my camera this would be such a neat picture!

Victoria takes pleasure in telling me about a *positive* association she has with the local nature and a region that she has also just told me can arouse anxiety and fear. This association is one of her youth, reminding her that in fact some things endure. Her remark about wishing she had her camera indicates her desire to preserve this moment, the experience of youth, in something she can hold on to. In many respects, her home has become her 'sanctuary', and there is a constant sense of permeable boundaries, of potential siege, or invasion.

For several participants, nature itself is a form of sanctuary that has been lost. For Victoria, the home has become the sanctuary, and nature is positioned as a threat or risk to be negotiated.

Possibility (open horizons, blue skies)

In addition to being associated with innocence and containment (sanctuary), it seemed the local nature and the water as experienced in childhood also evoked an open and untarnished world. Even Howard, who lived on the (highly polluted) Fox River and spent years swimming, boating and playing on it, experienced the river as dynamic and full of possibilities. It was a peaceful space to be on one's own explore, a state subsequently tarnished by "all the big houses on the river".

> In the springtime I'd walk along the river just to explore it, just to see what type of things got washed up from the ice and everything like that. It was always a relaxing place. That was before they got all the big houses on the river, like they have now.

For Howard, the loss of the river happened through development encroaching along the riverbanks, as the riverfront property went from being inexpensive real estate to desirable and high cost, and through his subsequent move out of the family home in his early twenties to a small bungalow formerly owned by his grandmother, "in town" in DePere. The loss is one related to access, rather than pollution, as the Fox River was already degraded. Howard contracting hepatitis in high school was a testament to its condition. However, he is ambivalent in making this causal assertion and skirts around it as one might protect a problematic but beloved relative, as many other participants do when it comes to discussing pollution impacts; he seems to know the river made him ill, and yet he is very attached to it. Howard moved only several miles into town, and the Fox River continues to flow close to his new house, but being in town entirely changed his mode of relating with the river. He experiences the river as lost in his shift from a "river rat" growing up in and around the river in rural De Pere to an adult living on his own. He tells me how he may take a few minutes of his lunch break and park near the water, looking out, and tells me in our second interview how after our discussion he decided to go spend a couple of minutes by the river during a recent lunch break. This practice of accessing the river through 'glimpses' and snatches is poignant in light of how important the river was in his youthful years.

For both Howard and Sally, sites of exploration and vista were lost in their respective moves: Sally's open horizon of Lake Michigan, a wild body of water with an endless horizon, and Howard's Fox River before the big mansions and his relocation to a bungalow in town. Howard retains an ambivalent relationship with his desire to return to the country and his beloved rural Fox River, as he cannot settle or feel at home in town. His relations with the water and river are in what seems to be a continuous state of melancholic longing. He is unable to return to the river and yet is unable to make a new home in town. Howard, Heather and Sally seem to have a melancholic relation to their earlier attachments with the water and nature, and their engagement with Green Bay's waterways as adults have found it lacking. Their camping and swimming activities have become sharply curtailed. When Howard tells me about how much he loves swimming and that he now uses a local indoor pool on special occasions, I feel sad. My sense is that swimming indoors cannot replace the unique pleasures of outdoor swimming and exploring the riverbanks.

Donald's accounts of being out in nature, boating and enjoying the water also indicated a sense of expansiveness and of open horizons: adventure. While Donald appears reconciled with his relationship with Green Bay, including the events concerning his father's accident at the paper mill, there is an undeniable melancholic tenor as he recounts the water and nature of his youth and the gradual erosion of these places. Environmental degradation has removed places where he sought sanctuary as a child; Baird's Creek and Bay Beach are no longer accessible, which he notes quietly, rather than railing against or complaining about. The sorrowful aspect suggests how anger may incite action and less so resignation. Environmental degradation is, for many participants, simply a matter of sad and irreparable fact.

Participants appear to shift their affective investments accordingly. The Fox River had always been and remained an abject object, a place where loss is a matter of course. Donald manages to retain a sense of possibility in the face of these developments. His shift of affective investments from Baird's Creek and Green Bay to the property in Two Rivers signals a form of reparation. He can care and tend for the newly acquired land. However, this is not a mere denial, minimization or disavowal of the existence of degradation. He is well aware, as are all of the participants. He laments the way the "city's forefathers" allowed the degradation and destruction of the water to take place and is clearly pained. Donald's growing consciousness of the threats facing the Great Lakes instils a genuine sense of personal limitation and vulnerability.

Object relations: Intermediaries between public and private meanings

What is it we have lost when our rivers, beaches and wetlands are degraded, have been developed or are altered? What aspects of ourselves are in the places in which we reside? In order to explore interrelated, intra-psychic dimensions underlying responses to local environmental issues, particularly those concerning local ecologies, we need to relate themes of loss, mourning and melancholia with the concerned objects of water, nature and industry. As shown, strong themes of loss are found throughout the interviews. These themes are strongly connected to specific places, sensations and memories specifically evoking a childhood associated with innocence, possibility and safety. If certain objects are like 'psychic keys' through which we articulate ourselves, I would like to now focus on the various meanings and significances that specific *environmental* objects may have in the context of loss.

The focus on environmental (nonhuman) objects is a relatively novel approach in psychosocial studies, in that the emphasis has tended to be to be primarily on interpersonal and intra-psychic dimensions and processes and on human relationships, without attending to the 'realness' of our object worlds and the spaces we move through. As I am drawing on three in-depth, free associative interviews per participant and not the outcome of psychoanalytic sessions or longitudinal interviews over months or years, my observations regarding internal and external object relations are limited. Even within these constraints, I have found it possible to identify a series of qualities, or dimensions, to these object relations, which are highly suggestive of the capacities to 'split' objects (and ourselves) in terms of 'good' and 'bad' qualities (e.g. pleasure, desire, escape; danger, threat, abjection) – a psychic process (I maintain in the final chapter) integral to industrialization and our experiences of industry as profoundly ambivalent and anything but straightforward.

To understand what has been lost, and what is being 'pined' for and what defences may thus be mobilized around the experiences of loss and pining, or longing, we need to take a closer look at the ways in which the environmental objects invoked are articulated: what is speaking through them, how we are to follow their traces.

In the following section, I discuss how certain bodies of water and places in nature are constructed as 'good' or 'bad' objects and the affective investments involved in the objects (see Figure 4.1): the focus tends to be on the Fox River, as the most central body of water in Green Bay, the site of much attention in

Figure 4.1 De Pere inlet, date unknown. (Provided by Howard [participant], 2009.)

the media and in the course of the interviews. Thus I focus on this in the following section. Far from binaries, these objects, like the Fox River, are 'shot through' with complicated, and at times contradictory, affective dimensions. At the centre of the contradictions, I argue in the following chapter, is the paper mill and industry itself, an object that casts a profound and complex shadow. I conclude with a discussion of the implications of 'the work of mourning' and ambivalence, a discussion continued in greater depth concerning reparation and bases for trust and belief in real objects in the following two chapters.

A "river rat": River as 'good' object

Perhaps more than any of the participants, Howard expresses great affection for the Fox River. Having grown up on its banks in rural De Pere, about 10 miles outside of Green Bay, Howard spent much of his childhood in and around the river (see Figure 3.1). Unlike participants interviewed whose associations with the river include abject pollution, abuse and neglect, Howard appears to have identified positively with the Fox River and associates it with play, exploration, curiosity, freedom and expansion, and indeed as a part of himself, telling me moments into our first interview that he was a "river rat" and confirming this perception in the second interview after speaking with his sister, who agreed, "Yep, I was a river rat." The passage at the beginning of this chapter reflects this identification, as Howard notes his emotional states are in rhythm with the river. The river is a 'good' object for Howard, in that it evokes a sense of himself, particularly his younger self as adventurous and autonomous from the family fold. To say the river is 'good', however, does not equate with it being idealized, although there may be aspects of this. I did not find Howard's relation with the river as idealized primarily because he was so keen to participate in the interviews based on his own concerns regarding water health and quality ("my way of making a difference"), however unconscious or distanced such concerns are from his conscious, everyday practices. Howard's environmental concern is actually very high, despite his presentation and responses in the survey indicating otherwise.[8] In addition, he mentions in the interviews that he contracted hepatitis C, a potentially devastating virus, which he strongly suspects was linked with his high exposure to the Fox River water.

However, even in noting this, he does not seem particularly angry or disgusted at the fact his health was so severely compromised through contact with the river; although he had to miss much of a year in high school and suggests the illness led him to pursue physical labour, working outside as opposed to indoors at an office job – perhaps tied with the trauma of being bed and homebound at the peak of his adolescent years – there is not a trace of bitterness or resentment towards industry or the river. The tenor with which he speaks of the river is instead affectionate and tender and borderline protective.[9] This is illustrated in the vignette he shares about the first time he became aware of the poor water quality in Green Bay. He is recounting a trip on Lake Michigan, which is often constructed as the 'good water' in many interviews due to its blue colour, open horizons and associations with fishing and boating, despite its own ecological issues as part of the Great Lakes system.

> The first time we went out on Lake Michigan, that we take the boat out, because you look at the back of the boat and it's coming out blue, blue water, as opposed to brownish water. Cos I had never seen that, we always boated on the river, and I cannot tell you exactly when it happened, but I, but I did, that's when I realised how clean water should be. . . . I distinctly remember the first time doing it, I can't tell you when or how old I was, but I do remember it being, "wow, I can't you know . . . I've never seen, that's what clean water is [laughs]. It's not the pollution that's making it that, it's the run-off of soil and different type of water . . . It would have been the point of recognizing clean from, clear water to cloudy water.

In contrast to those who found the water abject (e.g. Jeff, Donald and Sally, who would not want to touch it for fear of contamination), Howard didn't have a problem jumping into the water and swimming and water-skiing. He notes his mother wanted him to "Rinse off in chlorinated pool . . . and I agreed". But, he continues,

> I didn't worry too much about it. I mean, I keep, I had hepatitis when I was 17, and mom blamed herself for some food . . . I kept thinking I had better

chance of getting it from . . . I know that a lot of septic systems dumped into river, even ours did, I didn't realize that until I was older, but I kind of knew that when I was 15, 16, 17.

When I asked Howard about swimming in the Fox River in our first interview with a note of unintentional incredulity ("You didn't actually swim in it, did you?"), he responds, "I didn't even have a problem [going into the water] in my later years, I mean in the, in the last ten years, I was out there . . . but yeah, I swam in the river . . . Anything else? I kind of went blank there. Do you mind if I get a soda?" My sense was that he became slightly defensive at the suggestion there was anything unusual about swimming in the Fox River and quite literally came to a blank. The river and experiences with the water are so strongly a part of Howard's identity that it almost seems a part of him. He speaks about his claustrophobia living "in town" in the small bungalow and how he keeps the shades drawn most of the time: "From the minute I moved in," he says in our first interview, "I didn't like being in the city. I just, closed in to me. I have the drapes open and the blinds open for you, not for me, because I'd probably have them closed." He suffers being confined to the indoors and speaks of his enjoyment of the outdoors all year round almost boastfully, including the winters, when he has no trouble sticking his bare hands in the ice or snow (to his coworkers' shock).

While his mood fluctuates in sync with the seasons and the river's ice opening, he refuses to 'criticize' aspects of the river or the environment on account of its being cold, polluted or a sewage dumping site. These are arguably the 'good' aspects of Howard introjected into the river, so that in protecting and enjoying the river, defending it against critique, he is protecting and salvaging core aspects of himself. In this sense, it's vital to see the Fox River as inseparable from who he is as a person. He grew up literally in the water, even potentially contracting a serious illness from it, and found enormous respite and pleasure through his many years exploring, discovering and playing in it. His contact with it lessened in the move towards adulthood, via a move to town several miles from his childhood home and the interim development alongside the riverbank. This development virtually altered the river for Howard from a serene and natural area – despite its ecological woes – to a row of high-value properties, owned by the wealthy. While Howard still lives very close to the river, it's in town, and he notes that he has realized even more now how important it has been for him.

Being away from it makes me realize it more than had I'd stayed on the river my whole life. it might not be as noticeable to me, might be noticeable to other people that thought that, but it's when you interact with other people, that's why the term a "river rat" . . . I just talked to my sister today, actually I was going through this stuff and the interviews and I said, "well you know about me being on the river" and she said, "yep the river rat" . . . and I'm like, "yeah she probably had her time of doing that too" and ah . . .

Truly missing the river after moving from it, experiencing the loss of its proximity and thus self-experience in relation to it, echoes Sally's narratives regarding how deeply she missed and 'pined' for Lake Michigan only after the family had moved to Green Bay. For Howard, the river was his private space but also shared by his family: "The whole family was that way, we're kind of connected to it. Could be why we don't leave the area, I mean because if we left the area I think it would have to be near a body of water." Howard differentiates the Fox River from another body of water that was also polluted, Bay Beach. He notes in the second interview, "I mean, we heard stories about Bay Beach being closed down".

His relationship with the Fox River remains intact in terms of his perception of it as a river, not necessarily the site of a nationally recognized clean-up: "I'm for the cleanup they are trying to do, I feel the river has gotten cleaner since I was younger . . . so I think they're doing stuff to do it". Context matters for how degradation is understood and related to; for example, he tells a story about learning the cause of the PCBs from "a professor in a bar," which makes it all seem "less sinister." Unlike a waste dump nearby "where they knew what they were doing", the nature of the degradation as unintended consequences is what matters. This is a feeling also expressed by Donald when he notes how some businesses intentionally channelled wastes into the Fox River and expresses dismay and shock at such practices. Somehow if the PCBs are an unintended by-product of recycling processes, it's more palatable than outright and explicit harm being done to the watershed and its habitats.

Good water, bad water: "It's not something that I can change immediately."

In our second interview, after an initial glowing and jovial discussion of the region and the water (he refers to enjoying the water "glitter" on the surface of the Fox River in certain lights), Scott begins to disclose more about his feelings of sadness and disappointment when he became aware of the degradation.

R: Um, can you recall, the kind of um, the kind of feelings that might have, you know to learn that, that there are these problems with the river and with the bay?

S: I, I would be, it was more like, disappointment. You know cause, I, probably before then I was like, "hey look, neat water, you know, you drink water, you know," its stuff that . . . you know the bay isn't water, you drink water, you cook with water and all that and realizing that water could be dirty. You know. So that, that was probably, um, a point of when I went "oh, okay," you know realizing that you know, everything is connected. So why is the stuff that I use water with okay and the stuff that, that, that . . . outside the water is not okay to do with. Deal with you know and now I remember, um, when I was in school we took a field trip to the water treatment plant.

You know that, that site, the sewer treatment plant that's in Green Bay yeah I, I think I was in seventh grade, eighth grade, sixth grade, yeah, I remember, that might have been one of the things too would you know, going to the sewage treatment plant. Boy did that place stink. [Laughing]

R: What kind of impression did that have on you?

S: I don't know, just that you could turn bad water into good water. You know that, that things could be better. But you know, realizing that you know, when you go to the bathroom it has to go somewhere [laughing] yeah, okay, that makes sense. That, that and you know, my dad said and you know, when we went to the sewage treatment plant and when um, it was being built, you know, my dad was in construction at that time and he helped build the sewage treatment plant. So I always remember that too. Being that the one, the one section of the building is that seven stories, straight down and it's, and it's in the ground. You know just, that was always kind of neat. Mmm, yeah, I can still remember being inside the building. I betcha it hasn't changed much either. It's probably the exact same yellow paint [laughing].

Scott's realizing there is 'good' and 'bad' water, along with the fact you can not only turn good water into 'bad' but the other way round, signals negotiations with an object as neither all bad or all good, but mixed and even mutable. His recollection of the sewage treatment building, even the color of the paint on the walls, suggests this 'object' as having some sort of importance, an imprint in memory that is now recalled. For Scott, the sewage treatment center is "neat" and not abject, similar to his finding great beauty, adventure and relaxation in the Fox River, a site that many others found to be quite abject. I ask him to expand more on the disappointment.

S: I would, I would guess maybe it's disappointment that somebody could let that happen. That you know, water, you know that just because of what humans did that the water became bad, now, now I realize a little bit later that you know, it was more, it, it's not so much negligence, but being naive that "oh, I'll just dump it in the water and then it's, it's gone". You know, not knowing that some of the stuff that they used was potentially harmful. And then after the fact then they found out it was harmful and some companies tried to fix it right away and some companies must not of tried, they're just, "Okay, we'll just not say anything." Yeah, the Environmental Protection Agency must have been started for some reason you know. That's exactly it, environmental protection.

R: Yeah, so it's a sense of let-down?

S: Mmm hmm, yeah. Yeah, I've just, yeah sense of let-down with disappointment and just ah, you know, that's sad.

R: Mmm, were there . . .

S: Not so much anger. [Laughs]

I find Scott's absence of anger, just a sort of subdued sadness and sense of letdown by others, quite moving and curious. And, as suggested, it is what marks *environmental melancholia*. As I return to this topic in the following chapters, the role of anger and protest is potentially quite implicated in the capacities for creative engagement and response to our circumstances; a withdrawal into sadness and disappointment seems to suggest an internalized passivity that I find interesting. We continue, as I enquire into his feelings of disappointment and sadness:

R: Were there any other things that you can imagine that also contributed to that feeling?

S: Mmm, well it must have been with being, having so much fun with water and other places and you know, and then you know, the water up north is okay to swim in and stuff and then, you know, come down here and it's, not that okay. Maybe that's why we never really did much around here that we always went somewhere else to . . . You know, to the lakes or to the river or various other places.

R: So you weren't necessarily aware of other kinds of environmental issues –

S: Yeah, I didn't realize later in life that eating fish, you know if you eat too much fish then you know it's tainted with mercury because of air pollution. But yeah, actually it didn't really make that, make that connection 'til H. got pregnant, I was like, "You can only have fish once a week, why?" "Mercury." "Oh." [Laughs] but I, I, I must have known that ahead of time, that you know just, just that it would happen but didn't know that it was that predominate here too. You know cause, you know they had fish fries, is one of the big things around Northeast Wisconsin, every Friday fish fry (Yeah.) So, and you can only do that once a month.

R: Right, and um how does that make you feel, the idea that the fish is actually not entirely safe?

S: Yeah, it, it, it's, not something that I can change immediately.

We can see a shift in awareness from an object that has been largely 'good' ("having so much fun with water") to recognition of it having been spoiled in some way by others' negligence. However, in place of a sense of indignation or anger, we see a quiet sense of disappointment, followed by the admission that "it's not something that I can change immediately". This particular movement, between acknowledgement of a loss and sense of betrayal, as well as quiet admission of personal powerlessness, runs across the interviews.

The following examples illustrate a pervasive movement between participants' acknowledgement of loss, specifically in relation to a sense of powerlessness and efficacy. When I ask Howard how the idea of contaminated fish makes him feel, he responds instead with a comment that it's not something he can change; therefore, there is no point 'feeling' anything about it. The space for emotional processing of the losses or sense of anger is not available; rather, it has been short-circuited in the single expression, "*it's not something that I can change immediately.*"

What we observe as a lack of interest is likely a strategy for negotiating the painful experience of witnessing and not perceiving having agency to change it. Howard relates to the water's ecological issues as an 'engaged' activist or citizen. It does not refer to whether he sees the water as good or bad but rather to how he sees *himself* and his *agency* in relation to the particular object. In this case, Scott feels concern for the water, but it is not expressed as creative engagement; Winnicott suggests this is related to the lack of *contributing-to* that is so central for the animation of one's reparative and creative energies towards the world. It is possible, through an object relations analysis, to see that the river holds for Scott certain 'self-states', as Bollas (1992) describes his childhood swing holding certain associations of a particular time – and in this sense, perhaps certain environmental objects are 'frozen' in terms of evoking a sense of active reparation or engagement with them.

River as abject

In contrast to Howard and Scott, for Donald the Fox River seems to have occupied a site of abjection and loss. The two singular associations he has with the Fox River are when he lost a front tooth in an accident playing with friends and was hit in the tooth with a BB gun, and his father's traumatic experience of suffering an injury at the paper mill and subsequently losing his job after having worked his way up to a foreman over 20 years of working for the company. When Donald told me the tooth story (as I came to think of it) in the first interview, I was struck by how it arose – at the end of the first interview, as an errant association surfacing – and the language he uses.

> One other little incident in my life that has to do with our proximity to the Fox River . . . We were probably 11 years old. A group of guys decided we were going to go down to the Fox River . . . so we were down there horsing around, with BB guns, shooting at God knows what. One of the guys shot his BB gun, and the BB knocked out my front tooth. I paid for that for the rest of my life, cause I had to wear a false tooth, still have one as a matter of fact . . . but the trauma of wearing that crazy piece of hardware in my mouth all those years. I had to wear that until my mouth matured, until I was 18 years old, at which time they could put a bridge in. But that was a trauma, all tied in with the Fox River . . .

In the story there is a strong association with the river and the "trauma" that Donald experiences; although he is laughing a bit and recalling it as a light anecdote, there are indications of more to the story. The event takes place down by the banks of the Fox River, amongst old relics perhaps indicative of a more dignified time in the River's history, and for some "strange, weird reason" they started this game. The setting is already marginal, transgressive and a bit naughty.

I am most struck, as discussed in Chapter 5, of the phrases of paying for the accident for the rest of his life; like his father, a trauma took place associated with the river (the paper mill being directly on the Fox River) that was both recklessness and bad luck. While he may have trouble speaking about his father's accident or the paper mill, the story is a 'screen memory' in that it seems to bring together certain abject aspects of the river and associated brutality.

For Heather, having moved to Green Bay from Menominee (and more recently Oshkosh, which she describes as feeling like home, located on Lake Michigan), the Fox River seems to be a pale reflection of the waterways and nature of her earlier life. While, like Howard, she maintains that 'any body of water' has a similar soothing and relaxing effect, I was saddened and intrigued to hear her recount her experiences with the Fox River and how it is integrated with the 'life world' on the whole in Green Bay. Here she picks up the topic voluntarily when we meet for our second interview. She first recalls the affective associations with the beach and water, with friends and family, as "the days going on forever," and contrasts this with her life in Green Bay.

H: I know you were asking like, what did uh you know like being in the water and so what it meant to me up there and stuff and how I felt but um, of course I don't know if it was just because you know I was young, but I, you know I compare it to now I feel like that time was, um, going to the beach with my friends or being with my family um, the days went on forever you know? And like now cos I'm you know so busy working and doing other stuff and but um, so kind of, how do I want to say, not freedom but just being able to relax, not worrying (hmm mm) having to worry about anything you know. I guess that's one of the reasons a lot of times um [. . .] you know like here in Green Bay they have the Fox River Trails, I don't know if you're familiar with them or not? And like in the summer I mostly take her [dog] a lot between spring and fall and on the trails because it's nice it's kind of somewhat woodsy, you know you go by houses and some businesses at times but they don't have the traffic or the vehicles and stuff. And you've got the water and you can hear the fish jumping and stuff so it's more relaxing to me than just walking through town. Sit [talking to dog]

R: What do you think of the scenery along that walkway?

H: Um, it's nice I think it could probably somewhat be a little nicer in areas but um, you know, it's, I like kind of going where more of the residential part is because they do such nice landscaping of their land and stuff so that's really pretty, um, I you know it would be nice if there was a little more, um, access to go down like by the river maybe a little cleaner because there are a few spots where I will take her where it gets kind of mucky, and icky and [. . .] the one area where it's really accessible is down under 172. But kids, people leave their garbage you know down there they party or whatever, so there's broken glass a lot and stuff, um but there's certain times of the summer where you don't go too close to the river cos of the smell. [Laughs]

R: What makes, what causes the smell?

H: I don't know, I would just sense a lot of it is the algae and from the paper mill nearby and um but you know usually in Spring it doesn't look that bad but then you get to, by the end of June it looks kind of nasty, so, um. [She talks to the dog] gotta get your paws in too! Um. So that is probably the one thing about Green Bay that I do enjoy . . . is having those trails to, yeah walk or bike on or stuff so that's nice. I wish they were on this side of town so I didn't have to drive over there to get to it but you know, but yeah.

Heather's narrative about her walks down along the Fox River Trail is poignant. She says it is the one thing she likes about Green Bay; however, she has to negotiate bad smells, algae, broken glass and garbage. There is a remarkable ability to 'split' off the good and bad aspects of the river, thereby salvaging or protecting the 'good' qualities she associates and presumably experiences in herself in relation with the water and the river. She is unable to reject it completely, and in this sense is reminiscent of the 'depressive position' in her capacity to 'hold' both the good and bad qualities without splitting the object into being idealized or hated. However, despite the maturity demonstrated by Heather, I cannot help but sense something is being tamped down, a violation or anger in relation to the transgressions she witnesses on her walk (e.g. trash, broken glass, industrial trespasses leading to algae blooms). There is, as discussed in the following chapter, a mood of resignation or despondency even when speaking about gross levels of ecological degradation and her direct experience of the water.

Negotiating losses

In terms of loss and what the loss of the specific objects may mean for Heather, it is not the Fox River that has been lost but rather the sanctuary she found on the family farm and childhood associations with swimming and water that have not been recaptured. The sense is of someone wandering through life, not fully engaged, as if in a state of arrested mourning or, more accurately, melancholia. The loss is present but not clearly delineated; rather it seems a process of disappointments and losses that are affective and relational as well as tangible (e.g. the family farmland, the barn, the woods); the quality evokes melancholia as a loss that has unclear origins (Freud, 1917). Both Heather and Howard brought out photo albums to show me of times in youth in and around water and nature. The images were of family holidays and 'good times.' The Fox River is a 'good enough' object for Heather, as she suggests, but is it sufficient? How does it function as a 'transformational object'? What is being protected, defended, in the lack of affective engagement with the river? What would it mean for her to connect with the river as a body of water and site that has been degraded but which may have potential for renewal? In this sense, it would appear that to tolerate the river, walking alongside it but not fully engaging with it, is to protect something vital and 'good' that continues to be pined for. It is a preservation of a prior 'good object'; the physical sites of goodness have been lost but continue in the psychic, imaginal spaces. In the pining is a refusal, or inability, to engage with objects of the present. Rather, Heather continues to seek her 'home,' a place of love, security and nourishment, and she knows it is not in Green Bay. The Fox River does not call to her as it does not seem to call to most participants (with the notable exception of Howard), and it seems to mirror the unfriendliness Heather finds in Green Bay.[10]

For Victoria, her house has become the site and physical representation of 'sanctuary', a space of safety, containment and goodness. The home is the 'good breast'. However, as becomes evident, the good breast is also capable of producing ill effects; the drinking water is heavily filtered, the odours from large-scale farms come wafting in, the neighbours let their dog soil on the sidewalk by the mailbox. The garden needs weeding. The home, with its relational content of daughters and husband, is not impermeable to the forces of change. The daughters eventually leave home, the husband spends over 60 hours a week working at the nuclear plant on Lake Michigan, and the spectre of divorce looms as both siblings enter into divorces. The Fox River hardly registered in this world other than as something to cross on the bridge and the occasional news on the television about the PCB clean-up. As Victoria notes, because they don't use the river recreationally, its issues don't really impact the family. If anything, water, particularly rivers, register as sites of danger and threat, with a suggestion of risk. As she notes when discussing her contact with water as an adolescent, the *feelings* in rural settings are "more secluded, rustic . . . romantic." Maturing into adulthood is about becoming aware there are dangers in the world, "There were people who drowned in the lake, um, and so you knew there were, there were dangers . . . associated with it." The Fox River in her adult life has scarcely registered, although she mentions a boat ride on the *Foxy Lady* she experienced with a church group. In the first interview, she presents the ride as pleasant and fun, but in our final interview, I asked her about her impressions of the Fox River, and she mentions a boat ride her neighbours took her on that she seemed to enjoy, although found the scenery not very 'naturesque' due to the lavish homes lining the river. I revisit the vignette about her impressions on the *Foxy Lady*.

R: I was kind of intrigued because you said that it was very, you really enjoyed the scenery when you were on the *Foxy Lady*. Going down the Fox River.

V: I did?! [Incredulous] I guess maybe I was thinking about the river itself, because you're right! When I compare what we did with the neighbours on this part of the river, compared with what the *Foxy Lady* did, you're right! As far as the scenery off of the river, it's not very, um, very attractive. And it makes me wonder, why [laughs] why are people riding this boat?! [Laughing] And maybe, well just maybe just like to ride, whether you like the scenery or you don't and of course they serve drinks and food, so, maybe it's not about the scenery at all!

R: Why do you think that, I mean tell me more when you look at the scenery down the river? What does it, what kind of feelings does it – ?

V: I guess it makes me, um, sad in a way, that something so public as the river, and the shore would be used up, in a not a very attractive way.

R: What does 'not very attractive way' mean?

V: Um well. Like you said about some of the industries, and um, I noticed that a lot of coal piles, down there; I guess you'd rather see residential or recreational use along the river.

R: The fact that there is industry there, and that it is the way it is, um, how does that affect you?

V: Well it certainly doesn't make me want to go on the *Foxy Lady*. [Laughs a bit] I'm not a big drinker and their food isn't that good, and [laughs] I don't care to do that. Um. I guess it doesn't affect me in a real strong way, just like other things, thinking about, um, life for my children, it makes you concerned that all these, natural, um, natural um, [voice trails off] . . . conditions or natural . . . I can't think of the word. We'll just say phenomena, that ss- will be used up. But, I guess on the other, hand, you could look at some of it that wasn't, wasn't residential, and there wasn't necessarily um, industrial building and it, but it wasn't groomed or anything, looked ratty too . . . So it's, it's not something I think about a – a lot.

I ask Victoria why this may be, and if it may be related to a perception that there is not much that can be done about the situation.

V: I guess I just accept the way it is, and maybe there can be things done about it, industry that, industries don't always survive, um, businesses could go out of business they could sell the property and develop it in a more attractive way. . . . It's not something that I see on a regular basis so it doesn't . . . it doesn't effect me all that much. . . . And, . . . also I'm really interested in genealogy? And [sigh] so olden times interest me, too. And, I guess realistically these industries that . . . you know are on the river, they're probably the founding industries they were what made this city, get established. (Yeah.) And grow . . .

R: So how does that affect the way you see it?

V: Kind of as a nec- a necessary evil?

R: Uh-huh.

V: That this negative things come, come along with progress and prosperity for the community.

The Fox River, it seems, is an object that has been 'used up', is beyond repair, unless industries or businesses literally disappear. This is a surprising image that conjures up a more futuristic, possibly dystopian fantasy than I was expecting. The possibility for change as presented does not allow much in the form of reparation or agency. It reflects a highly passive subjectivity, of one literally watching from the sidelines. As Victoria admits, she is more anxious and concerned about life for her children and the idea of "nature" being "used up". There is a tacit acceptance of using up and debasing nature – the view of the river and its condition as being part of a "necessary evil" for the benefit of the human community in the region, e.g. progress and prosperity lying at the nub of the difficulty in coming to terms with the experiences of both sadness and appreciation of the benefits. This is ambivalence, as discussed in the following chapter. She is able to dissociate from the environment and displace engagement with it on to others, as she states in the third interview:

> I think it's, my, feeling of being somewhat removed, from, like you asked do I consider myself, do I realize that I'm living on the Great Lakes, do you consider yourself living on the Great Lakes. You know, and it, it doesn't occur to me. So I feel somewhat *removed* from this, this situation. Um, it doesn't impact me on a day-to-day basis. But I'm sure there are others, you know, who make their living, um, in these areas, who live in these areas. That would be more moved to do that than I would.

Occupying this ambivalent position, Victoria remains exempt from affective involvement with the Great Lakes as such.

In the conflicting affective dimensions of sadness, disappointment (to be discussed) and appreciation are likely to be unconscious levels of guilt. Guilt and ambivalence go hand in hand. In recognizing degradation, there is the recognition of transgression and practices that have somehow violated a sense of ecological integrity. Whether it is the visibility of trash and debris or the lack of fish and other aquatic life basic to a healthy, ecologically viable river or the presence of PCBs on the river bottom, environmental issues are essentially about crossing the line and doing harm. This ambivalent dance around environmental damage includes, on the one hand, sadness and disappointment and, on the other, acceptance of the "necessary evils" of industry that allowed Green Bay to thrive and become such a "good community" to raise children. Donald is aware of the darker aspects of this beneficent entity of industry (the paper mill) that treated his father with brutality, essentially emasculating him at the prime of his middle-aged years, so that he had to seek work as a precarious laborer for years. Donald is also aware, as someone who worked and thrived in a local industry, of the responsibilities and ease with which business can take liberties with its surrounding ecologies (illustrated by his discovery of the errant pipeline that once sent waste directly into the river). He expresses loss and sadness at the current state of the waters in Green Bay and the Great Lakes, and he is aware of the costs of disrupting one ecosystem (the Fox River and the Bay) for the entire system. While Donald is affectively connected positively with the Great Lakes, his ambivalence towards the Fox River is evident. It has robbed him and his father of vital organs, in a sense. It is the site of the tooth story but also the site, by association, of his father's injuries and symbolic 'castration' by the mill. Yet Donald lives alongside the Fox River Trail, and the mill can be seen from his back window.

Why ecological mourning matters

Freud asks, "So what is the work that mourning performs?" (1917, p. 204). This question is central for understanding the relationship between loss, mourning, melancholia and engagement. As illustrated in the data, how we respond to particular environmental issues can be shot through with powerful and inchoate affective investments, memories, desires and losses. This complexity is lost when we reductively equate environmental engagement and action with care, concern or deep affective investments in the natural environment. Rather, the external 'presentation' of apathy, appearing as an *absence* of action, may in fact be related to loss. These losses may be inchoate, unconscious to some extent or at least not well understood and experienced as 'stalled out' or frozen in certain aspects. As environmental losses are usually not explicitly articulated in many social or cultural contexts as experiences that need 'working through,' such losses may go 'underground.' Environmental efforts are quick to direct people into action but do not address the complex nature of coming to terms with industrial environmental degradation. However, there is a high price for the lack of naming the loss. These unspoken dimensions, and more precisely how they are negotiated socially and psychically, inform our choices from political engagement to what products we buy. For a viable environmental engagement, we need to understand how losses have been sustained, worked with psychically and socially, experienced, survived and mourned in order to see how they can be more constructively integrated or used creativity. Arguably one of the keys to this is the act of naming, speaking to it, giving it life outside of the unconscious domains, so it can be processed and 'worked through'. This can take place through a number of surprisingly mundane ways, from publishing editorials in the paper to designing messaging and framing that acknowledges loss while pointing to what is taking place to repair and restore.

In addressing the affective and psychic dimensions of loss and apathy, I am not suggesting these are processes restricted only to the subjectivity and interiority of individuals. I view these processes as both psychic and social. I do wish to highlight the role that biographical influences have in helping us understand some aspects of how loss influences our choices, including how we respond to chronic ecological issues. Based on the data, I situate loss as central for understanding the absence of agency and the forms of engagement that environmental advocates desire so deeply from their communities. In making this crucial shift, we can begin to appreciate that where there is presumed to be a lack of affect, in fact there may be a surprising surplus of affect to explore. In the following chapter, I continue this discussion with exploring responses to loss and mourning as forms of ambivalence, splitting and managing contradictions. Addressing loss and responses to loss can then enable a fuller appreciation for what constitutes and enables reparation, concern and creativity – capacities a sustainable, ecologically healthy future depends on.

Notes

1 As I argue, surveys eclipse much of the affective content of the issues as explored through the interviews.

2 This point regarding the seeming ease with which the category of 'apathy' is embraced and accepted as a viable interpretation of the lack of public will or engagement with these issues raises issues regarding how apathy functions and performs politically, socially and psychically; I return to this topic in Chapter 7 when I discuss the possible construction of apathy as a means of projecting internal and disowned aspects of the self, e.g. selfish, destructive or aggressive aspects.

3 For example, after Ray described the large rubbish heap in the middle of the Pacific Ocean, I asked how it made him feel. He responded, "Small and insignificant." I could not argue with this; higher levels of environmental literacy can arouse justifiable senses of powerlessness.

4 Ulrich Bech, writing on "industrial reflexivity", argues the consequences of our industrial processes are often displaced and disavowed through complex systems and networks precluding "reflexivity", so that actual effects surface in the form of breakdown, ruptures, illnesses and events (Beck, 1992, 2009), but this process is not theorized (psychologically or psychoanalytically) in terms of its affective and unconscious dimensions, such as how anxiety, loss and fear may contribute to how industrial impacts are disavowed and disassociated.

5 I did, however, find it useful during my data analysis process to, at certain points, present how certain topics appeared in interviews and how they changed across the three interviews; I created tables to help illustrates these objects and the associated stories, meanings and associations – a form of object "mapping".

6 Bollas (1992) writes about *mnemic objects* as the way a child "may associate a conserved self state with certain actual objects that were part of his early experiences" (p. 19). Bollas describes an example of how he "nominated" a swing to conserve some aspects of a self-state associated with his parents' marital conflicts (an object formally producing joy now "empty and unoccupied"). He writes, "These 'subjective objects' to use and yet extend Winnicott's term, are a vital part of our investment in the world. Through this particular type of projective identification we psychically signify objects, but as they retain their own intrinsic value they can be said to occupy an intermediate area between the conventional use or understanding and our private one" (p. 20).

7 As Klein points out, "The object which is being mourned is the mother's breast and all that the breast and the milk have come to stand for . . . namely, love, goodness and security. All these are felt by the baby to be lost, and as a result of his own uncontrollable greedy and destructive phantasies . . ." (Klein, 1986, p. 148). I was struck by the similarity in how the participants recalled their experiences with and in nature as children, and the subsequent loss of such good objects. This is seen most vividly in Heather's narratives of the farm, a land of milk and honey, however it is seen across the interviews in varying forms.

8 The disconnect between what appeared in the survey data and what emerged through the three interviews is striking, suggesting the need to consider our methods extremely carefully in relation to what we actually want to uncover.

9 The stance of 'protective' towards the degraded and fragile ecosystems runs across the participants' interviews.

10 Arguably the Fox River can also be interpreted more psychoanalytically as a symbol of internal states: the water as an 'objective correlative' of a self that has been perhaps neglected, abandoned or beyond repair or 'recovery'. The river can be viewed as a symbol of life, as something that inevitably becomes ruined or degraded and is therefore beyond reprieve (or repair). I have resisted this level of interpretation as taking the analysis to a potentially more specious level; however, I do feel such interpretations are worth exploring.

References

Beck, U., 1992. *The Risk Society: Towards a New Modernity*. London: Sage.

Beck, U., 2009. *World at Risk*. London: Polity Press.

Bick, E., 1968. The experience of the skin in early object relations. *International Journal of Psychoanalysis* 49, p. 484.

Bollas, C., 1987. *Shadow of the Object: Psychoanalysis of the Unknown Thought*. London: Free Association Press [reprinted 1991].

Bollas, C., 1992. *Being a Character: Psychoanalysis and Self Experience*. London: Routledge [reprinted 1997].

Britton, R., 1992. *The Oedipal Situation and the Depressive Situation*. In Anderson, R. (ed.), *Clinical lectures on Klein and Bion*. London: Routledge, p. 103.

Caruth, C., 1996. *Unclaimed Experience: Trauma, Narrative and History*. Baltimore, MD: Johns Hopkins University Press.

Felman, S., & Laub, D., 1992. *Testimony: Crises of Witnessing in Literature, Psychoanalysis and History*. New York: Routledge, Chapman and Hall.

Freud, S., 1917. *Mourning and Melancholia*. In Strachey, J., et al. (ed.), *Standard Edition* 14. London: Hogarth Press, pp. 204–258.

Fromm, E., 1941. *Escape from Freedom*. New York: Rinehart & Co.

Klein, M., 1940. *Mourning and Its Relation to Manic-Depressive States*. In Mitchell, J. (ed.), *The Selected Melanie Klein*. New York: Free Press, pp. 146–174 [reprinted 1986].

Kristeva, J., 1992. *Black Sun: Depression and Melancholia*. New York: Columbia University Press.

Kunziar, A. A., 2006. *Melancholia's Dog: Reflections on Our Animal Kinship*. Chicago: University of Chicago Press.

Leader, D., 2009. *The New Black: Mourning, Melancholia and Depression*. London: Penguin, p. 155.

Lorenzoni, I., Nicholson-Cole, S., & Whitmarsh, L., 2007. Barriers perceived to engaging with climate change among the UK public and their policy implications, *Global Environmental Change: Human and Policy Dimensions* 17 (3–4), pp. 445–459.

Nussbaum, M., 2001. *Upheavals of Thought: The Intelligence of Emotions*. New York: Routledge.

Sànchez-Pardo, E., 2003. *Cultures of the Death Drive: Melanie Klein and Modernist Melancholia*. Durham, NC: Duke University Press.

Santner, R., 1993. *Stranded Objects: Mourning, Memory, and Film in Postwar Germany*. Ithaca, NY: Cornell University Press.

Winnicott, D. W., 1960. The theory of the parent-child relationship, *International Journal of Psychoanalysis* 41, pp. 585–595.

Bridge on Fox River, November 2009. (Photo: R. Lertzman.)

You know, it's a classic, what goes around, comes around. It might not next month or next year, but the contamination, wherever it is, everybody is going to have to contend with it, eventually, on the planet. You know, for a lot of my career I sold machinery that cleaned up waste paper pulp, and they start with a big tub, got a big mixer on the bottom, and they throw all the waste paper in there, beats it all up, makes it this big, gooey, looks like a brown milkshake, if it's not white paper, usually, you know, I'm talking about box paper, and everything goes in that, so there's plastic from these boxes, and there's staples from these boxes, and there's Styrofoam from these boxes, and, all the stuff gets, of course, all beaten up, and gets taken out by various methods, in the process depending upon what they are, if they float they get skimmed off. But I read recently where in the Pacific Ocean, I guess it is, see now, in the middle of one of these tubs, you know, you have this vortex, right, and it's all swirling, and one of the removal methods is they make a rake, they throw a rope in that's got a bunch of barbed wire on it, they just throw it in, and this, it's a rope maybe about twelve feet long, about this big around, and it wraps around inside this tub just by the motion of this stuff swirling around, it wraps on this rag, and then every, every few minutes you pull this rope out by about six inches and this continues to build from this plastic, and you can continue to do this then, as long as, as long as you continue to put waste paper in you can continue to pull this rope out of this plastic, and it'll be this big around, hard packed, it's like a rope. In the middle of the Pacific Ocean, there apparently is this huge, if you want to call it a vortex of junk, contamination, plastic, only it's like what I just described, only on a much larger scale, apparently this thing is just miles in diameter, imagine this big island of plastic junk, just floating in the Pacific Ocean.

– Ray, Interview 2

Chapter 5

Ambivalence

Negotiating industrial rewards and environmental losses

Conducting a narrative analysis that incorporates an object-relational approach offers arguably more dimensional insights than conventional ('frontal') interviews and surveys. This approach (1) provides a richer investigation into the complexity of how people experience and respond to local ecological degradation caused by industrial practices and (2) suggests that complex psychic processes inform the ways in which ecological issues are negotiated and repaired. By highlighting affective dimensions of loss and longing, environmental engagement becomes more complicated than whether or not people care enough to act. The emphasis shifts to a consideration of unconscious processes, both psychic and social and to the very real dilemmas occasioned by immediate and chronic ecological problems. The experience of ambivalence is one such dilemma.

Ambivalence in the form of vacillating between talking about objects positively or negatively, notably associated with industry in the region, emerged in the narrative data. Such vacillations point to a reluctance or inability to acknowledge a source of distress, illness or health problem. This ambivalence presents clues for understanding the nature of environmental subjectivities and responses to chronic issues, particularly those which arouse concern and yet are not 'repaired'. Ambivalence also marks a critical dimension of environmental engagement that experiences industry as fraught, involving both well-being and destruction. As environmental issues *are* largely consequences of industrial processes, how the relationship between the two evokes dilemmas that lead to feelings of ambivalence is worth investigation. In light of Klein's theories of the coexistence of aggression, hate and love in infancy and the achievements of the depressive position as integrative of these aspects, I argue that ambivalence towards industry and the environment contributes to a *melancholic* mode of response to ecological degradation. Protest and anger may not be possible to direct towards the source of this loss for fear of possible repercussions, such as job loss, social ostracizing or appearing 'ungrateful' for the fruits of industry. Ambivalence and melancholia thus comprise a constellation of defensive strategies that inform agency, response and engagement.

To consider what may foster reparation and concern in response to ecological degradation, we need to account for the ways in which the objects in need of 'repair' are in causal relationships with objects that are 'repairing'. For example, while industry may degrade valued ecosystems and recreational opportunities, it also provides livelihood and community resources and prosperity. The "conflict of ambivalence" (Freud, 1917) is a precondition for melancholia. And, as discussed, melancholia as a response to loss presents profound implications for capacities for action and constructive responses to environmental degradation. As I will argue here and in Chapter 7, approaching environmental engagement and advocacy in terms of the 'trifecta' of values, behaviour and attitudes is insufficient. Focusing on values and attitudes as driving behaviours, as well as the quest for the right alignment of these three aspects, overlooks the complex picture that reveals itself when ambivalence, melancholia and loss are considered. As long as communications stimulate defensive strategies, the ongoing efforts for mobilizing actions will be thwarted.

I illustrate the process of ambivalence by showing the tendency across participants to assert that Green Bay is a 'good' place to live, as well as its legacy of multiple industrial effects, resulting in serious air and water quality issues. Green Bay, primarily the Fox River and the surrounding waterways, tends to be split into a good object and a bad object alternately. It is imbued with both loving and aggressive attributes. The ambivalent relations suggest powerful affective needs for security, afforded by jobs, home and community, which can override concurrent and potentially distressing awareness of ecological degradation. This results in a complex capacity to recognize ecological degradation but to choose to focus on the 'goodness' of the place. This capacity splits objects into partial objects.

Further, the need for security in its various forms harkens to the infantile quest for containment and is one of the driving forces for a return to a site of love and nourishment (Klein, 1945). I regard this phenomenon as symptomatic of an ambivalence experienced in relation to local ecology and primarily how industry is perceived and experienced as both 'good and bad'. Following the discussion of Green Bay as 'good and bad', I focus on degrees of ambivalence and conflict in relation to causality of environmental health issues and the presence of toxins and risk in the immediate environment – that is, a simultaneous recognition and denial of industry's complicity in ill effects. I suggest this ambivalence constitutes a much broader and endemic ideological dimension that views industry as simultaneously celebrated, protected, blamed, hated and loved.

Matters of love and hate

Ambivalence matters for how melancholia is understood through the coexistence of love and hate (or aggression) towards the lost object. As Freud theorized, this coexistence can lead to unconscious guilt, which in turn leads to the lost object being introjected and internalized in the subject. It is as if the self has become fused with the lost object. In the case of industrial ecological issues, object relations appear similarly complicated; while natural damage may be experienced as a loss, the causes of the loss (e.g. industry) are also imbued with benefit, achievement or surplus. We partake of the fruits of industry whilst we may experience sadness or longing for the losses it incurs. As discussed, I found strong affective dimensions throughout the interviews regarding specific environments, such as affection, longing, even love and tenderness. This presence of loving affect was surprising, given the lack of involvement with organized activities associated with environmental engagement such as with local watershed or environmental groups or otherwise recognized environmental action.

Ambivalence is psychoanalytically conceptualized as simultaneously holding competing affective investments such as the classic example of 'love and hate' experienced towards one's parents or the breast (Freud, 1926; Klein, 1935). In many ways, ambivalence characterizes the mood with which participants tended to relate with Green Bay, the local industry and the local environments. On the one hand, many openly expressed disgust and shock towards the level of local water and air pollution, yet on the other hand they quickly shifted modes and contradicted themselves to provide excuses or rationales for the very issues they just expressed unhappiness over. It was difficult to obtain a straightforward and simple narrative about the local environment. In this sense, there was considerable 'movement' across the interviews around the topics of environmental issues, shifting from a subject position of blame, victim and disengaged citizen. The movement could be tracked within a single interview and particularly across the set of three interviews. These subject positions are reflected in statements such as "I don't know how they could let this happen," "Green Bay is a good place to live" and "I guess I see it [industry] as a necessary evil." Such positions are also reflected in the ambivalent feelings towards environmental health concerns which were initially acknowledged, then disavowed, acknowledged again, and so forth.

As discussed in the previous chapter, melancholia does not solely relate to loss of human relationships, as is commonly interpreted, but may include other forms of deep and inchoate loss of object and identity. As Freud (1917) observed, this can

> include all those situations of being slighted, neglected or disappointed, which can import opposed feelings of love and hate into the relationship or reinforce an already existing ambivalence . . . This conflict due to ambivalence, which sometimes arises more from real experiences, sometimes more from constitutional factors, must not be overlooked among the preconditions for melancholia.
>
> (p. 250)

We can take from this that melancholia can be triggered by *situations* as opposed to direct and specific losses, e.g. the death of a loved one. These 'situations' include slights, neglect and disappointments, which can "import opposed feelings of love and hate" or strengthen an existing ambivalent relation. This distinction suddenly widens the view in terms of what can be considered loss and what may trigger or reinforce the experience of ambivalence.

Most germane for this discussion is how ambivalence can fracture or divert psychic energies in terms of adequately processing a loss. Recognizing the existence of ambivalence, its source, naming it (acknowledgement) and coming to terms with it is part of the eventual 'work of mourning'. In melancholia, ambivalence towards the loss can divert the sense of anger and resentment felt towards the external object inward, such that the love and hate presumably felt towards the lost object is internalized. The external lost object is 'rescued' from the wrath of anger, and it is thus turned inward with its aura of longing, "pining" (Klein, 1940, p. 151). The result is a narcissistic, inwardly directed impoverishment, unresolved and static. In the extreme sense, it is as if the individual has internalized the dead or lost object. Most significantly, grievances experienced as a result of the loss and disappointment (e.g. contaminated water, the pollution of a beach, the muck of algae) are not directed outwardly but rather remain private and contribute to a subjectivity that may be incapable of action or repair.

Why would ambivalence be a 'precondition for melancholia'? It is suggested that the experience of both hate and love for an object can arouse intolerable guilt, which is then directed inwardly, making it impossible to withdraw the 'libidinal' affective investments that can foster (healing) mourning. In order to mourn, as Freud points out, the subject needs to be able to recognize the loss, make it 'real' through reality testing of its absence. If there is an unclear origin of the loss and an inability to articulate this socially, as suggested in the previous chapter, it may not be possible to undertake the work of mourning which is the basis for action, repair and creativity. As I argue, the presence of ambivalence in relation to environmental degradation may constitute a form of *melancholic* subjectivity, impeding what might otherwise be seen as viable and active engagement with the issues. It is not that people lack concern or awareness about these specific issues but rather that a psychic 'dance' is taking place, suggesting a form of ambivalence. Engagement or the lack thereof is not a straightforward expression of valuation or attitudinal positions. The presence and process of ambivalence reflect the highly complicated nature of our deep investments in practices that are both life-affirming and life-degrading.

As discussed in Chapter 3, observing splitting in the context of the interviews helps bring into relief the ambivalent positions I am describing. I therefore begin with the concept of 'splitting' as the mechanism for understanding ambivalence and its central role in environmental engagement. Ambivalence is difficult to illustrate because it is an internal state; however, splitting is identifiable in narrative discourses by noting how the same object is referred to alternately in different terms. In the following sections, I present examples from the interviews that illustrate the kind of splitting I suggest is representative of ambivalence.

Green Bay: Good object, bad object

There is little question at this juncture that how people relate to and perceive their local environment and the ills caused by industry is complex. In contrast to a stance perhaps more aligned with a 'paranoid-schizoid' position in which the world may appear as quite black and white, in the interview data I found degrees of complexity with regard to how both place and its industry are experienced. There was the capacity to switch modes between viewing Green Bay as a polluted and abject site (e.g. Jeff and Sally's "shock" at the water pollution when relocating from outside the area) and viewing it as full of nourishment and a good provider (not unlike a benevolent father or a loving mother). The object in this case has multiple dimensions. What matters here is how ambivalence presents the capacity to simultaneously hold competing, conflicting views, attitudes and affects about a place, practice, experience or relationship. We are literally 'pulled' into tensions, like a tangle of yarn. It is the texture and nature of this 'tangle' that I examine more closely.

Green Bay as an external and internal object appears to encompass these respective qualities of 'good and bad', mutually coexisting. Across the interviews, I found a striking juxtaposition between expressions of affective attachment with Green Bay as a community and the acknowledgement of its irresponsible industrial practices and environmental quality issues (notably air and water quality). Jeff, a former nuclear plant manager and boating enthusiast, tells me he regards his move to Green Bay from Sheboygan as "one of the best moves of my life." As he says in the first interview, "Ah, Green Bay is a nice town. I really like it." He mentions its virtues as a place for raising a family, the schools and sense of community. At the same time, he is aware of its chronic pollution problems, concentrated primarily in the Fox River, and chronic air pollution issues (he mentions working in town and not being able to breathe during his lunch break walks due to the stench from emissions). He describes his experience of the water on arriving from Sheboygan:

> The river, when we first moved here, twenty-two years ago, was quite polluted . . . ah in fact you couldn't see, you know, you couldn't see the bottom. At least now you can see the bottom. They are cleaning it up which is nice . . . well, [sighs], I think it's EPA. There are all these paper mills up the river, dumping crap, they got them to stop . . . most of what they are putting in, the sources have pretty much stopped. There are PCBs that are still a problem, especially if you want to eat the fish.

Jeff then mentions the clean-up efforts:

> They are talking about pumping sediments out of the bottom of the river to clean it up. Which would be really nice. If it was really clear it would be really, really nice, it would be a lot more usable for recreation, I mean people are still fishing out there, I'm not sure I'd eat any of the fish. They do. I like looking at it . . . like, like I say when the water was higher I'd take that little sailboat I have out here, and sail up and down the river . . . it, ah, I don't know, I think it's, it's nice.

At the end of our first interview, Jeff continues to talk about his appreciation for the Fox River Trail, which runs directly behind his house, as being a "neat" mix of industry and nature: "If you get south, just, well by the reformatory, you're out in the middle of the woods, in the woods someplace, you know. Which is kind of neat, I think. The contrast of industry and population and non-population." The comments about the Fox River Trail echo sentiments across the interviews, although few people actually used it much. However, it was regarded largely as a civic achievement. At the end of the second interview, as I was leaving the house, Jeff said it was interesting that I had asked him why they chose to stay in Green Bay despite its polluted condition – a question I had never actually addressed to him. This 'imagined' question suggested our conversation about the pollution in Green Bay had stimulated an internal process of questioning or reflecting on why they would stay in a place that he acknowledged was polluted and whose waterways they could not use (in contrast to Sheboygan, where Jeff was very active with racing boats). In the third interview, I raised this topic again with him and asked why he brought it up.

> I guess talking about, you know the environment, and I thought about some days you couldn't breathe, and some days the water was so bad it looked like you could walk on it . . . And I guess I asked myself why did I stay in an environment like that. And I guess the other things that were going on here, overcame that. [. . .] I mean the university here, ah, well I went out there for several years. I had gone to school before, but I never finished, so I started going part-time here. Ah. I guess the assets outnumbered the bad parts. Because otherwise why would a person stay. I mean why do coal miners keep going down that hole [laughing], just do I guess. So I don't know.

As someone who refrains from any environmental activism, it is important to recognize Jeff's simultaneous awareness of local ecological issues, including visceral experiences of polluted water and air, and his appreciation for the 'good' qualities that he feels outweigh the 'bad'. In his way, he is able to appreciate the river despite its abject pollution and (as Donald also recounts) takes some pleasure in reporting his observations of the water becoming clearer on his walks on the Fox River Trail. In imagining my question regarding his decision to stay in Green Bay despite its pollution, he presents the contradiction and complexity of this dilemma beautifully in his example of the coal miner going down into the hole. His laughter signifies the lack of words to articulate what appears as an incoherent situation: the act of willingly going down into "that hole," which he is likening to his arrival to Green Bay.

Yet throughout the interviews, it is clear that Green Bay has afforded Jeff remarkable opportunities in terms of personal development and career challenge, as he thoroughly enjoys learning new skills and was able to be a part of a large-scale nuclear power plant construction project as a project manager. Even in the case of the nuclear plant, Jeff brings his concerns and sentiments together in an unlikely combination in writing an in-depth report on the plant (which he lovingly displayed and provided a copy for me, dug out of the attic) for his environmental studies course at the University of Wisconsin in Green Bay (UWGB), one of the first universities in the United States to offer environmental studies. His pride from his involvement in the power plant is palpable, and he regards the experience as a highlight of his professional career. In his work on the plant, Jeff was forced in some ways to background his environmental concerns, as he alludes to in the final interview. When discussing environmental engagement, he notes that he would not "be quiet" in the context of his workplace but that he learned over time that it was important to know when to speak out and when not to.

For example, in discussing how certain environmental issues affect him emotionally, he responds:

> Well I'd just, it's like, ah, today's world I mean if you think about the war or other things that aren't going right, you think about our political situation, I mean it's depressing, what do you do you do what you can, influence what you can and other than that you have to go on with your life. It's like a lot of things. Ah. We had an issue that came up, ah years ago, EMF or electromagnetic fields on high voltage lines, I don't know if you are familiar with that at all.

And then he continues with a long story about an uncle who had been involved with research on electronic long-wave risks. The point of the story is the importance of being aware of risks, even if they may not be certain. He then relates this to his experiences working on the nuclear plant project:

> When we were arguing that point, ah, I made myself heard, that at least let's acknowledge that there is something there, and we're looking at it. And do look at it. Which they did and I don't – and again I doubt if it's just cause they were listening to me, but I was one of those, who was saying. And that was not in my realm of work field at all, but I did . . . maybe that's why they stuck me in Antigo for the last three years! [Laughs]

In certain respects, Jeff reflects a particular subject position in which environmental concern – in the Winnicottian sense of having moral responsibility – is present but expressed in quite specific channels, as is the case throughout the participants in the study. The demonstrated capacities for regarding the positive and negative attributes of particular objects, such as the water and environment in Green Bay as both life-giving and risky, appear to work in concert with channeling environmental concern in particular ways. It may be necessary to 'split' objects in order to then live with and manage environmental concern in ways that are expressed in very particular formations. For example, boating is culturally and socially sanctioned, but being outspoken politically is not. The splitting, then, not only is about how objects are related with but reflect internal forms of splitting and disassociation as well – from self-states of deep concern and care that may not have adequate outlets or, as Winnicott says, opportunities for "contributing-to."

Staying connected with the 'good': The Snoopy fishing pole

Participant Scott's perceptions and relations with the local environment, as both loved and recognized as slightly damaged (not unlike a loved but slightly pitied relative) illustrate the ways in which water can be viewed as 'good and bad' but also the sense of possibility that 'bad water' can be turned into 'good water'. Scott is a 31-year-old father of a small girl he was looking after during my visits. He and his partner lived in a small modest home, both of them doing shift work, so that they could take turns looking after the baby, but having limited time together. His father had been in the United States Air Force, and the family moved around the United States frequently until Scott was 13, when they settled in the Green Bay region. Through the G.I. Bill, his father received a degree in communications; however, as Scott points out, employment opportunities were limited at that time, so he ended up training as an electrician. His mother, who had not worked while he grew up, was due the following week to receive a college degree. In the first interview, about halfway through, we begin discussing his feelings about Green Bay and the water. As with Howard, Scott tells me with some pride about someone he knows who moved away to a supposedly more desirable place, only to return. It seemed important for him to emphasize Green Bay here as 'good', a common tendency in many first interviews:

S: Well, living in Green Bay, you know I've, I've heard some from many people that have lived here, moved away and came back that this is such a great area, you know that, not so much that, I, I know somebody who lived in Florida, came here, went back to Florida and then came back, you know just because they, they like the area so much.
R: And what is it –
S: Um I think it's, I, I, I think you know, overall you know, like um, the quality of jobs that are available, I mean the pretty good economy. Um, the friendliness of the people. That, that goes a long way. Um, . . . you know, yeah, I'd like to say climate but you know [. . .] There's much better places than Green Bay if you want to talk climate. [We both laugh.] But [. . .], yeah, it, it's . . .

Scott refers to human qualities, friendliness and the economy, as the positive attributes, downplaying the non-human environment (e.g. the climate). I ask him to expand on how the local water influences his experiences of the place.

R: Do you think the water adds to this area?
S: Well definitely, um, if it wasn't for the water, um, wouldn't have any of the paper industry that is growing up and built the economy. You know because

you need water for the paper making process. Um, and, and you know, historically you know, people are always drawn to where water is. Um, so, ah . . . it, it, it's a good thing to be near water, you know because, you know when, when ah, Green Bay was first starting out everybody got their water from the river, you know a hundred and thirty, a hundred and fifty years ago . . . And then, when they started going more to the groundwater and, which is better, and, and now, now, you know there's a big push not too long ago for, and everybody is getting their water either from the bay and getting it treated or . . . yeah, um, there's a coalition of governments around the area that are piping water from Manitowoc, so, it's getting treated, and getting piped here so . . . I think that, you know, [paused] you know water is important to life, I mean we're, what seventy-percent water? So, yeah . . . What was your question? [Laughing]

Here Scott relates a somewhat incoherent string of associations with water, ending with a moment of dissociation ("What was your question?") – a pattern that also occurred when Howard spoke of swimming in the river and when Sally was speaking about the contaminated water. Scott's free associations suggest the connection with industry, water and its "importance to life", bringing it back to the human body. If it was not for the water, there would be no paper mill and industry that support the economy; however, if not for industry, there would be no need to treat the water from the Bay and pipe in drinking water from elsewhere. Scott is aware of the interconnected nature of the Great Lakes and the relation of Green Bay with the Great Lakes and at the same time is able to both celebrate the local economy and acknowledge that the water is both 'good' and 'bad', preferring to focus on it being 'good'. In the following passage, he describes water as calming and how he is able to enjoy the "glitter of light" on the Fox River, as well as the fog rising in the early mornings, without distinguishing between industrial and more 'natural' areas. He does not wish to split the object in this way, but rather he is able to hold simultaneously conflicting or different affective relations with the water, calming and pleasurable but also "dirty". He then mentions the "Snoopy pole", a good object from his childhood that he wishes to pass on to his daughter. The 'good' in this case subsumes any 'bad' qualities that may be present.

S: I, I think you know, being that it's calming, you know, being that it's pretty, you know, no matter what time of the year there's always something neat to look at . . .

R: Everywhere, or certain parts of it?

S: Yeah, pretty much anywhere. You know, well, downtown, it's so industrialized you know but its still, there's still, you know it, when the light hits it just right you know, you can get all the glitter of light coming off [. . .] I, you know, if, if, things were cleaned up and you know wouldn't think of it as a dirty river you know . . . Um, we would, yeah, I don't know if we would do anymore recreation on it than we do . . . You know, just because you know, you know boats can be really expensive. But you know, taking walks along the ah, Fox River Trail or over at the park, you know, yeah, well we do that now, but you know, maybe do a little fishing you know, that would be a little more fun. You know, I, I'd love to teach my daughter how to fish eventually. You know. Everybody's got to start out with a Snoopy pole some time. [Laughing]

The Snoopy fishing pole is a poignant invocation, bringing together childhood associations with the centrality of fishing in his family (despite the fact that, although he seems either unaware or disavowing, the fish caught in any waters near Green Bay are potentially contaminated). As Bollas notes, "The object world is, in many respects, a lexicon for self-experience, to the extent that the selection of objects is often a type of self-utterance" (1992, p. 30). Objects can hold both positive and negative qualities, can 'contain' (and thus evoke) aspects of the self and experiences we wish to protect, savor or disown. Green Bay on the whole is a strong *positive object* for Scott that provides essential needs such as "friendliness" (love and affection) and work (security). Affectively and discursively, there is little space for the 'bad' qualities, similar to Sally and her need to put aside the experience of Green Bay as flawed in any way, despite her ongoing acknowledgement of its serious ecological issues. It is not a denial but a capacity for *splitting* off 'good and bad' qualities so the good object is not contaminated.

To put into context Scott's ambivalence surfacing around industry and the water, we need to attend to the positive affective qualities conveyed in the interviews. For Scott, because he had moved around frequently as a child, notions of *home*, *security* and a sense of *belonging* are central themes, and he spends much time discussing the minutiae of his domestic situation in Green Bay. For example, he talks about how he and his partner had been displaced from an apartment building so that it could be renovated into an assisted living development, and although speaking lightly of it, they were essentially forced to leave along with other residents who had been living in the building for decades (including a 91-year-old, he notes with irony). The ability to purchase a small, modest home was a huge achievement, and he enjoys telling me about all of their work involved with the house, particularly extensive renovations done by Scott and his friends. In this sense, they were able to make the house their own and had strong affective investments in the home itself, similar to the way Victoria invested reparative energies into the home, as a site for modification and reflection (and expression) of herself. As with Howard, who lived with his parents as long as feasibly possible, Scott stayed living with his parents until he was in his early twenties. He was forced to move when his partner told him, "I can't marry you unless you move out on your own." While Scott jokes and laughs often, I sense in the narratives a distress around the frequent moves in childhood but an inhibition to express (or consciously feel) this distress. For example, he recounts the time when they were living in Utah and his affection for the landscape:

You know and I, I always remember looking at that, and especially you know, in, in the early evening when it would turn orange and purple in colors you know, my mom said she would just catch me just staring up at the mountains. . . . And then the move back, you know it's, I'm, the way I look at it now is that, you know I was like, 'okay, we're going somewhere else,' you know, left a few friends behind and, but didn't really bother me . . . You know because I was going somewhere else [uses higher pitch voice].

The ambivalence about environmental issues is related to the focus on security. The first verbal association Scott makes with Green Bay in the first interview is with the local economy. This is significant, for as Klein points out in her discussion of livelihood and security, "The satisfaction of our self-preservation needs and the gratification of our desire for love are forever linked up with each other, because they are first derived from one and the same source". She continues, "Security attained by satisfaction of our essential requirements is therefore linked up with emotional security, and both are all the more needed because they counteract the early fears of losing the beloved mother" (Klein 1945, p. 108). The point is that Scott's prioritization of the local economy and the ability to work and afford a home reigns affectively significant and may serve to elide or override other, less desirable qualities or traits. In actuality, Scott demonstrates in the interviews a surprising level of environmental literacy, as with many of the participants, thereby dispelling the potential misconception that he either is not aware or does not care. But how this is negotiated in relation to additional, admittedly complex, variables is what requires attention.

For Scott, loss and mourning are not explicitly expressed or conveyed until the second and third interviews. However, the experiences of loss via frequent relocations as a child until age 13 likely inform his mode of relating with his current residence. Through a 'jolly' affective exterior, there is an avoidance of negative or mournful affect. He seems genuinely happy and at peace with his life and circumstances. There are hints of recognition of a reality that could be improved: the water would be seen as "less dirty" if cleaned up, which may afford him and his family more opportunities for recreation and enjoyment of it. With regard to the river and the water, it's viewed as both 'good' and 'bad' – glittering and dirty. In our final interview, I revisit the topic of his feelings of sadness about the compromised water quality in the region and see the refrain echoed across the interviews:

You know shrimp isn't from around here so but still it means, everything is, you know, everything is affected by pollution somewhere. You know, and around here is little different than, you know in the middle of the ocean because I think it's a little more concentrated around here. Because of the . . . overly industrialized area we have. But you know it's what the economy was built on. You know, Green Bay is the number one toilet paper producer in the world. So it mean it's . . . that accounts for a lot of things. You know and . . . generally sometimes when you have [. . .] progress you have you know ya, there, there's a cost to that . . . be it you know, monetary or government or . . . or ah, environment.

We can clearly see the ambivalence in relation to industry. At one point in the interview, Scott acknowledges sadness about the water quality issues, as do all of the participants at one point or another in the interviews. The sadness about the environmental issues that Victoria expresses as acute 'disappointment' mainly in herself for "choosing to come here" and Sally's disappointment in others for allowing it to get "so bad" are continually tempered with the need to highlight and defend the good qualities provided by the same industry responsible for the degradation and loss.

Industry may be seen as a "necessary evil", but what is the affective function of this sentiment? What does it perform affectively, psychically and, ultimately, politically? This stance may be viewed as an expression of the 'depressive position', the capacity to integrate both the 'good' and 'bad' qualities in the particular object. In the depressive position, the anxieties experienced by the potential loss or absence of the object are 'depressed'. This arguably enables us to direct the sense of guilt for causing potential harm to the object, towards a grounded and mature basis of concern and reparation, even creativity. And yet if this is the case, would we not be able to observe more evidence of reparation and creativity in the form of active attempts to make right, repair and contribute to the environment that has been so degraded? For this reason, we must appreciate the form of splitting that is taking place, a process that neutralizes any prospect for further involvement or sense of concern for the environment. In order to act on concern and view the environment as an object requiring intervention in some way, there would need to be the recognition of some harm or damage that has taken place.

This is where the participants consistently stop short; they come close to signaling their distress over the environment – indeed their participation in the interviews signaled some sort of affective investment – but withdraw when it approaches what may seem as a critique or anger towards industry itself. In this sense, we need to look again at Freud's insights into melancholia and the role of ambivalence. The inability to express hate or anger towards the loved object can arrest mourning, which is the most constructive and appropriate response. To truly call out industry as degrading appears to be a betrayal of some form. Industry has taken the role of a 'father' who is both beneficent and brutalizing, and it may arouse too much guilt to confront the transgressions of the providing father figure who has made Green Bay "what it is". As Scott notes, "It's what the economy was built on". As the economy is security, and as Klein notes, security takes us back to our hunger for the sense of complete love and protection from the mother, we may begin to appreciate what is actually at stake in making environmental redress in this region (and others). However, Klein points out the interaction between the aggressive impulses and the libidinal ones: "The course of libidinal development is thus at every step stimulated and reinforced by the drive for reparation, and ultimately by the sense of guilt" (Klein, 1945, p. 410). Reparation is a result of the confluence of the opposing instinctual drives rather than merely a displacement of an impulse onto some socially acceptable representative (Hinshelwood, 1989, p. 414). For Klein, reparation is the cornerstone of the maturational processes that forge a way out of the depressive position.

In these cases, we see profound ambivalence and inability to 'make reparation' towards the environment. However, the issue warrants a closer examination in terms of both Freudian melancholia – an arrestment of mourning and paralysis – and Winnicott's concept of contributing-to to include concern and creativity. For both Klein and Winnicott, there is the paradoxical need to have integrated or tolerated aggressive and destructive capacities. The infant must see that the mother can withstand her attacks. It is when such impulses are not tolerated that guilt may become so overwhelming as to impair capacities for concern. In the case of the local industry, which has provided jobs, the civic economic base and international cache as a paper processing empire, it is the destructive capacities that are not necessarily fully addressed. The consequences are felt, observed, even in some cases experienced as illness. Yet deep ambivalence remains, causing an inability to come to terms with, and potentially to grieve and mourn, the impacts of the local industry. Perhaps not surprisingly, this capacity is displaced and projected onto environmental advocates and scientists, who thus 'hold' these experiences and are able to mourn, grieve and ultimately make certain reparations to the ecological systems. As we will see later in the chapter, environmental engagement is cordoned off as a zone for others and constructed as constituting those who see the world in black and white – indeed, what Klein would refer to as the paranoid-schizoid position, mobilizing manic defences.

Disappointment and the melancholia of illness

Expressing genuine distress towards those who have despoiled or degraded the local ecologies appears to be fraught for many participants. In contrast to what we may consider an environmental subject position, full of anger or rage against the perpetrators, in this case I notice reluctance to 'go there'. This is not the same as denial. In the context of health, we see in the next example of Victoria the articulation of disappointment, a common response to environmental issues. Disappointment is a variation on the melancholic theme and suggests a lack of options for agency or action. In disappointment, the locus of accountability is both external and internal; it is directed outwardly but also inwardly, as if one must assume some measure of responsibility and guilt for risks. For several participants, various health issues are either actively present or discussed. In some cases, the participants allude to health issues linked with the environment. The way in which illness is articulated, however, reflects a dance around issues of causality. Most often there would be mention of a particular health issue, a light suggestion of its being caused by local pollution or environment and then a retraction and possibly movement forward again. There was considerable ambivalence about the sources of illness. This registered, affectively for me listening to the accounts, as a need to protect a beloved object from attack or blame. There was a process of internalization to protect the external object – in this case the region, industry, the city – from attack. This could be viewed in the cases of Howard contracting hepatitis, Victoria and the respiratory infections experienced by family members, and Sally's discussion of the drinking water contamination.

I first noticed the capacity for both acknowledging and disavowing industrial causes for health problems during the interviews with Victoria. When asking Victoria to free-associate about Green Bay in our first interview, she first mentions the health effects:

> I know that when we first came here, we felt healthier before we came here. I, my kids never had sinus infections, um, my older daughter never had an ear infection, in fact we moved to Green Bay when my younger daughter was just two- two weeks old. And I don't know how old she was, if she was five months old or what, she wouldn't sleep laying down, the only time she would sleep would be if I would hold her. And, you know being a new, um, new mom, but just having the baby, I was tired too. Felt really frustrated and I took her to the doctor and the doctor said, M'aam, your daughter has an ear infection. And I just kind of looked at him and said my kids don't get ear infections! But she had probably three of them, as an infant. . . and then it seemed my husband would get sinus infections and we had never experienced that before. And lots of people would say, 'Welcome to Green Bay,' they really felt the paper industries had, had a big effect on that.

During the third (and final) interview, however, Victoria has retreated from acknowledging the environmental effects on their health. In the following excerpt, I have asked Victoria to reflect on what she had meant in the previous interview when she said she felt "disappointment" about the various water quality issues in the region.

> What is the disappointment . . . Somewhat in ourselves, that you know, we made this choice, to come here. And then we find out that, you know, it is like this. You would hope for better, you would hope that, you know that the air would be pure and the water would be pristine and, and, that you were not somehow endangering your, yours or your children's health or safety. Um. Disappointed that somehow, along the lines, sss- somebody allowed this condition to come about, and it wasn't always that way, um, so disappointed, um, unfortunate, were my feelings, and then when, when unfortunate things happen, you just do your best, to combat that. And I, you know the water thing was easily remedied, with um, water systems, or buying, buying water. And the air issues don't cause, uh, daily irritation, it's not like, it's not like these problems that we've had have been chronic, its just things that we have not experienced before, and now are and I suppose I can say that there is no guarantee that that is what did cause

it. I mean for my husband and I we can just say we are getting older and our immune systems aren't as good and your health isn't as good as when you were younger. Disappointed when you are making a change in your life, and you're buying a new home . . . there is such excitement about it, and it's kind of a, let-down, when you find out you've got water in the basement, it's like oh I just got this new house that I think is perfect – and it's not. And I guess that's the same way in our world, you want it to be perfect but it's not.

Victoria's narrative of disappointments, both in themselves and others, signals the psychic processes of melancholic 'pining', acute disappointment and the capacity to internalize this disappointment. She cannot remain disappointed or angry for long towards others (e.g. those responsible for the unclear water and air) and directs it towards herself, the sense of guilt quite discernable. It is a narrative of a mother coming to terms with having moved her family to an environment that may pose health risks. It is also a narrative of lost ideals and the quest for perfection (as discussed in the previous chapter, the loss here is ideal rather than tangible). "You want [the world] to be perfect but it's not", she says. As the depressive position marks the capacities for recognizing that the world (mother) is not perfect and that it indeed is flawed, or absent, it also signals mourning for the loss of an idealized object.

Particularly striking in Victoria's narrative is the way in which she retracts from her previous statements about the illnesses linked, likely, to the paper industries. It becomes now less focused on the externalities but the interiorities, specifically their immune systems. Victoria displaces her disappointment in the environment and a sense of betrayal (for allowing the environment to become degraded, potentially "used up") onto herself and her husband, e.g. their being older and more vulnerable to illnesses, and questions the link with environmental factors: "I suppose I can say that there is no guarantee that that is what did cause it." Why is Victoria now, in our final meeting, vacillating on her previous assertion of the area as contributing-to their respiratory illnesses? She is expressing profound ambivalence towards Green Bay and their home as both a loved and hated object. In a sense, she has been betrayed, and yet she must maintain her affective investments. As Klein notes, when we feel we have been betrayed in terms of loss of livelihood or security, the sense of sorrow can be ever more profound as reflecting the conditions of our earliest experiences, of our needs not having been adequately met (Klein, 1959). The affective tenor of Victoria's narratives, combined with shifting around causality of environmental ills and her actual feelings about these issues, suggests a degree of psychic conflict. As a result, she pulls away and focuses on the 'good' as she can, trying to keep out the 'bad' as reminders of how she has failed to fulfill expectations of the good and perfect life. The decision to focus on the 'good' unless proven otherwise (e.g. ignorance is bliss) is illustrated next in her comments about the drinking water quality. Victoria lives in a region known to have experienced chronic water contamination due to the proximity and practices of local concentrated animal operations (CAO). The following excerpt is from the second interview:

> There have been other communities in surrounding areas that have had severe issues, with farmers. Um. And it's been on the news [tone of voice changes, becomes higher], and you can see them, you know, filling a glass with this filthy looking water, and um, I, there, it's obvious that there's something wrong. I guess if, if our neighbours said they took their water to some lab or some sort, and they knew that there were harmful chemicals in our water, then, I would question ours too. I would say well, we live next door to each other, and if you know that, then maybe we should have our water tested too. I mean maybe ignorance is bliss, but as long as water looks good and tastes good, I think we are alright.

Victoria establishes her parameters clearly in terms of what would be required for alarm, regardless of rationality or logic. If other communities in surrounding areas have severe issues, then it stands to reason her locality may have similar issues. This can be viewed as a form of defence against the knowledge that would require some form of action or tangible response. As noted, the ability to split objects into 'good and bad' qualities and to overlook the bad ones is central for understanding the appearance of apathy. In contrast to attributing a lack of engagement with a lack of concern or ignorance, what we may observe in the illustrations provided is the capacity for a simultaneous recognition but refusal to engage any further.

There is splitting between an idealized object (industry perhaps) and a hated object (illness, infection). As Klein notes, "Idealization is bound up with the splitting of the object, for the good aspects of the breast are exaggerated as a safeguard against the fear of the persecuting breast. While idealization is thus the corollary of persecutory fear, it also springs from the power of the instinctual desires which aim at unlimited gratification and therefore create the picture of an inexhaustible and always bountiful breast – an ideal breast" (Klein, 1946, p. 182). I argue that the splitting taking place in the self and environment, reflected in the Green Bay water and industry, is about preserving certain 'good and bad' aspects and the ability to gain trust in 'real objects'. Not being reflected in the narratives are levels of care or concern – recognizable as environmental activism or advocacy – as much as the ways objects are split off into ways we can cope with. If we pay attention to the *affective economy* of what is taking place, we may appreciate that in fact certain objects call out or act upon the participants in complex ways. Bollas (1992) notes how we use objects, but they can also use us; in other words, the degraded or risky environments call forth qualities that cannot be tolerated or processed. In fact, what appears to be the case is a strong sense of resignation when faced with the evidence and circumstances of loss. The point is to place this resignation of affect into some context, so we can gain a more useful understanding of why people withdraw and what practices and techniques may be effective for inspiring active response – that is, to provide permission and make sense of the impulse to *contribute* to one's environment, with its limits, damage and imperfections.

Based on the data and theoretical analysis, ambivalence is a key factor in conceptualizing environmental subjectivity in light of how we live with industry. Specifically, experiencing industry as both benevolent and brutalizing contributes to a peculiar type of 'industrial ambivalence' in which we can be deeply attached to the very practices that are recognized as harmful and even damaging. Contemporary environmental subjectivity – the experience of, perception and response to chronic ecological threats and degradation – arouses or evokes a form of 'non-dialectical opposition' that produces splitting and makes reparations emotionally arduous. In other words, experiencing ecological issues, particularly in an industrial region like Green Bay that owes its development and prosperity to highly polluting and resource-intensive industries, can be fraught with contradictions and dilemmas.

Environmental discourses perform and produce commensurate subject positions of disassociation and ambivalence, for example by not acknowledging the paper and ink used for producing campaign materials, the carbon emissions from the computers used for generating online advocacy and so on. There is a presumed 'out there' from which we speak of environmental issues, and nature itself is cleaved into the 'good' kind and the 'bad' kind. The Fox River is an ecosystem and a dumping site; it is abject and glittering, a gem or place of trauma. It contains shopping trolleys, PCBs, algae, fish, and mayflies. These constructions of the river depend on particular subject positions, experiences, cultural and social contexts and affective investments. The river *is* both an ecosystem and a waste site. It is both industrial and natural. It makes sense that there are marked narratives of ambivalence in the interviews with regard to Green Bay and various negative effects from industry. However, this matters in the implications for understanding what is actually required for reparative impulses and energies to be tapped into. In the experience of degradation, ambivalence leads to melancholia, and melancholia has profound consequences for political engagement.

References

Bollas, C., 1992. *Being a Character: Psychoanalysis and Self Experience.* London: Routledge [reprinted 1997].

Freud, S., 1917. *Mourning and Melancholia.* In Strachey, J., et al. (ed.), *Standard Edition 14.* London: Hogarth Press, pp. 237–258.

Freud, S., 1990 [1926]. *Inhibitions, Symptoms and Anxiety (The Standard Edition), Complete Psychological Works of Sigmund Freud.* New York: W. W. Norton & Company.

Hinshelwood, R. D., 1989. *A Dictionary of Kleinian Thought.* London: Free Association Books.

Klein, M., 1935. A contribution to the psychogenesis of manic-depressive states. In Mitchell, J. (ed.), *The Selected Melanie Klein.* New York: Free Press, pp. 262–289 [reprinted 1986].

Klein, M., 1940. Mourning and its relation to manic-depressive states. In Mitchell, J. (ed.), *The Selected Melanie Klein*. New York: Free Press, pp. 146–174 [reprinted 1986].

Klein, M., 1945, Love, guilt and reparation. In Klein, M., & Riviere, J. (eds.), *Love, Hate and Reparation*. New York: W. W. Norton, pp. 57–119 [reprinted 1964].

Klein, M., 1946. Notes on some schizoid mechanisms. In Mitchell, J. (ed.), *The Selected Melanie Klein*. New York: Free Press. pp. 175–200 [reprinted 1986].

Klein, M., 1959. Our adult world and its roots in infancy, *Human Relations* 12 (4), pp. 291–303.

Bay Beach, November 2009. (Photo: R. Lertzman.)

We never had a lot when I was young and but, we'd always find something to do. And my aunt and my grandma both had chests up in the attic and boxes, old clothes from the early 1900s and old baby clothes and things like that, we'd go and get dressed up and go up into the field and play or whatever and we'd kind of go off and make our own fun . . . so at times my grandma had to do her chores and stuff and to keep us kids occupied, um, you know, she'd get out a thimble and hide it and we'd have to go find this thimble you know, or we'd go hide and she'd come find us, but that gave her you know 10–15 minutes to finish doing her dishes or whatever it might have been you know, she played 'Go Fish' with us or she had a big chalkboard, to me back then it was big cause I was little. I'm sure it's not really that big, she'd get that out and you know, have us write words you know and teach us and stuff.

– Heather, Interview 1

Chapter 6

Reparation

Reframing environmental engagement

The concept of public apathy is often invoked in response to a perceived absence of care towards environmental quality or protection demonstrated by either the absence of certain practices or an apparent disregard for conservation. Some such practices include buying eco-friendly products, reducing carbon footprint and participating in political efforts and campaigns. These contrast with a life-style that includes a high carbon output and continuation of ecologically damaging practices. An apathetic subjectivity is characterized as one that is numb, tuned out or simply does not care about issues beyond one's immediate sphere of influence. As this book argues, apathy is a psychic defence for managing intolerable primitive anxieties and is the result of a peculiar combination of helplessness, fear and omnipotence (Segal, 1997). The helplessness at the root of apathy is in part actual – in some cases, the ecological threats we face are too large to confront on our own – and in part manufactured and result from projecting accountability and responsibility onto others (e.g. governments, industry, previous generations). In other words, individuals may experience a sense of helplessness ("there is nothing I can do"), but how they cope with that feeling can fuel the problem if responsibility is shifted to others. In the data, disappointment emerges in close relation to helplessness insofar as it contains elements of both loss and resignation. However, common to both helplessness and disappointment is the recognition that something *is* in fact not right and that things are not as we would wish them to be. I found an embedded and often unrealized element of longing and nostalgia. This complex of emotions is an expression not of apathy but of something entirely more complicated.

As discussed in previous chapters, apathy is ultimately a superficial assessment because it simplistically equates external acts with internal states. The concept does nothing to further our understanding of how chronic environmental issues are subjectively experienced and negotiated. In critiquing the apathetic subject, I reframe understandings of agency, creativity, concern and reparation as altogether more complicated than a matter of concern for certain environmental values. I commence with the premise that people care. The question then becomes one regarding the nature of such concern. For example, what limits its expression? And what are the optimal contexts for facilitating its expression?

Rather than presume an absence or of certain 'barriers', I take a *lateral* approach to explore agency, creativity, concern and reparation. A lateral approach interrogates underlying psychic and social processes as potentially informing what may shape particular expressions of reparation and creativity. In relation to the data, a lateral investigation attends to the ways in which participants express reparation and concern that are not straightforward, or 'frontal'.

Focusing on how concern is *constrained* (not absent) places creativity at the center of the reparative impulse (Winnicott 1963). In contrast to focusing on what barriers exist and how to remove or overcome them, this orientation emphasizes reparation as a form of creativity, *as well as* a product of negotiating guilt and destructive, aggressive impulses towards loved objects (Klein, 1940). As we shall see, loss, mourning, melancholia, ambivalence and reparation are inextricably linked and mutually influencing processes. Continuing from the previous chapter, we now turn to the role ambivalence plays in reparation.

Ambivalence and reparation

As discussed in Chapter 5, there are contradictions about industrial development in general. This contradictory nature can give rise to ambivalence, a capacity to hold and experience simultaneously conflicting desires, drives and investments. Water can be 'good' and 'bad', damaged and irreparable, glittering and valued. It provides relaxation and respite, but perhaps only if one is positioned in a certain way and the light falls at a particular angle. It provides recreation but also illness. Green Bay as well is a contested site of contradictions. It is home to dominant industry that provides both jobs and despoliation. In spite of the efforts on behalf of environmental advocates and scientists in the region, such as Sea Grant and the Lower Fox River Alliance, considering how complex these object relations are, it is hardly surprising the public response is less than enthusiastic. However, evidence of present concern, showed in the previous chapter, suggests that something is arresting or impeding reparative energies, or what Winnicott (1963) frames as "concern and creativity". This is ordinarily analyzed as a 'gap' between what people say and do. Again, I reject this notion of the gap because, in fact, the particular space between what people say and do is fraught with psychosocial complications and constraints. It is not a gap at all but a tangle of often competing desires, drives, commitments and investments.

As a researcher, the quality of environmental engagement has felt almost viscous, like a substance or fog surrounding the issues concerning water and air quality. I often felt confused, inchoate and vague about the ecological issues in the region during my initial field visit. I found myself colluding with both the sense of resignation for reparations to Green Bay and with the recognition of the waters as ecosystems worthy of repair. The capacity for splitting objects into 'good' and 'bad' qualities as part of the process of ambivalence has been signaled as symptomatic of the paranoid-schizoid position (Klein, 1940), otherwise perceived as defensive mechanisms against the experiences of intolerable guilt, aggression, and destructive impulses (Segal, 1972). Most salient for this discussion are the relationship between splitting and paralysis and understanding how this relationship informs a melancholic mood surrounding environmental reparation. Seeing splitting and paralysis as a "revolt against mourning" (Freud, 1917) – as strategies for managing distressing or uncomfortable truths about our way of life, industrial progress and its consequences – raises profound implications for how we think about reparation and concern.

I argue that while reparations may be impeded by ambivalence and melancholia, they are simultaneously present in more intimate practice. Reparation, therefore, is not absent but rather lacking a 'home' for broader expression. The industrial presence in Green Bay constitutes an object that cannot withstand anger or redress without arousing intolerable levels of guilt in community members. The refrain, "Green Bay is a good place to live" is true but only partially so. The loss and disappointment, poignantly expressed by the participants, is not a loss that can be socially processed and recognized, which is essential for the work of mourning. In this way, the loss is *melancholic* (Freud, 1917). It has unclear origins and is thus cathected internally into a mood of sadness or vague disappointment. However, there are unique qualities to this form of 'environmental melancholia' best understood in social, economic and political contexts because such contexts provide 'affective homes' for our losses and grief. This relates to there being fewer expressions of self-flagellation (e.g. self-hate as the internalized hated lost object) in relation to environmental damage and loss. Rather, we find a more generalized guilt that may lead to a collective form of paralysis, as well as ideological defensive structures, such as equating environmental practices with being non-capitalist and "un-American", or viewing environmentalists as only wanting money, which I will discuss in the next section.[1]

I frame the discussion of reparation by first focusing on certain activities engaged in by a few participants. This is a deliberate emphasis because central to my argument is the assertion that while there *appears* to be an absence of activity or response, reparative activities are taking place. Although activities such as home gardening, switching to LED or CFL bulbs at home and other related intimate practices often fall short of moving beyond a certain sphere of influence, they are reparative nonetheless. Understanding these reparative activities as contextualized by social, biographical and affective influences, such as identity, unresolved loss, sense of helplessness and disenfranchisement help further destabilize the set of prescribed reparative activities generated largely by environmental professionals. I then examine how several participants articulate their own levels of involvement and, in some cases, recount negative experiences and associations with sanctioned environmental activities. These narratives raise the issue of *contribution*, a critical concept articulated by Winnicott in the context of the capacities for concern, e.g. taking responsibility for oneself and one's environment, which I shall discuss and thus conclude the chapter. As I argue, a focus on *contribution* has the potential to radically reframe our strategies, tactics and orientations to environmental engagement.

Ambivalence as achievement: The emergence of concern

In order to address reparative capacities, we need to revisit ambivalence and its role in understanding the emergence of concern, or what Winnicott refers to as *ruth*. Hanna Segal, in writing about "socio-political expressions of ambivalence" highlights the central role of ambivalence in the capacities for both loving and mature engagement with the world, as well as a capacity for splitting the ego and objects that can lead to manic defences (Segal, 1997). Segal usefully distinguishes between the "achievement of ambivalence", which is essential to the integration of split object and feelings, and "the recognition of reality, which is both gratifying and frustrating. The achievement of ambivalence, so to speak, also brings with it a new range of feelings, such as the fear of loss and guilt (p. 159). In optimal circumstances, when ambivalence is recognized, the ensuing aggression felt as damaging to a loved and necessary object can mobilize loving impulses and the wish to repair and restore (p. 159). For example, the infant may attack the mother, but in the mother's withstanding, the child can begin to experience the desire to repair. Likewise, feeling our anger towards industry for polluting and destroying our ecosystems may, in fact, give rise to the capacity to access the desire to repair. This is precisely why emerging platforms for convening open and honest conversations about our environmental predicaments and challenges presents such profound potential (Randall, 2009). Being able to work through our aggressive and angry feelings and accessing love and repair form the basis of constructive sublimation, in Klein's view. However, as Segal points out, we must look at what can impede or impair this process. The guilt and fear of loss is extremely painful, and powerful defences can set in if there is not an adequate sense of containment or security by which to 'work through' the ambivalence.[2] The presence of a 'safe space', where one is free to express mixed-up, complicated, confusing and angry experiences without fear of attack or threat, can be accessed in a number of ways, which I discuss in Chapter 7. Although the context for this theoretical framework is set in infantile development, we can apply similar concepts to the mature person's capacities for coming to terms with ambivalence, loss and aggression. As Winnicott suggests, recognizing our destructive and aggressive energies in relation to repair, concern and creativity may provide a wholly more grounded and psychically astute approach to social and individual forms of environmental creative response. In other words, allowing the expression of a full range of emotions from frustration, annoyance and anger and not sanitizing them in favor of a "happy-happy environmental solutions politics" (Lertzman, 2011) may allow for a far greater range of authentic engagement. The depressive position, per Klein, is often cited as a basis for concern and for effective psychic integration. It marks the human capacity to tolerate loss and to develop capacities for integration and empathy (versus splitting into good/bad binary thinking). Another way of looking at the relationship between aggression and reparation is through Winnicott's discussion of *ruth* (1958):

> What is the so-called depressive position about, or better, what is it? The helpful approach perhaps to this problem starts with the word ruthless. Ruthlessness, of course, has to come into our lives constantly if we are to be alive and clear. At first the infant from our point of view is ruthless. There is no concern yet as to the result of instinctual loving. This love is originally a form of impulse, gesture, contact relationship, and it affords the infant the satisfaction of self-expression, and release from instinctual tension. Furthermore, it places the object outside the self . . . suggesting that there must be a recognition and engagement with our ruthlessness, in order for concern and 'ruth' to emerge. This is what is missing.
>
> (p. 265)

He continues:

> At some time or other in the history of the development of every normal human being, there comes the change over from pre-ruth to ruth . . . the only thing is, when does this happen, how does it happen, and under what conditions does this happen? The concept of the depressive position is an attempt to answer these three questions, and, according to this concept, the change from ruthlessness to ruth occurs gradually under certain conditions of mothering during the period of around five to twelve months. And its establishment is not necessarily final until a much later date, and it may be found in analysis that it has never occurred at all . . . The depressive position then is a complex matter, an inherent element in a non-controversial phenomenon. That of the emergence of every human individual from pre-ruth to ruth.
>
> (p. 265)

As Winnicott points out, the depressive position is inseparable from the ambivalence that marks our relationship with the loved object: from one of primarily need fulfillment (pre-ruth), to something altogether more integrated and mature (ruth). Segal helps distinguish the potential "flight from ambivalence" as leading to primitive mental mechanisms of the paranoid-schizoid position (e.g. denial, splitting, projection and fragmentation) from the "achievement of knowing one's ambivalence, accepting it and working through it" (Segal, 1997, p. 159). For Segal, this is accomplished primarily through the recognition of guilt and of loss brought about by ambivalence that "leads to the capacity to mobilize restoration and reparation" (p. 159).

Paradoxically, the capacity to express aggression and anger is part of (despite the current trends to focus on 'positivity' and hopeful discourses) developing ruth, or care. Rather, such a capacity and the guilt attached to it become proportional to the cause. In psychoanalytic object relations, resolution of the 'ambivalence conflict' depends on how parental objects cope with infant destructiveness. It may seem a stretch to translate this to an environmental engagement context. However, we need to look at how society or social contexts provide 'good' experiences for tolerating ambivalence and guilt. Most environmental advocacy campaigns are working to either put a happy face on sustainability or scare people into action. Many parallels have been made between climate change threats and nuclear threats. Segal (1997) suggests such threats evoke "the most primitive psychotic anxieties about annihilation, and mobilize the most primitive defences" (p. 163). How often do we see honest, mature, straight-talking campaigns and engagement strategies that give expression to what many may feel but dare to express – such as outrage, disappointment, loss, the spectrum of emotions expressed so vividly in the interviews? Most campaigns function to manage collective anxieties and tamp out threatening or potentially disruptive affects, including grief, guilt or aggression, by smoothing over ambivalence and anxiety and focusing on aspiration. Connecting this back to the practice of communications for mobilizing and involving people in environmental engagement, it raises the question of how well our communication practices foster a process of 'working through' ambivalence and fear, rather than using fear incentives and cajoling a socially constructed apathetic audience to action.

Splitting as basis for agency: Some considerations

While it would appear the emergence of the depressive position is a psychic achievement, the "emergence of every human individual from pre-ruth to ruth" (Winnicott, 1958, p. 265), there is also the question of whether certain forms of splitting are conducive, indeed a prerequisite, for agency and action. It has been suggested that the depressive position may be a mode of being that can neutralize or impede forms of resistance essential for political action. This point, (Hoggett, 1992, pp. 47–51) in relation to political agency, presents a different angle on the depressive position as "achievement". As opposed to viewing a progression from paranoid schizoid to depressive, Hoggett suggests that the positions are dynamic, shifting and in oscillation. In addition to seeing the positions as dynamic, he suggests that a form of splitting which would be considered the paranoid-schizoid position may be required for action.

Based on the data analysis presented, the participants who express the most developed sense of a 'depressive position' – a capacity to recognize and integrate both the 'good' and the 'bad' aspects of environmental objects and the place of Green Bay (as both provider of life and nourishment and source of toxicity and degradation) – may paradoxically be the least able to mobilize a political subjectivity in response to the ecological trespasses they are so acutely aware of. There appears a potential complacency, similar to what Britton (1998, p. 82) writes on the complacent patient in analysis (and in everyday life), where treatment can remain at a sort of stasis. This sense of complacency, he notes, is nourished by a belief that all things seem to have a purpose and a reason, so that life's circumstances are presented to test us. This 'Panglossian' attitude, Britton notes, can fuel a complacency challenging to the work of analysis – and of course, in relation to political and social actions. He notes treatment tends to move forward at the moment the patient is able to express outrage – not only anger but genuine outrage – occasioned by a rupture in their sense of peace with how things are. That is to say, if one accepts the good and the bad as coexisting, there may be a diminished capacity for engaging with the truth of what is really happening (in this case, the devastating effects on the water quality caused by myriad human practices from unregulated ballast waters bringing in invasive species to the leaching of agricultural sites into precious water tables). This is a provocative argument suggested by Hoggett, who queries if we require some degree of splitting in order to be activated (cf. Hoggett, 2011). Further, Meltzer, Bremner and Hoxter (2008), in discussing autism, discusses the limited ways in which Klein conceptualizes splitting as always incurring damage to the object and therefore always an occasion for guilt and remorse, and suggests,

> It is also perhaps true that splitting processes are *necessary* for the kind of decisions that make action in the outside world possible. Every decision involves the setting in motion of a single plan from amongst its alternatives; it is experimental, involves risk, a certain ruthlessness toward oneself or others.
>
> (p. 241; italics added).

I agree with Meltzer, Bremner and Hoxter (2008), Hoggett (2011, 1997, p. 47) and Britton (1998) in recognizing both the necessary dynamism of the positions – that is, the so-called paranoid schizoid (Ps) and depressive (D) vacillation that is essential for effective agency – and the capacities to recognize and respond to external exigencies. I can also accept the idea that splitting processes are necessary for the kind of action and response required to take direct and authentic, effective reparative action on behalf of the natural environment. Signaling the depressive position as an achievement, as I have done and following Klein, is admittedly a crude mode of engaging with what are highly complicated and nuanced psychic and social processes, often largely unconscious in both individuals and groups.

And yet the reason I do signal the depressive position in contrast to the splitting in the paranoid-schizoid position is that it suggests the capacity for a mature and integrated psychic structure to integrate both 'good' and 'bad' – that is, the ability to resist the temptation, when faced with the unknown and uncertain, to retreat into a mode of splitting – easily recognized as denial, projection and blame, especially in relation to threats of climate change – both internally and externally. This is particularly relevant for environmental issues and degradation, a context in which gross splitting of 'good' nature and 'bad' nature is prevalent and presents serious challenges towards more effective environmental engagement and agency. The perception of an oscillation between these modes of being and that a form of splitting may actually be constructive and a prerequisite for action does not preclude the recognition of the need for a more integrative psychic engagement with chronic environmental issues.

Rather than assert the argument that splitting is required for action, as Meltzer does, which may or may not be accurate, I prefer to frame this problem in terms of mature, resilient integrated subjectivity in relation to chronic ecological degradation and destruction. Rather than a form of 'splitting', I prefer Winnicott's formulation, as discussed in the next section, on the capacities for care and concern that do *not* require a conceptualization of splitting. In my usage, splitting refers to a departure from what is real and actual, a retreat into the psychic processes that Segal describes as a turn from authenticity. It depends on how we are defining and engaging the concept of splitting. I maintain what is constructive is to consider more integrative, mature and authentic modes of engagement with environmental issues that may involve but are not predicated on 'splitting' in the sense of cutting up the world into discrete and concrete objects.

Intimate reparation: Books, food and water

It is inaccurate to suggest that the participants do not engage in reparations towards damaged environmental objects simply because they do not engage in recognized practices such as joining an environmental group or signing a petition. In the case of Sally, for example, I was moved by certain uses of objects and practices that were reparative in nature. Sally expresses potentially reparative practices in her relationship with food, for example how she and her parents will consume only organic, locally produced meats and dairy. She seemed quite pleased about her involvement with organic farming and even showed me her freezer full of organic meat and procured the ranch's business card for me. On my third visit, I came into her kitchen to find something simmering in the slow cooker, which she proudly informed me was organic beef stew. By carefully monitoring what she takes into her body, Sally is 'repairing' the damages caused by unsafe agricultural practices and bringing into her world 'good objects' in the form of organic meats and dairy. Likewise, Sally possesses a large library of books on herbs, vitamins and alternative health, although she does not necessarily ascribe to the lifestyle any longer (the books as objects, like the Save the Whale cards, reference a previous time and self). She mentions owning a book about endocrine disruptors, *Our Stolen Future* (Colborn, Dumanoski & Meyers, 1997). The discussion of this book illustrates some ambivalence on her part with regard to 'knowledge' and awareness about environmental health risks. Her first comments about the book are:

> And I started reading that and I couldn't handle it. Because the ramifications from all of that knowledge, once you have the knowledge you have to change your behaviour. You know you can come to the precipice and you

have a choice, of learning the knowledge and once you learn the knowledge you have to do something with it. Or you can step back, and just leave it because you don't want to do anything different. So. With that book, I started reading it and realized, I have so many limitations with what I can eat, and food allergies, and all of this other stuff already, I don't want to know more, I don't want to know.

She continues to say the book is up in the library "and I'm not doing anything with it. [Laughs a bit] I think the best thing I should do is donate it to a good cause! [Laughs] So that other people that want to, and really need to, because if your health is effected that badly by what they have to say *you have to make the change*".

The book itself becomes objectified knowledge, containing attending risks of knowledge, and her ambivalence about becoming more literate and aware of environmental health risks is reflected in her possession and rejection of the book ("I should donate it"). What is at stake, as Sally articulates, is her own responsibility to take action based on what she knows, and she would rather not know, as she states very clearly. And yet she continues to own the book and perhaps feels guilty for not reading it (it would benefit someone else).

In another surprising example, Sally tells me, in a free associative way at the end of an interview (having just remembered a memory fragment not related to our current topic of discussion), about her neighbor purchasing pheasants for the back lot shared among the neighbors. She does not seem to want the interview to end and is pleased to share this story with me. While it appears trivial, I am quite moved by this little vignette, as it speaks clearly to me about the importance of being able to *contribute* and find a 'home' for one's reparative impulses for expression:

S: You know what? I just . . . My neighbor, he loves the wildlife in the back, behind our house. And, he used to feed the deer, but that's illegal to do so he had to stop doing that [laughs] and we're neighbors so I don't say anything, you see it but you don't say anything, so he decided to go and raise money and buy pheasants. He bought one rooster and five hens. And um, we had five to one, and he bought several of them, and set them loose in the back here. And you know, for our environmental whatever, and um, he thinks it's a good thing and he's going to be putting corn out and stuff and if we want to, will I? Probably not, because I'm off for four months without pay right now, feeding other critters is not, I've got three critters and me to feed right now, so that's kind of my priority right now, I'm not going to feed them out there. It's interesting, I did contribute to buying some of those. And um, it's kind of exciting, knowing that there's a nice variety of critters in the background, and not just the mice and the rats [laughs].

R: Why did you mention that now?

S: I don't know! I don't know! It just popped up so I thought I'd bring it up real quick. As you were saying that it just popped in my mind, I don't know why. So kind of support, you know give the neighborhood support, you know here's some money, go buy some [laughs].

My reading of Sally's sharing of this story that "popped into her head" is her desire to demonstrate her reparative, environmentally 'contributing' energies, as demonstrated in her modest participation with her neighbor acquiring pheasants. We can see in the story an opportunity, or a 'home', for Sally's affective concern to take root or at least find a temporary expression. Her enjoyment of her back garden and of nature was able to connect effectively with her neighbor's activities, although she drew boundaries about feeding the birds on an ongoing basis. It was enough for her to help buy them.

Saving the whales: Expressions of reparation

The sense of not being able to contribute is poignantly reflected in Sally's discussion about her involvement with Save the Whales in our third interview (I present the excerpt at length):

S: [Laughs] After you left, I was rather, um, I thought about it a lot after you left the last time.

R: About what?

S: All the different things I talked about. I hadn't thought about Save the Whales in years and I still, like I said I still have three of those cards that you can, and you know, it's just really nice cards with envelopes you can mail out, I think I may even still have the T-shirt, and all the different environmental issues that came up, that I remembered, it was [. . .] interesting to remember them all. And just, be that animated about it because, when you can't do anything about it, a lot of times, after a while, it's just, yeah, okay. Well there's nothing I can do. And, like for example, with the water thirty years later they are saying get going, there's nothing I can do in that thirty years. You know. So, sometimes you can just watch and see how things happen and what, what happens. So it was kind of, um ... fun to touch back on that, how [. . .] intense I was at one point with the save the whales thing. And all the environmental stuff. And over the years you just kind of realize there's nothing you can do and you just go on, so it was, kind of um,

R: What does it mean to you that you were once passionate about those issues?

S: Hmm! Somebody once said when you're young you need to have a heart, and when you're older, you need to be able to you know, have heart, be passionate over those things when you're young because when you're older your priorities change a bit, and as you're, in your 50s to 60s you start thinking more about retirement, and how you're going to live out your final years, things like that, and if you can help out you do. But on the whole, your priorities change. So. Um. It was [. . .] actually, I was glad. I mean everybody knew about the save the whales thing, I mean, my family thought it was hilarious that I would just, [laughing] get into that. But, it um, I don't know.

It brought back good memories. I don't know if that's answering your question or not.

R: Yeah. Well, I guess I'm wondering, how, what it means to look back and to see that you were once really engaged with those things. And, I mean I hear you saying that you kind of have to move on, at a certain point. And realize –

S: Yes.

R: What you can and can't do. But that's kind of like, um, that's, that's analyzing it, um, from your perspective now. Whereas, I guess when I ask what does it mean for you, when you look at yourself as a younger person, really passionate and, I guess I'm wondering what feelings come up around that. If you feel maybe, do you feel you lost something, or –

S: Yes and no. Because, when you're young and you're not exactly sure which direction your life is going to go, how you're going to go, what your calling is in life, I guess calling, I don't know if calling is the right word, but what your abilities are, and where you can make the difference. You look, you know when you're young you're just kind of looking at everything trying to figure out where do I fit into this whole, where's my path, where's my thing and that was it for a little bit, but as I got more into the music that consumed more of my time. So priorities changed, because of, with music there's practice, and there's rehearsals, you know there's performance, things like that. So priorities. Knowing that I have the ability to do different musical things, I can play guitar, I can play viola, I can sing, and having those abilities, not using those and focusing on total environment things, is not a good use of the talents and the abilities that I have. And there are other people who, don't have those talents or not willing, it's not their passion. Music is my passion. So I think over the years, it just, it was a matter of, the music taking over more and more of my time.

R: Hmm hmm. [. . .] And did you find you thought about environmental things less? As you became more focused on other things?

S: Not so much less, but you pay attention, you read it like I would have read the article [referring to the one about the Fox River clean-up] and I would have looked at it and saying, I hope they start it soon. I hope they really don't let them out of it. I hope, you know, that they will follow through and really make them do it this time. And that's about as far as this time, and otherwise it would go. Because there's nothing I can do.

There is a powerful assertion in the passage where Sally feels her concern and contributions lie. She became involved with the Save the Whales campaign and still possesses the cards and T-shirts as desired and cherished objects, indicating her desire to hold on to and retain this aspect of herself – a reparative aspect. She mocks her involvement, particularly in the second interview, as being frivolous and suggests fantasies of omnipotence in her desire to make an impact on something as remote as protecting whales from extinction. It is also suggested that her family did not take her environmental commitments seriously. To better understand if Sally experiences a sense of loss or nostalgia for herself as a young, impassioned woman collecting whale cards and T-shirts, I press her to articulate a possible sense of loss, which is quickly glossed over in her rushed narrative about her process of finding where she can adequately contribute and make a difference in a particular sphere.

What becomes clear is her decision at a certain point, to *contribute* in an area in which she feels reasonably competent, even gifted, and to choose to withdraw affectively from those areas in which she does not feel able to make a difference. As she repeats frequently, "There is nothing I can do". My reading of the involvement with the Save the Whales campaigns when she was younger expresses something quite powerful and important regarding her impulses for addressing ecological degradation, even if it was not channeled locally; in fact, the way she focuses on the whales in distant regions, in the context of her "shock" at the polluted environment in Green Bay, is notable. If we view reparation as expressions of the desire to repair and to contribute-to – and not only defined in terms of environmental activism that is sustained – it is clear there is a presence of concern, or *ruth* in this case, directed towards vulnerable and endangered large sea creatures. Perhaps Sally is identifying with the whales and seeks to repair an internal sense of vulnerability or fragility. Regardless, how she expresses her contact with Save the Whales indicates that the whales were important objects and safe enough to direct such creative impulses. However, there was not an adequate sense of contributing-to, and so she moved on to spheres of influence and efficacy more intimately focused. The intimate sphere therefore can contain and harbor reparative impulses that may not feel 'at home' or safe in the larger world of activism, politics and social movements. We must not assume that the concern is absent but rather that it may be seeking a home.

Lost opportunities for reparation: Environmentalism as black and white

The recognition of limits of oneself as an individual and of the failure to find a 'home' for reparative impulses is reflected in Howard's narratives as well. He begins the interviews with a strong declaration that his participation in the study itself is an expression of "having some influence", which he suggests is more effective than voting. At the end of the interviews as well, he considers himself "very lucky" for having been selected as one of the participants. He is overall enthusiastic about the process and followed up the interviews with sending vintage photographs he discovered of the family home on the Fox River in De Pere. When Howard begins to acknowledge his own pro-environment feelings, he notes that he is not "fanatical", an expression echoed in almost every participant's case, in which they seem to equate environmental activism or agency with fanatical, extreme, rigid behavior. Most striking is when Howard projects onto me a query as to why he does not take more environmentally active behavior and proceeds (without my asking) to outline what such environmentally active behavior would look like and how he has chosen not to pursue that avenue. He describes a local environmental issue, which he suggests by association rather than full assertion is connected with his bronchitis. Howard begins mentioning his bronchitis, which he first suggests is from being in the city ('bad object'). Then, with the added "And it's not", he discounts this assertion. It initiates a discussion of environmental issues that bother him, which he claims are many. He remarks that he is "more sensitive" than other people seem to be, especially since he has gotten older.

> I've got some bronchitis, the first time I've ever had it is this year. I've always said, when I moved into town, I wanted to get back out of town, because I always felt the air quality probably wasn't as good. Twenty years here, and I've never had any problems, I get one year I have bronchitis and I'm like, yeah it's from living in the city, you know the pollution in the city! And it's not. So I, it's, but I do believe the valley uh, is more polluted than outside of the, once you get above the ridge on the end either side, and tend to think the west than the east side, because you can't be burning as much coal in the power plant and I know, years ago the solution, because they, they do tests air quality tests around the area, and they didn't pass, I remember seeing that in the news, I don't know how many years ago it was, their solution was to build another, how many feet on the tower [laughs] to disperse it a little farther out. I'm like, no, to get it up so it doesn't fall down into where they are testing. I'm going, [sigh] I understand about how scrubbers work, they are expensive but they work- but it's cheaper to build on and build a little taller and that way they pass the testing on it. But I'm like, you're still putting as much in, you're just spreading it over a larger area! That kind of stuff, I keep, I keep thinking, don't people see that? [Laughs] Um, I guess I'm not as much of an advocate to actually go after, and doing anything about that, but I end up having my opinions.

I then ask, "What does it mean, 'doing something about it'?"

> Going out and getting petitions, or to um, join any organizations that might be involved in it, or even to the point of starting organizations that would you know, take something an issue like that, and just bring it to the public going how can we let this, you know, let this go this way? So I'm not, active in that, in that way. On stuff like that.

When I press him to discuss this subsequently, in the third interview, he says, "I keep thinking that you're wondering why that even though I have all the knowledge , . . . to do something about it, what would have to happen for me to [. . .] take that step to actually do something?" And then says:

> I think that it probably has to do with my feeling that people who get this involved tend to be fanatical about it, obsessive, um, this is the way it's got to be over everything else, everything else is completely wrong, this is

right . . . to kind of get to that point you have to be black and white, you can't be gray at all . . . and that I don't want that, I don't . . . I understand the other part and the, and why people do it that way to turn around and, to be and to do that I think you have to be definite about it, you can't go in and say 'well I think this is what you should do' and it'd be good you know, to do something like that but I understand that you don't do it', to be part of the organization it has to be . . . this is the way it's supposed to be done . . .

To do it that way is wrong, this is why it's wrong, this is how it's wrong and this is what you should do, that's not my personality, and I, and so I wouldn't go that direction except as a very small part of it.

Howard goes on to describe the local environmental group, Wisconsin Citizen Action Council, going door to door, how focused they were on fundraising and how he "has a problem with fundraising" and again associating this with being obsessive. As with Scott, he perceives this as controlling and lacking attunement to the needs and concerns (ironically) of others, hence appearing as obsessive or manic.

In light of the interviews and related issues that come up for Howard regarding agency and action, in his own personal life *and the fears of making the wrong choice or decision* (discussed at length in all three interviews, notably around his paralysis to move into the country despite the fact he has never felt at home in town and has never settled into his current home after 20 years), it is evident he is able to make contributions in particular contexts. For example, in the workplace, if there is something to do, he "has no problem getting it done" and taking whatever risks are necessary. His environmental concerns and sentiments are essentially sequestered into a manageable area "as a very small part" of anything that might be taking place.

This contrast between his high levels of knowledge and awareness with his actions and behavior is compelling. For Howard, as for others, he primarily channels his concerns into small actions, such as recycling and entreating others to (e.g. his boss) do so, drinking bottled water (which he feels is morally superior to drinking Great Lakes water from the tap), using the truck or outside for keeping things cold, not using salt on the sidewalks for de-icing, and expressing his views through discourses with friends, coworkers and acquaintances. Sadly for me, Howard refers to himself as an "apathy-type person", a remark that shows an individual internalizing the public-political rhetoric. His concerns have not found a suitable 'home'. Howard remarks that "[t]o go beyond his 'own little world', that's a step, that's a different, different thing . . . I guess I never got along with people who did that because of the fact that they tend to be, I think in the ones I've met, I hate to be opinionated too much on things, but ah, that they tend to be better-than-thou people". However, despite his characterization as apathetic and his responses in the surveys, in the third interview Howard admits that environmental problems are *"always in the background, for me . . . On a personal basis"*.

Scott is another participant whose feelings about environmental groups and advocacy are quite painful. There is a sense of having been either unseen or not approached respectfully. One of the reasons I selected Scott as a participant was based on his short answer responses and a comment he made regarding Greenpeace, signaling some aspect of environmental concern, even if it was not particularly 'active' for various reasons. In our second interview, Scott relates to me a particularly painful story about an initial attempt to connect with Greenpeace when he was about 12. His "hate" for Greenpeace is rooted in the organization's gross lack of appropriate or adequate response to his effort to connect and 'contribute' in some meaningful but non-monetary way. Most participants perceive environmental organizations as primarily wanting only money or signatures on a petition and very little else. Scott recount reflects how this soured his perceptions of environmental groups from that point on, characterizing them as inflexible and "forcing people to do things" instead of offering options.

S: I really hate Greenpeace [laughing]. One time I was um, doing research because I was really interested when I was in middle school about seventh or eighth grade and I wrote to Greenpeace and asked to send some informational brochure and all they wanted was money, you know and I, oh I sent a nice letter and said I'm doing research and I'd like to do a report on Greenpeace, da, ta, da, ta, da, please send us money. (Hmm.) No, [laughing] so then I decide, whatever.

R: Was that the last time you reached out to an environmental group?

S: Yeah, because there's, you know, there's different, there's definitely other environmental groups out like Sierra Club. And just some of the things that you know they, some of the tactics that those environmental groups use you know are, not productive, they, you know, they'd rather, just, you know, try to force people to do things instead of just offer options.

The perception of the organization as a totalizing and controlling entity is the result of a radical misalignment between Scott's needs and expression for contributing-to and the response of the organization.

Finding a home for concern

In light of this discussion, I make three central arguments. First, I argue for an approach to environmental engagement that can allow for ambivalence, contradiction, concern and anxiety and equally for the presence of loss and the sense of *disappointment*. I suggest that a lack of active engagement with environmental practices may not reflect a lack of care or concern. Rather, it may be the result of an inability to process loss and ambivalence in relation to the environment and industrial practices, as well as a failure to find an adequate 'home' for contributing and participating *creatively* with ecologically reparative practices. The failure to contribute-to, to animate aspects of concern which may be present but dormant, is a theme running throughout the interviews. In many cases, the participation in the study itself was a form of 'contributing-to' which appeared to provide participants a great sense of relief, enjoyment and pride.

Second, I argue that the presence of ambivalence, notably towards the damaged environmental objects, is bound up with feelings of guilt and conflict regarding industry and the act of feeling anger towards the 'provider' of the city. The ambivalence seems to have the effect of neutralizing anger, producing instead an acute sense of disappointment and inchoate sense of loss. This loss is related to the lack of contact with one's own sense of creativity and agency in the world. It appears to be a form of the depressive position, without the capacities for maturation into reparation.

Third, I argue that the quality that may best describe the mode of relating and experiencing ecological issues, particularly those affecting loved objects (e.g. the dunes, the Fox River, Bay Beach), is *melancholic*. My employment of the term *melancholic* is a direct reference to Freud's formulation in *Mourning and Melancholia* (1917) that distinguishes mourning from melancholia and that attempts to address what may interfere with the 'work of mourning' essential for the capacities for concern and reparation. There are two central features of melancholia relevant for this discussion: the unclear origins of the loss and the "extraordinary reduction of self-esteem, a great impoverishment of the ego" (Freud, 1917, p. 204). As Freud wrote, "[W]hen the loss that is the cause of the melancholia is known to the subject, when he knows *who* it is, but not *what* it is about that . . . he has lost". Conceptualizing one's relationship with ecological degradation as melancholic may have the capacity to shift the normative frame away from the trifecta of behavior, attitudes and values to considerably broader psychic and social processes of loss and agency. I argue that the lack of sanctuary, the 'home' for contributing-to, can result in a profound sense of melancholic affect, leading to a withdrawal of affective investment (as evidenced by Scott's ill-fated contact with Greenpeace). The acute experience, so prevalent when it comes to environmental issues, of not being able to contribute (e.g. Sally's "There is nothing I can do") forces any affective investment to shrink down, as the world becomes very small. Any available reparative energies are then directed in the most intimate and manageable spheres, e.g. food, water, recycling and so on. Or they are disavowed altogether.

The importance of contributing

The concept of *contributing-to* offers a productive lens for thinking through the dilemmas of apathy, concern and care. For Winnicott, the ability to 'contribute' begins in infancy, as the child learns to smile or gesture, which in turn evokes a response from the mother or adults. Parents humanize the terrors of destructive and aggressive instincts by withstanding, tolerating and processing (or assimilating) the infant's experiences. The infant needs a context, a frame, for fears. The ability to express the range of impulses and desires, according to Winnicott, sets up a "benign cycle" in which the contributions of the infant can be received and enjoyed. I relate this dynamic in infantile development to what is being expressed in the interview material, notably an absence of a site for contributing, and the subsequent withdrawal or sublimation of the reparative or creativity energies elsewhere, or quite possibly resulting in a melancholic or depressed affect. With Sally, for example, she has effectively chosen to channel her contributions to music where she feels she can make an actual contribution; her efforts and produced effects are valued, appreciated but, most importantly, employed. In her participation in an orchestra or choir, she is part of a group, a *contributing member*. Sally articulates this in terms of focusing on her talents, but there is an important subtext in both her and Howard's sentiments regarding their environmental commitments and actions. Both perceive themselves as lacking in certain skills for contributing in a particular way. This is dictated by the constraints and contexts provided, e.g. Howard's ability to list the various activities in which he could be involved. There is a discounting of one's own offering ("I'm not an expert"). Donald removes himself from any political context in asserting his need to keep these issues "close to my person", as if to make them public would be somehow unsavory or unacceptable. Scott experiences a radical 'mal-attunement' in terms of his needs and those of the organization's, based on his contact with Greenpeace, where he sought affirmation and a 'good experience'. Instead he was treated as a donor, which only reinforced the sense that he had nothing of value to offer their efforts.

The question becomes how much takes place in environmental outreach efforts and communications to reinforce such experiences of feeling either unwanted or unwelcomed (due lack of finances, usually), other than in particularly circumscribed ways? What in our environmental communications overwhelm people with the magnitude of the problems and result in a perceived insignificance of oneself, which in turn may lead to a withdrawal or shutting down of affect and concern altogether? There is a well known battle between informing and overwhelming, and the recourse tends to be to focus on 'here is what you can do, this little thing'. We also know that focusing on the 'little steps' can be equally counterproductive, as it appears as too tiny and insignificant. The point here is that there is often little opportunity for *engagement not determined by compliance* – sign this, pay that, show up here. Genuine engagement, as discussed in the following chapter, involves creative participation. As Klein asserts, guilt is the basis for reparation if it can be tolerated and processed adequately ('worked through'), which requires a series of good (environmental) experiences. If this does not take place, guilt can surface as sadness or depression, complacency and resignation. On the other hand, in light of the more positive concept of concern, tapping into creativity means "seeing the world with new eyes all the time" (Newman, 1995, p. 109). This suggests a critical need for environmental communications practices to consider new forms and venues for fostering and facilitating creative contributions, opportunities for participation, rather than compliance.

Reflections

Klein suggests that a direct and active involvement with nature helps preserve the desire to make reparations, whereas a disconnection with nature, e.g.

through industrial practices, may actually disrupt the processes of guilt leading to reparation:

> [T]he struggle with nature is therefore partly felt to be a struggle to preserve nature, because it expresses also the wish to make reparation to her (mother). People who strive with the severity of nature thus not only take care of themselves, but also serve nature herself. In not severing their connection with her they keep alive the image of the mother of the early days. They preserve themselves and her in phantasy by remaining close to her – actually by not leaving their country. In contrast with this, the explorer is seeking in phantasy a new mother in order to replace the real one from whom he feels estranged, or whom he is unconsciously afraid to lose.
>
> (p. 110)

In the context of industrialization, we may perhaps extend this analysis of the explorer to include the need not only to "replace the real one", but to then dominate, control and extract from. Feelings of vulnerability and the terrors of dependency are transmuted into a relationship of service and exploitation. However, there may be psychic costs and well documented ecological cost to this dynamic, namely, the sense of guilt that may arise in the face of our actions. When people are confronting the severely polluted water, the sense of guilt combined with loss may be too much to bear consciously – for example, in the shock registered by Jeff and Sally on apprehending the polluted water in Green Bay, Howard's realization of "what clean water looks like" or Scott's sadness and disappointment when he learns as a child about the dirty waters. Anger is required to move us into action, healthy, constructive anger, not "losing one's temper" but the ability to say "NO!" (Newman, 1995, p. 112). Winnicott prefers to think that it is in living creatively that we "can allow ourselves to become concerned with our destructiveness and come to do something about it. Reparation here is not for him a sufficiently generous word to describe how we might make up for the damages we do: he thinks of *creating something new*" (Newman, 1995, p. 108; italics added).

For Winnicott (1963), "*Immorality for the infant is to comply at the expense of the personal way of life*" (p. 93). Conversely, morality is the creative response to wrongdoings. When not complying, we may experience the results of own destructiveness: concern, sadness, depression. This is an achievement. The sense of loss, sadness and depression detected in the interviews *is* positive; it signals the ability to register transgressions and loss. What happens, however, is a stasis or inability to move through these results into a creative mode, which is the basis for repair. In the following and final chapter, I conclude with the implications of these arguments in the practice of environmental communications. Specifically, I discuss the importance of environmental outreach and communications strategies informed by a complex environmental subjectivity that can contain ambivalence, loss and mourning, melancholia and dilemmas of contradictory desires and impulses.

Notes

1 This is a much larger topic beyond the present discussion. Numerous emerging studies have been focusing on political and religious ideology as a barometer for how environmental issues, and climate change in particular, are engaged (Haidt, 2013); (Markowitz & Shariff, 2012). However these studies overlook what leads to this ideological rigidity in the first place. Along these lines and suggested by Welch (2008), such ideological fixations are psychic strategies to negotiate unspeakable and thus unthinkable loss, anxieties, fears and concerns.

2 Related to the point about conversation-based engagement strategies, this is precisely why I argue for the need to actively create and produce more 'safe spaces' in environmental engagement, messaging, branding and communications. See Chapter 3.

References

Britton, R., 1998. *Belief and Imagination: Explorations in Psychoanalysis.* London: Routledge.

Colborn, T., Dumanoski, D., & Meyers, J., 1997. *Our Stolen Future.* New York: Plume.

Freud, S., 1917. Mourning and melancholia. In Strachey, J. et al. (ed.), *Standard Edition* 14. London: Hogarth Press, pp. 237–258.

Haidt, J., 2013. *The Righteous Mind.* New York: Vintage.

Hoggett, P., 1992. *Partisans in an Uncertain World.* London: Free Association Books.

Hoggett, P., 1997. Contested communities, in Hoggett, J. (ed.), *Contested Communities. Experiences, Struggles, Policies,* Bristol: Policy Press.

Hoggett, P., 2011. Climate change and the apocalyptic imagination, *Psychoanalysis Culture & Society* 16, pp. 261–275.

Klein, M., 1940. *Mourning and Its Relation to Manic-depressive States.* In Mitchell, J. (ed.), *The Selected Melanie Klein.* New York: Free Press, pp. 146–174 [reprinted 1986].

Lertzman, R., 2011. What it means to be green. *Meeting Professionals International.* Available at: http://www.mpiweb.org/Magazine/MPINews/20111111/What_it_Means_to_be_Green.

Markowitz, E., & Shariff, A., 2012. Climate change and moral judgment, *Nature Climate Change* 4 (2), pp. 243–247.

Meltzer, D., Bremner, J., & Hoxter, S., 2008. *Explorations in Autism.* London: Karnac.

Newman, A., 1995. *Non-compliance in Winnicott's Words.* London: Free Association Books.

Randall, R. 2009. Loss and climate change: The cost of parallel narratives, *Ecopschology* 1 (3), pp. 119–129.

Segal, H., 1972. A delusional system as a defence against the re-emergence of a catastrophic situation, *International Journal of Psychoanalysis* 53, pp. 393–401.

Segal, H., 1995. From Hiroshima to the Gulf War and after: Socio-political expressions of ambivalence. In Segal, H., & Steiner, J. (eds.), *Psychoanalysis, Literature and War: Papers 1972–1995.* London: Routledge & Institute of Psycho-Analysis, pp. 157–169 [reprinted 1997].

Welch, B., 2008. *State of Confusion: Political Manipulation and the Assault of the American Mind.* New York: Thomas Dunner.

Winnicott, D. W., 1958. The depressive position in normal emotional development. In Winnicott, D. W. (ed.), *Collected Papers: Through Paediatrics to Psycho-analysis.* London: Tavistock, pp. 262–277.

Winnicott, D. W., 1963. The development of the capacity for concern. In Winnicott, D. W., *The Maturational Process and the Facilitating Environment.* London: Karnac.

Bay Beach Wildlife Sanctuary, Nature Center, July 2006. (Photo: R. Lertzman.)

I keep saying yeah if there was a way that I could help out in a smaller matter rather than getting totally involved with it, I think if I go to that website and I have to sign my name or, or email I'm gonna to get petitioned for, for money of some sort. I believe that so when I go there if they request an email address or something for contacting um, I probably won't sign it. Because it's like, okay, you asked for a little bit, I'm going to give you some, now I have to give everything, and you know, why can't I choose how far along I do. They always say the worst person to be around for moral superiority is someone's who quit smoking. Because they'll tell you all the bad things. And so, I don't want to become that, I think I would, I don't know if I would, I might end up becoming like that if I got that involved in environmental issues. Environmental issues, I think it's always there, in the background. On a personal basis . . . I'm trying to think of ah, salting the, the sidewalk, I don't think putting a lot of salt is [.] that good for the environment so I don't put that much salt out, I don't get that many people coming here, I will salt my sidewalk, but it's no good to do it now because it's just going to melt and refreeze.

– Howard, Interview 3

Chapter 7

Moving from loss to engagement

A new environmental subjectivity

> The stubborn refusal to accept that latent acts are psychic in nature can be explained by the fact that most of the phenomena in question have never been studied outside psychoanalysis. Those who . . . accept that the 'slips' of the tongue are accidental, who are content with the old saying 'dreams are froth' need ignore only a few more riddles of the psychology of consciousness to spare themselves the trouble of postulating unconscious psychic activity.
>
> – Freud, *In Defense of the Unconscious*

Taking account of unconscious psychic activity complicates how we conceptualize environmental subjectivity. No longer can we focus on the 'gap' between values and actions and presume that how we behave is a straightforward expression of our concerns, beliefs and values. Postulating unconscious psychic activity is, indeed as Freud notes, "trouble". Trouble because it potentially throws our methodologies into question. Trouble because it takes us into the less certain, messier terrain of decoding, sleuthing and feeling our way into how we construct meaning. Trouble because researching unconscious processes is fraught. And yet investigating "beneath the surface" (Clarke & Hoggett, 2009) affords the opportunity to innovate and extend our thinking about the most effective means of inviting greater levels of reparative actions on behalf of our natural environments and ecosystems.

This project began with my experiences at university in the late 1980s, moving between environmental studies, psychology and cultural studies lecture halls. As my environmental awareness grew, so did the chill of paralysis brought on by anxiety and a sense of powerlessness. Ulrich Beck's (1992) description of the risk society maps onto this affective landscape, as "an epoch in which the dark sides of progress increasingly come to dominate social debates . . . What no one saw and no one wanted – self-endangerment and the devastation of nature – is becoming the motive force of history" (p. 2). He asks the question that has been on my mind for years. "Why is nothing happening, or why isn't more happening? What does it mean for everyday life to believe the problems exist and to take them seriously?" (p. 12). The question of how we integrate into our everyday life our awareness of industrial impacts on life systems has been the guiding theme of both this book and my work as a researcher and communications professional. How can we best support people in this integration? How can we facilitate the basis of concern that Winnicott (1963) asserts is core to who we are as human beings? What does it mean to apply insights of psychoanalytic work to the practice of environmental advocacy and engagement?

As discussed in Chapter 2, I applied an 'analytic attitude' to illuminate complex ways humans are caught up in nettings of affect, hopes, fears, anxieties and losses in relation to industrial degradation and ecological threat.[1] Bringing these sensibilities into the context of an empirical qualitative study presents strengths, challenges and limitations, as others have attested (Hollway, 2006; Frosh, 2007; Frosh & Baraitser, 2008). However, psychosocial approaches to environmental engagement complicates our conceptualizations in the right kind of way. Introducing affect, unconscious processes and the role of object relations to how we understand engagement arguably enables us to meet people with far greater levels of attunement, compassion and authenticity. This project makes the case to take into account not only people's values, attitudes and practices but also the ways in which we are stitched into our social worlds in often contradictory and paradoxical ways. We can both love and care for our earth, water and nature, as well as for our cars, vacations and long hot showers. Our capacities to understand the nature of our investments and anxiety, the primary role of ambivalence and what is required to support reparative practices is essential for anyone working actively in the environmental sectors today.

Environmental Melancholia offers a critical analysis of how we construct people as 'apathetic' and provide an alternative to constructions of environmental subjectivity in popular media and environmental communication sectors. This research reframes current debates, which focus on 'barriers' and 'how to get people to care', in terms of how attachment and concern to threatened or lost ecological objects can be impeded by various psychic, social and biographical contexts. By re-shifting the conceptual frameworks about environmental concern as a *presence* or surplus of affect to be tapped, rather than as an *absence* or lack to be refueled, new opportunities emerge for how communicators, educators and activists can design and tailor messaging and outreach efforts. From the vantage point of *presuming a presence of care* in people, perceived 'barriers' shift and dissolve into new configurations for effective environmental engagement and citizenry. This includes the need to consider how we offer and invite opportunities for reparation. Applying psychoanalytic insights regarding mourning, melancholia, ambivalence and reparation, the way forward appears to center on ways to enable people to experience themselves as true agents – with opportunities to contribute-to, create, be heard, respected and valued. The greatest resource we have access to is the human desire and need for efficacy, impact and influence in some sphere of our world.

In turn, the study problematizes how research is conducted in environmental fields. The heavy reliance on quantitative and cognitive-based approaches in environmental psychology is but one component of the broader methodological landscape in which we work. Where most studies investigating environmental concern or 'engagement' are conducted using larger samples and tools such as surveys, polling, focus groups and one-off interviews, this study employed in-depth approach, spending approximately three hours with each participant, in addition to the use of an online survey. The interviews were conducted with attention to safety and 'containment' and encouraged free association. The analysis was also conducted using a combination of psychoanalytic narrative analysis and object relations approaches, with qualitative data analysis in which the material was systematically reviewed. As a whole, the project has sought to destabilize 'apathy' as a trope: a taken-for-granted concept that carries assumptions regarding subjectivity as rational, unitary and self-conscious and importantly about the nature of reparation, concern, grief and loss. In designing the research in this way, to allow for more expression of these contradictions and ambivalent relations with industry and nature, I seek to re-establish some measure of dignity for those who may be labeled as 'apathetic' based on certain criteria.

Psychoanalysis and psychosocial theoretical research presents tremendous resources to serve and support environmental scholarship. In particular, the valuable work in British object relations psychoanalysis and, to some degree, relational analytic work in conceptualizing the researcher–participant relationship. I have found the work of Christopher Bollas to be particularly useful in his work on the 'object', specifically how to read our object relations – that is, our relations with the nonhuman, environmental object world – as manifest of unconscious processes and meanings. Bollas (1992) represents one of the few psychoanalytic thinkers to turn his attention to the material object work, in a similar spirit to Searles, and as such informs how objects are theorized. Hanna Segal has been a fundamental inspiration for the project and its aims, particularly her work on terrorism, nuclear threat and political engagement, as well as her theorizations of apathy as a primitive manic defence.

In order to garner broad environmental actions, they ways in which we understand engagement require a critical capacity to examine our conceptions of agency and the role of affect. As I have explored, there is such a thing as 'good agency' (i.e. political action) and 'bad agency' (i.e. more private, personal forms of reparation) from the viewpoint of environmental advocacy. The interviews illustrate examples of reparations, as expressed in very specific contexts and practices, that are coherent and affectively manageable by the participants – for example in Donald's case, attending courses on local ecological history, instilling respect for nature in children, spending much time outdoors enjoying the country property. He claims he is "not an activist" and yet demonstrates considerable engagement with the issues. These practices are on his terms. He may not be engaging in forms of agency focused on by environmental organizations, such as taking more explicitly political action, or involvement with community-based activities. However, these practices would not be felt as appropriate given his particular identifications and affective relations with the place and industry. To do so may be experienced as a betrayal of the (good/brutalizing) father (industry) that has provided so well. The interviews portray in rather vivid terms how what may appear as 'apathy', if defined via specific behaviors and practices, falls far short of the level of concern, care and attention that may be present. The cost of this situation is for many individuals to internalize a sense of their own engagement as less than, lacking, deficient and flawed – leading to even greater levels of withdrawal from more public forms of engagement.

A different picture emerges when surfacing affective themes of loss, mourning and melancholia, ambivalence and splitting and capacities for concern and reparation. This is one that places affect and unconscious dimensions as *underlying* particular attitudes, beliefs or opinions. When we view specific forms of environmental engagement as expressions of – not as separate from – complex affective, psychosocial processes, it necessarily shifts our frameworks in how we analyze behaviour change strategies and theories of engagement. Our focus moves away from 'gaps' and 'barriers', as discussed in Chapter 2, to examining the contexts and influences informing how people make sense of and respond to chronic ecological threats. In line with social practice theory, the emphasis is on the systems at play that inform behaviours; however, in this case the emphasis is on the *affective*. It is arguably our affective investments that drive our practices, as well as the interplay of culture, uneven distributions of resources, social norms, identities and infrastructures. Ideally, this supports a less reductive mode of analysis, one that can appreciate how early childhood experiences and associations, as well as the way certain objects 'hold' particular self-states and impressions inform our practices. This orientation also supports the recognition of contradiction and ambivalence – our abilities to hold competing and contradicting values, beliefs and desires quite easily. We can both love certain objects and find them abject. We can have deeply ambivalent feelings about our natural environments, particularly when they have been degraded and wasted. This recognition of the affective complicates how we conduct our research, design strategies and create messaging. It is a complication that can hopefully spur innovations and developments in environmental scholarship and specifically how human dimensions are conceptualized. We need to see how certain modes of environmental practices are strategies to manage our need for safety and security and to consider ways of inviting more creative and genuinely participatory modes of engagement. Several participants noted that opportunities for environmental engagement were so circumscribed and prescriptive – donating, petitions etc. – that they exercised their creativity by *not* participating in practices they did not wish to.

The research thus criticizes an approach that focuses exclusively on attitudes and behaviors that tend to show a gap – something missing – and thus implicitly blaming people for their lack of action or practices. The gap or barrier discourse tends to place the problem with the individual and fails to recognize that, in fact, environmental outreach can be often alienating. It also misses the fact that people may care a great deal about specific environmental issues but feel insignificant in relation to the problems that the notion of repair naturally becomes transmuted into private acts. What is often on offer by environmental groups – signing a petition or donating money – may not feel adequate or appropriate, and more creative aspects of reparation and concern are entirely missed out on. Further, studies on behavior, attitudes and the 'gap' between values and actions do not take into account the problem of ambivalence and guilt in relation to environmental problems. They presume a particular subjectivity predicated on a rational mode of being. In fact, as my data suggests, notions of good and bad, right and wrong, reparation and destruction are more likely to be confused and mixed up because we live in a context that continues to reap benefits from damaging systems.

Implications for engagement

If we are able to transition towards more ecologically sensitive practices at a scale to meet the challenges ahead, it is imperative to understand how people experience environmental issues and how affective unconscious processes such as anxiety, loss and fear may impair or complicate effective modes of agency. This is no longer the province of those in the mental health professions; rather, environmental professionals must begin to collaborate and incorporate human-centered insights into their work. As much of environmental communications as a discipline of research and a practice-based sector is concerned with outreach, advocacy and developing effective means of mobilizing particular forms of responses – from the corporate stakeholder level to community engagement in economically challenged cities – understanding how people manage and negotiate anxieties and loss is paramount. There are, at least, four clear arenas of impact for this work to have in communities of practice. All four arenas draw from the following insights developed through the study.

1. **We need to innovate our methodologies.** Data derived concerning environmental attitudes, values and behavior does not always adequately reflect 'what is really going on' in relation to environmental problems. Particularly, data derived through surveys, polling and focus groups must be critically interrogated. Psychosocial research methodologies, which tend to focus on carefully designed in-depth interviews and a variety of ethnographic methodologies, offer enormous potential for extending and deepening our insights into the affective and less conscious dimensions of environmental engagement.[2] We need to encourage our governmental agencies and research funding bodies to support and invest in research innovations, that move us beyond a metrics-based, quantitative behavioral focus to one that is more culturally, socially and psychologically systemic (Shove, 2010).

2. **We cannot measure levels of concern by actions alone.** Levels of concern regarding specific ecological issues or degradation, both locally and globally, are not commensurate with levels of action or otherwise observable forms of agency. This fundamentally calls for a shift in how we conceptualize

subjectivity and that we manage often coexisting, conflicting and paradoxical views, drives, desires and commitments. With this orientation, we are better equipped as researchers, educators, communicators and practitioners to recognize that where the concern may 'live' may not be readily obvious.

3. What presents as 'apathy' is a defensive strategy. The concept of public apathy misleadingly portrays people who are disengaged from environmental issues as lacking emotional or affective investments. Apathy describes a particular affective state that is likely to obscure difficult, painful or conflicting feelings, thoughts or beliefs, and is not an adequate descriptor for environmental subjectivity or political engagement. Denial of climate change and related ecological threats is a psychosocial strategy by which intolerable information is managed, often unconsciously. How we approach denial and apathy must be informed with insights derived from psychodynamic practices, such as the creation of a 'safe space' and containment via group conversations. This can and should inform how we design messaging, branding and outreach platforms.

4. Engagement is about creating contexts for creative, authentic participation. For cultivating capacities for reparation or what Winnicott (1962) refers to as "concern" and reparative impulses, we need to look more carefully at how the environmental sector, through its communications practices and its structures for action, allows for creating contexts for contributing and creativity.

In Chapter 4 I argued for attending to the undercurrents of sadness and loss and the implications for mourning and melancholia. I suggested that if unresolved mourning exists, particularly in relation to the loss of specific environmental objects, whether the objects signify certain memories, feeling-states or appreciation for the objects on various levels, this would present potentially profound implications for the capacity for reparation. More specifically, the emergence of *melancholia* as a core affective theme and psychic process in relation to environmental losses complicates the issue of environmental engagement. This problematizes epistemic and ontological assumptions concerning subjectivity. The overwhelming focus on attitudes, values and behavior that currently informs much of environmental communications research is but one part of the picture. The notion that a mood of mourning and loss may be running throughout much of how environmental issues are experienced has implications for how communications are conducted. If we look to psychoanalytic literature on these often unconscious processes, the 'work of mourning' is supported through various practices in psychotherapy and community activities. As Leader (2009) points out, mourning is often a social phenomenon, and without the social context including recognizing and acknowledging the losses, mourning can be impeded. Communications practices enter the arena in terms of developing means for acknowledging the loss and possible sadness, so it may be brought to awareness and perhaps processed more effectively.

The most powerful and moving observation to have emerged from this research, starting with the first interviews, was how complicated and often unstraightforward ways *concern* and *reparation* can be expressed. I became aware of how reductive and superficial most analyses of environmental concern tend to be, given that they often are not based on in-depth methodologies that, again, are labor intensive but yield richer data. With this in mind, I began to critique my own internal constructions of the 'apathetic subject' and to see it as full of cracks and fissures. The construct of the apathetic subject crumbled before my eyes as I met with people who clearly struggle on various levels with often deeply held and painful associations with their local environmental situation. Environmental activism as a construct became reworked, and I began to see how much environmental engagement work is predicated on frameworks that may not be helpful or psychologically accurate.

Perhaps most significant is the recognition of how vital it is to invite creativity as a basis for engagement. I believe, therefore, that campaigning strategies must begin to take account of the issue of contribution – what Winnicott (1963) refers to as the basis of concern, the ability to 'contribute-to' – and offer up a more collaborative mode for engagement (reparation) that can allow for *creativity, concern* and *contributions* to be animated.

Taking a psychoanalytically informed approach to the study and research of environmental advocacy, communications and outreach, as demonstrated through this study, necessarily draws on conceptions of subjectivity that allow for ambivalence. It is a conception of subjectivity that allows for fluidity, for contexts and biographical backgrounds, and for the ways in which our early life experiences often deeply inform important object relations, including nature, ecology and existential belonging. Such an approach gives credence to the presence of unconscious processes as informing attitudes, values and behaviors and recognizes them as dynamic and context specific. As I have argued (Lertzman, 2008a; Lertzman, 2012a, 2012b), a cogent environmental communications theory and practice *must* account for unconscious defences to anxiety, such as denial, projection, splitting and paralysis, and it must account for the ontological and existential dimensions of environmental problems and their consequences and impacts.

Using a psychoanalytic approach to communications and political actions also raises the ongoing question, addressed in this study, of the 'portability' of the theory to practice. If psychoanalysts are describing processes and dynamics coherent in the clinical context and consulting room, then the capacities for translation into different contexts are complicated. While we wish to avoid simplistic attempts to 'cut and paste' certain theoretical positions and clinical practices into non-clinical contexts, I believe there is a tremendous opportunity. For example, if the view is taken that perhaps one strategy for helping to soften defences is to provide a supportive, non-judgmental space, e.g. the holding environment, then we can creatively consider communications in the context of support and containment. This can be achieved through the actual formation of groups, conversations and workshops (Randall, 2009), particularly those facilitated and convened by skilled psychotherapeutic professionals. This is also potentially achieved rhetorically in acknowledging possible emotional responses, for example stating either explicitly or implicitly, "We know it is scary (overwhelming, frustrating, upsetting, etc.), but we are in this together". Further, if we are to take seriously Winnicott's work on capacities for concern and the vital role of creativity and contributing, then campaign efforts can incorporate modes for engagement that draw on and *invite* creative participation, rather than transmitting prescriptive and directive actions such as donating, signing a petition or showing up for a rally – actions which may not 'work' affectively or practically for many concerned populations (as illustrated vividly in the narratives of Howard, Scott and Donald).

What is required is the opportunity to pilot actual environmental communication campaigns and strategies informed by the preceding suggestions and thoughts and to evaluate them accordingly. As yet, there has been no large-scale psychosocial research study to provide more comprehensive data regarding the role of unconscious processes and affective investments in environmental issues. In fact, the field of psychosocial studies has yet – at the time of this writing – to adequately engage with the domain of environmental issues. The need for future research in this area is urgent, and psychosocial research findings cannot be adequately conducted on a small scale to attain the necessary level of impact. For informing policy decisions and governmental leadership for designing more effective public information and outreach campaigns, there would need to be larger projects, comprised of research teams, ideally in diverse regions, demography and populations. This requires adequate funding levels. Further, the psychosocial research endeavour in relation to environmental issues and concerns would be strengthened through the use of interdisciplinary teams, drawing from geography, ecological sciences, environmental history and social theory, anthropology and humanities. In terms of researching affect and environmental threats, the arts and poetic fields must be incorporated more actively, as the work of Cape Farewell and related arts projects can attest (Lertzman, 2008b; Jeremijenko, 2009).

It is my hope this work can serve as a provocation and rallying cry to the field of psychoanalysts and psychosocial researchers, as well as a bridge connecting to the field of environmental communications practice. There is evidence that this connection is already underway: the newly formed Climate Psychology Alliance in the United Kingdom[3] and events such as *Engaging with Climate Change* convened at The Institute of Psychoanalysis in London and the subsequent proceedings, edited by Sally Weintrobe (2013) which received considerable media attention (Revkin, 2010; BBC, 2011; Karpf, 2012). We are starting to see more active engagement linking psychoanalytic and psychosocial insights with our environmental threats, sparked by the rising focus on climate change issues (Dodds, 2011; Marshall, 2014). However, we have a ways to go. Until the environmental sector begins to fully come to terms with the human capacities for unconscious responses to anxieties and threats, as articulated a century ago by Freud, I am afraid it will be limited in its ability to reach out to those with deep concern, creativity and reparative energies, which need active facilitation and support as well as respect and compassion.

Notes

1 Schafer's definition of an analytic attitude is helpful: maintaining an atmosphere of neutrality; avoiding either/or interpretations; an interest in analysis (that relies on interpretation); and the aim to be helpful (Schafer, 1985).
2 The recognition of the need to develop how we can 'research affect' has been growing, as evidenced by the 2010 ESRC funded project Researching Affect and Affective Communication Seminar Series, convened by Valerie Walkerdine: workshops and symposia that brought together psychoanalytic practitioners and qualitative social science researchers to innovate and explore this emerging focus. The same needs to happen with regard to environmentally specific contexts and affective dimensions.
3 For more information, visit www.climatepsychologyalliance.org.

References

BBC, 2011. In Denial – Climate on the Couch. BBC Radio 4. 10 February. Available at: http://www.bbc.co.uk/programmes/b00y92mn.

Beck, U., 1992. *The Risk Society: Towards a New Modernity*. London: Sage.

Bollas, C., 1992. *Being a Character: Psychoanalysis and Self Experience*. London: Routledge [reprinted 1997].

Clarke, S., & Hoggett, P., 2009. *Researching Beneath the Surface: Psycho-social Research Methods in Practice*. London: Karnac.

Dodds, J., 2011. *Psychoanalysis and Ecology at the Edge of Chaos*. New York: Routledge.

Frosh, S., 2007. Facing political truths, *Psychotherapy and Politics International* 5, 29–36.

Frosh, S., & Baraitser, L., 2008. Psychoanalysis and psychosocial studies, *Psychoanalysis, Culture and Society* 13 (4), pp. 385–396.

Hollway, W., 2006. Paradox in the pursuit of a critical theorization of the development of self in family relationships, *Theory and Psychology* 16 (4), pp. 465–482.

Jeremijenko, N., 2009. The art of the eco-mindshift. *TED*, October. Available at: https://www.ted.com/talks/natalie_jeremijenko_the_art_of_the_eco_mindshift.

Karpf, A., 2012. Climate change: You can't ignore it. *The Guardian*. 30 November. Available at: http://www.theguardian.com/environment/2012/nov/30/climate-change-you-cant-ignore-it.

Leader, D., 2009. *The New Black: Mourning, Melancholia and Depression*. London: Penguin.

Lertzman, R., 2008. Love, guilt and reparation: Rethinking the affective dimensions of the locus of the irreparable. In Willard, B., & Green, C. (eds.), *Communication at the Intersection of Nature and Culture: Proceedings of the Ninth Biennial Conference on Communication and the Environment*. Chicago: College of Communication, DePaul University, pp. 8–13.

Lertzman, R., 2008a. The myth of apathy, *The Ecologist* 34 (4).

Lertzman, R., 2012a. Researching psychic dimensions of ecological degradation: Notes from the field. Psychoanalysis, Culture & Society 17 (1), pp. 92–101.

Lertzman, R., 2012b. The myth of apathy: Psychoanalytic explorations of environmental degradation. In Weintrobe, S. (ed.), *Engaging with Climate Change: Psychoanalytic and Interdisciplinary Perspectives*. London: Routledge, pp. 117–133.

Marshall, G., 2014. *Don't Even Think About It: Why Our Brains Are Wired to Ignore Climate Change*. New York: Bloomsbury USA.

Randall, R., 2009. Loss and climate change: The cost of parallel narratives, *Ecopsychology* 3 (1), pp. 118–129.

Revkin, A., 2010. "Shrinking" the climate problem, *The New York Times*, 28 October. Available at: http://dotearth.blogs.nytimes.com/2010/10/28/shrinking-the-climate-problem/.

Schafer, R., 1985. Wild analysis, *Journal of American Psychoanalytic Association* 33, pp. 275–299.

Shove, E., 2010. Beyond the ABC: Climate change policy and theories of social change, *Environment and Planning A* 42, pp. 1273–1285.

Weintrobe, S., 2013. *Engaging with Climate Change: Psychoanalytic Interdisciplinary Perspectives*. New York: Routledge.

Winnicott, D. W., 1962. The theory of the parent–infant relationship: Further remarks, *International Journal of Psychoanalysis* 43, pp. 238–239.

Winnicott, D. W., 1963. The development of the capacity for concern. In *The Maturational Process and the Facilitating Environment*. London: Karnac, pp. 37–55.

Appendices

Introducing the participants

To introduce the participants, I will present the brief snapshots to orient the reader for the voices that appear and constitute much of this study. I interviewed in the following order: Donald, Jeff, Victoria, Sally, Howard, Heather, Dana, Ray, Scott and Jessica. For a more in-depth case study of one participant, Sally, please see Appendix B.

Donald (focus of case study, Chapter 5) was the sole participant not selected from the survey, but instead from meeting in an adult education course on the history of Wisconsin energy and water; our interviews initially were a pilot I decided to include in the data. Donald grew up in Green Bay and had retired as a successful manager of a vegetable canning company; he and his wife lived in a subdivision overlooking the Fox River, adjacent to the Fox River Trail, and had three grown children and grandchildren, who lived out of the area.

Jeff, 67, grew up in Sheboygan Wisconsin (on Lake Michigan) and had moved to Green Bay in 1966; he and his wife raised three grown children and lived in a large, ramshackle Victorian house on the Fox River, directly behind the Fox River Trail. He had spent much of his career working as a project manager for a large-scale nuclear power plant nearby and had been retired for about 10 years. His sharing of documents from a university term paper on the nuclear plant for an environmental studies course constitutes one of the 'objects' in the study (see Appendix G). His dog Rudy was an active presence in the interviews, often nudging his head into my lap.

Victoria, 47, was a stay-at-home mother and housewife, living in a semirural area in De Pere, in a large, well kept house very close to the Fox River. Her older daughter had left home for college, and the younger one was in her final year of high school, preparing to leave the following year. Her husband worked for a nuclear power plant on Lake Michigan about an hour away. Victoria was very active in her church community and was beginning to look for casual part-time work.

Sally, 46 (focus of case study, Chapter 6) was a rural postal carrier, recovering from a work-related surgery and had grown up in Sheboygan before moving to Green Bay with her family at age 15. She lived adjacent to her parents in a duplex (houses that are adjoined) with a large shared back garden, very close to the Bay. She had three cats present through much of the interviews.

Howard, 49, grew up in rural De Pere, on the Fox River, and worked primarily in construction as a manager, along with various odd jobs. He was living in a small bungalow in the town of De Pere close to the university, and our interviews took place during a few snowstorms. Howard shared with me photographs of the region during our meetings and sent several later via email (see Figure 4.2 on page 000).

Heather, 40, lived alone with her dog and cat in a small house in the east side of Green Bay. Heather worked as an administrator for the state (at a mental hospital) and had grown up in rural Wisconsin.

Dana, 48, worked for the state government and requested we meet in her office. She had always lived in Green Bay and had a husband and two teenage sons.

Ray, a stay-at-home father, had Crohn's Disease and had to be drinking fluids and snacking continually. He had worked as a distributor for machinery used in paper mills and recycling plants. He and his family lived out in a semirural area about 10 miles from central Green Bay.

Scott, 31, had lived in Green Bay since he was four years old and had lived in different areas prior as his father was in the military. He was married and had a small toddler daughter, whom he was minding during our three interviews, as he and his partner had shift schedules (she worked days and he worked nights).

Jessica was the youngest participant, 23, and had grown up moving between divorced parents in Green Bay and Milwaukee, Wisconsin. She worked as an emergency call operator (e.g. 999) on shift schedules and lived on her own in an apartment on the east side of town. Whilst she seemed engaged in the first two interviews, she did not show for our final interview.

Case study: Sally

I have included the following case study, focusing on one participant, whom I am calling Sally. This piece provides a more in-depth review and analysis of the data from our interviews. In providing a case study with longer excerpts and analysis, I aim to illustrate the range, depth and breadth afforded in conducting multiple in-depth interviews using free association and a dialogic style. As with the excerpts throughout the book, the data has not been "scrubbed" or edited to remove pauses, corrections and repairs.

"Waves" poster. (Provided by Sally.)

As I crested the hill leading to Sally's subdivision, I was struck by the sudden panoramic view of the Bay, which I had not seen until then. When I shared this with Sally later in the interview, she whispered dramatically, "Isn't it awesome?" When asked if she spent time by the Bay, she responded, "I don't do it as much as I used to, or as much as I would like to. Lot of times I will just go by . . . on my way home, I'll just stop there for a while and just stare at the water, but you just, you see businesses, you see factories all over. You have to really angle yourself so you don't and then you just see land on the other side. Which is different than, the Lake. Um. But it's still water and I still love it".

The "Lake" is Lake Michigan. Sally grew up swimming and playing in its dunes as a young child in Sheboygan about 65 miles from Green Bay. She mentions the Lake moments into our first interview, in relation to the Bay (which is seen as inferior and polluted), as a place she deeply misses. It was only after the family left Sheboygan and moved to Green Bay when she was 15 that she claims to have started to miss Lake Michigan and its open, expansive horizon: "Actually, after we, after I was an adult and I was out on my own, I actually went out and bought myself a picture of waves. Because I didn't get enough, you know you don't get quite enough of the Lake and driving to the Lake is different from the Bay . . . Looking at the Bay is not the same as looking at the Lake! The Bay is calmer, the Lake you don't see anything, you just see water as far as the eye can see. The Bay you can see across to the other side, and it's not as rough. It's not as, what is the word I'm looking for? *Wild* isn't the right word, but it's more nature, the Lake, where the Bay is more subdued".

Sally both loves the Bay and is disgusted by it; she takes pride in living near the Bay and yet hardly goes down to the shores, and when she does, she "angles" herself so she is not facing industry and land on the other side.

At the time of our meeting, Sally was in her late forties, divorced, living in a duplex shared with her parents (the houses connected by a doorway and a shared garden). She has a physically intense job. She was recovering from cervical spinal fusion surgery, a result of a workplace injury lifting heavy boxes and was wearing a brace, and was two months into a six-month leave of absence from work. She had quite an expressive, at times dramatic style of communicating, and her discourse was often punctuated with laughter. She spoke rapidly, which I found challenging and initially intimidating, but we settled into a comfortable rhythm together.

Sally's parents uprooted the family from Sheboygan when she was 15, in the middle of her penultimate year in high school (junior year), a move Sally was opposed to; she jokes, "I was going to move in with my Aunt Margie [laughing] but she moved to Milwaukee [laughs] so I didn't have a choice, I had to come up here. I didn't want to come. It was the unknown!" She spent her early years growing up in a trailer park a few miles from the beach of Lake Michigan. As if anticipating judgments about trailer life, she says, "Back then, trailer parks were *very* nice, it was, you know, it was a very nice area". The family outings seemed to revolve around trips to the dunes of Lake Michigan and visits to Terre

Andre State Park (on the Lake Michigan shore). The outings mainly involved her mother, brother and the dog; her father worked long shifts at his mechanical factory job and her mother did not work while the children were very young.

When she was about 7 years old, the family moved from the trailer park to a ranch-style home across town, where they lived until moving to Green Bay in 1977. It was during this time on the east side of town that Sally seemed to have more autonomy; of this time, she says, "I mean, you know from little kids who are totally dependent on their parents to kids who are older have their own friends. And being able to say, 'I'm going over to my friends' and you know, bike off [laughs]". Her life changed abruptly when her parents decided to buy a motel and run their own business when she was a teenager. When asking Sally about this decision, following up in the second interview, she says, "We all talked about it, but we were the kids, and really, they made the decision that was best for them, the family". The family moved into the motel, which they ran as a family business. As Sally describes it, there was little privacy, the phone and doorbell were ringing at all times and she and her brother had to help with cleaning rooms, answering phones most weekend mornings. When I asked Sally if the motel was in any way a step up from the ranch house in Sheboygan, she says dryly, "Uuhh, only in the fact that it took that many steps to go up there, no [Laughs]" and then describes in great detail the Sheboygan ranch home with its basement and bar.

Sally expresses her relation with Green Bay in terms of what she was missing: "I know that after we moved to Green Bay, I missed the Lake a lot. The Bay is not the same. First of all, it was so *polluted here* that we couldn't go swimming in it". The move to Green Bay becomes strongly associated, at least in the context of our interviews and her awareness of environmental issues, in terms of how polluted and degraded the water was and the inability to go *in* to the water (e.g. immersive, entering into it). However, despite the "shock" and abjection of the polluted water and overall disorientation of the relocation, Sally remained in Green Bay and eventually moved into her own apartment soon after high school. She seems very close with her parents. She recounts a story that conveys something about her struggles with establishing autonomy from her parents. While living in the apartment, an intruder broke into the apartment: "He was there when I got home and that was a little exciting." Although it sounds like a terrifying experience, she tells the story with levity and laughter, as she ends up giving the burglar a lift when she leaves the house, and comments on her handling of the situation. "But I think some of that is our personality and how we react or not panic. You know, it's like I didn't really panic that much." However, following this incident, despite the fact she didn't "panic" she moved back in with her parents and stayed for the next couple of years. In her early twenties, she travelled abroad on an exchange program working in a German post office for a few months, where one of her uncles was working, and on her return began working for a delivery service. She then bought a condominium and eventually sold it a few years later and moved into the duplex she shares with her parents; connected by a doorway, the two homes share a large garden, full of trees and plants. She has lived there since and referred once to the fact she was married for several years and recently divorced.

At the time of mentioning her two months in Germany, in our second interview, Sally tells me her parents were both born and raised in Germany. Both parents grew up in Berlin and lived there during World War II. Of her father, she says, "He came over in '54 or '55 and my mom came over in '59". In the third interview, I follow up on this topic, and Sally describes the severe deprivation her parents lived through during the war. (As I will discuss, her parents' experiences in Germany may help us understand how she has learned to negotiate difficult circumstances and experiences, significantly the unhappy circumstances of her involuntary move to Green Bay as a teenager.)

Sally's rather frenetic activity had come to a standstill as she recovered from her surgery, and she found it a time for reflection; hence her desire and time to participate in the study. Her lifestyle has been 'filled up' with a physically demanding full-time job (e.g. her vehicle has two steering wheels and two sets of pedals for maneuvering post and country roads), music and adult education. As she told me, breathlessly, "Um I have rehearsal two nights a week, I take another, because I sing with the [X], I play with [X] Symphony, so have those rehearsals two nights a week, Monday is usually a ten- or eleven-hour day, because there's a lot of mail on Mondays, because we're not delivering on Sunday! So Mondays I don't want to do anything but I also take a workshop class every other Monday right now. Monday, Wednesday, Thursday, so you know three nights a week I'm already gone. So the other kind of, the other two times, and on the weekends, I you catch up. Which I need to catch up during the week so I can have my weekends free so I need to change that [laughs] goal for next year, new year's resolution!" I am already feeling exhausted and a bit of out breath just listening to her.

I am most struck by the way she consistently gets close to a topic clearly of great affective investment and then retreats or backs away into a mantra or litany that repeats itself through the interviews: "There is nothing I can do". It is this dynamic I am most interested in, in terms of what it may tell us about her subjectivity in relation to environmental issues, the topic of 'concern' and 'engagement' and how we can adequately assess someone's level of engagement if what we are looking at, e.g. specific practices, are seen as heavily negotiated strategies which have their own psychic logic and contexts.

In the analysis that follows, I begin with Sally's recollections of the sand dunes in Sheboygan (as 'good' objects) and the affective associations. As with several other participants, when describing her childhood, she falls into a sort of reverie. I then turn to the move to Green Bay, a 'turning point' in the narrative, a crucial 'plot' turn and informative for subsequent relations with ecological issues and her perceptions. As I discuss, the move ushers in a new era, in which childhood ideals are lost, things become topsy-turvy and a new order must be constituted. In paying close attention to the 'incantations' of adjustment and adaption to conditions, no matter how toxic or chronic, I explore her narratives about water and its risky quality. Water (as object) seems to be a source of love, affection, nostalgia, disgust, risk and danger; it connects her with something vital and potentially lost and yet is impure and sullied. I then address the core themes of adaptation and adjustment, in the context of both the acute shock (and trauma) of the move and the parental authority it represented, as well as her parents' survival in a deprived wartime and postwar Berlin. There appears to be the sense of extreme vulnerability; no protection, no ability to be safe (e.g. "There is no more quarantine"). In this light, I suggest her attempts at environmental reparation, e.g. through the Save the Whales campaign, are heavily qualified with a sense of impotence. I finally discuss Sally's participation in the interviews and survey as an expression of concern, reparation and engagement and conclude with final reflections.

Affect, environmental objects and memory

I begin by asking Sally to tell me "what comes to mind in terms of where you grew up", the prompt I used opening all of my first interviews. She tells me they lived in a trailer park and then says: "Back then, the sand dunes were *all sand*. Now there's a lot of growth. I don't know if you were over there at all, but it used to be pure sand, just sand. And now there's other stuff growing up out of it". The narrative is a story of loss, of the pure sand dunes. I ask if she would go out to the beach with her brother or on her own; she responds:

> Oh my parents would take us, and we had a dog also, so we'd all go down, we'd all be playing in the sand, in the sand dunes. And go swimming in the Lake, and you know that the Lake is pretty cold in June and July and May, if you want to freeze that's your choice! And then by August it warms up. And um, so we were used to that. Yes so we'd be out there, we'd play out there, we'd run to the dunes and the dog would go running with us. It was a lot of fun. And, just jump in the Lake, cool off, spent a lot of time – and I love looking at the Lake. I just love, what it . . . Looking at the Bay is not the same as looking at the Lake!

I am given a vivid account of family trips to the shores of Lake Michigan – the cold waters, the sense of freedom and playing in the sand with the family dog. She also invokes the Bay as inferior to Lake Michigan; she loves looking at the Lake, whereas she does not enjoy looking out at Green Bay. My feeling is that she is somewhat embarrassed by the Bay; it is not as 'wild' or 'natural' as her hometown waters of Lake Michigan. I ask how the Bay is different, and she responds:

> Bay is calmer, the Lake you don't see anything, you just see water as far as the eye can see. The Bay you can see across to Oconto over there to the

other side, um, and it's not as rough. It's not, what is the word I'm looking for? Wild isn't the right word, but it's more nature, the Lake, where the Bay is more subdued.

The Lake is more wild, less "subdued", not as rough; the Bay is associated with settlement, towns, industry, whereas the Lake seems untouched by all of that, is just wide open, wild and has rough waves to gaze out on. I then ask Sally if she has any particular memories or stories (I am probing for a Particular Inducing Narrative [PIN]):

R: What is your, what are some of your earliest memories of going out to the Lake?
S: Well in summer of course, being on the beach, going swimming and playing and that. And sometimes, just um, enjoying it. Being young and knowing, not knowing that there's anything wrong, you know the world was a safe place.
R: So you felt safe –
S: Oh yeah!
R: And at ease
S: yes safe and at ease. Yeah. Calm, peaceful.
R: Are there any, it's a bit hard to do this but can you imagine any particular moments or incidents that you can describe that really stand out to you.
S: Well, with the sand and you're young kids, you, we did a lot of um, sand-castle stuff. And making a lot of different sandcastles and the waves would come and wash them away and start over and try to build a really nice big one, all that kind of stuff. Building sandcastles, and just having lunch and relaxing out there, playing in the water and going swimming and going as far as we'd be allowed [laughs] and coming back in.

She articulates what it meant to enjoy the water, the sand, the warmth and the cold water and, "Being young and knowing, *not knowing that there's anything wrong, you know the world was a safe place*". This is a world *prior* to adult concerns, where the future was as open as the horizon of Lake Michigan. It is this identi-fication with the dunes and the outings to Lake Michigan as feeling "safe" and "not knowing that there's anything wrong" that exists in contrasts to the life in Green Bay, which is clearly not safe and where there are things that *are* "wrong". Also of note is the reference to swimming also being a monitored activity, as they would go out "as far as we'd be allowed" and coming back in. This reflects both the sense of freedom and innocence, as well as containment and a sense of limits (which I observed in Donald's accounts as well; nature was wild and open but within certain limits. The exception to this was the accident at the Fox River for Donald, and with Sally, the polluted waters signify a sharp lack of protection and containment, as will be discussed). I have a strong sense of her mother's presence during these outings, as her father was often absent due to his shift schedule.

In the second interview, Sally corroborates her memories of the Lake with her brother, and she brings him in to collude (on the part of Sally) in the experience of the dunes and of the shock at the pollution of the water in Green Bay. (It is also worth looking at what it means for Sally's brother to corroborate her own memory retrievals.) For Sally, the move to Green Bay signaled the end of swimming in nature (e.g. not in swimming pools); for her brother, as a 'guy', the polluted water didn't pose as much of a threat.

> I talked with my brother and um I asked him what he remembered from that time, and he agreed, he remembered we spent a lot of time playing in the dunes in Lake Michigan-in Sheboygan. And um running into, and we had a dog Cleo too, and running into the water and doing some swimming and you know playing in the dunes you get all dirty and you need to go jump in the water and rinse off. So he remembered a lot of that. And then his shock, and too, that when we moved to Green Bay, that um, you couldn't go swimming! And then, several years later, you know he did go swimming in there, a bunch of guys went out there, I mean they're guys, and they went swimming and he said now I know you don't go swimming in the bay, you don't want to. [Laughs] Cause it's polluted and it's just not, worth swimming in.

When describing the dunes and the waters in Lake Michigan, Sally recounts memories of a more idyllic time in childhood, running into the water, playing with the dog, as capturing a certain quality or moment when they were young. In the narratives about the pure sands and the clean, clear and wild waters of Lake Michigan, she is also indirectly referencing the polluted and degraded waters of Green Bay. She does not mention one without the other; each is articulated in relation to the other, to something prior, unspoilt, pure. I am interested in the way she articulates her life in Sheboygan and the dunes because it helps me make sense of her account of the "shock" of the pollution of the waters in Green Bay and how this can be seen in the context of the shock of the move itself. In the second interview, I wanted to know if Sally's experience of the dunes as overgrown with grasses had led her to learn more about the ecology.

R: And you mentioned that the dunes were very high –
K: They were very sandy. Very sandy. And now there is more vegetation.
R: And why is that?
S: Don't know.
R: The change in –
S: Ww – I have no clue.
R: Okay.
S: I just know that way back then there was not that much vegetation, it was sand all over for as far as the eye can see. Just once and a while you'd see a little bit of vegetation.
R: But now there is more grass.

There is a prickly quality in her responses, as if I am suggesting she ought to know more about the issue, or perhaps she is projecting onto me an idea of what she should know. In this case, it is difficult to ascertain if the grasses that seem to have become more prevalent in the dunes are native species, and perhaps Sally doesn't recall their being there (e.g. her selective memory is of "pure sand") or if they are invasive grass species, which do plague many areas of the Great Lakes wetlands and beaches.

However, the dunes, for Sally, are no longer pure and sandy. The water is no longer clean, and she cannot swim at the beach as she once did. She speaks of Sheboygan and of her childhood prior to the move to Green Bay in affectionate, idealized terms. In order to understand more about how Sally relates and experiences the water and environment in Green Bay, as the interviews progressed, I wanted to explore her life prior to the move to Green Bay. I was curious if her nostalgia and feelings about Lake Michigan were connected with the subsequent dislocation and trauma of the move to Green Bay, which occurs when she is about 15. By the time they left Sheboygan, how central was Lake Michigan to her life; that is, when she says that she missed the Lake intensely after the move, is it possible the Lake comes to represent something vital, pure and innocent she has lost. In the second interview I ask how much she spent time at the Lake, after the move across town to the ranch house.

S: Not as often, as when we lived closer by. Cause there were other things, and you know we were getting older too, I mean, you know from little kids who are totally dependent on their parents to kids who are older have their own friends, and you know, do things like that. So. And having bicycles and being able to, "I'm going over to my friends" and you know bike off. [Laughs]

R: Right. So would you say the Lake, um, you know, what, would you say that actually the move, there was a shift where you spending less time there, or did that happen not necessarily by the move, but more your age, getting older.

S: You know I can't quite remember exactly. I can't really. That would be a question my parents would be able to answer better. Because you know, you're just a kid, 10 and younger, and 10 and 16, you just really don't, or 15 you don't think about that kind of –

R: Yeah you just kind of are doing your thing

S: Yeah! As a kid the world revolves around you! [Laughs]

R: As an older person getting into your teens, would you all go out to the Lake?

S: My dad worked a lot of hours. So, my mom, my brother and I probably would, yeah. And then dad probably would, you know, if my dad would be available on the weekends.

Again, a prickly quality to the responses; I then add, "Yeah you are just kind of are doing your thing" as if to say, "It's okay, I am not judging you". The Lake seems to have receded in Sally's memories and life by the time the family moved to the ranch house, as she gets older and has more autonomy. At the same time, the world "revolves around you" as a kid, which also suggests how, prior to the move to Green Bay, she still enjoyed a sense of innocence and freedom associated with childhood. The way she mixes up the ages, going from 10 to 16 to 15, suggests the time between 10 and 16 as when this progression took place; it is also the time period when she lived in the larger ranch house prior to the move. By the time Sally moved to Green Bay, she was spending less time in the water, by the Lake (which was largely associated with family outings) and was mostly consumed with teenage preoccupations of socializing along with church and school activities (orchestra). It was when they were moved – while she was in high school, to Green Bay to run a motel – was when she began to long powerfully for the water, the Lake and the ability to look out on to an open horizon; this is the narrative she provides in the context of the interviews. As she says, she didn't begin to appreciate the Lake until they moved.

From the beginning, Sally's narratives concerning the dunes and her early experiences in and by the Lake are clearly powerful and strongly associated with childhood innocence and family. As it becomes clear throughout the interviews, Sally expresses very strong concern and awareness of environmental issues in Green Bay, specifically relating to the value of quality drinking water, clean water for swimming and the value of the Great Lakes as a resource. However, she does not participate or 'look' like an environmentally engaged individual; music is her passion and focus. However, there remains a vital energy present with regard to issues concerning water. I now explore the move to Green Bay as a pivotal event in her life story, one that may offer clues as to how and why Sally responds and engages with issues in the way she does. Specifically, the move to Green Bay may signal an end to innocence – from 'idyll' to abject, from the omnipotence of childhood to the imperfections of adulthood, from safety to risk. The move to Green Bay dovetailed with Sally's emergent adolescence, and the perception of Green Bay as shockingly polluted and abject may be affectively associated with the shock of leaving life in Sheboygan. Her experience of the water and environment in Green Bay may operate as an "objective correlative" (Eliot, 1921) of unconscious processes and intra-psychic dynamics.

Moving to Green Bay: The shock of the water

In the first interview, as discussed in Chapter 4, the main focus is on eliciting free associations with the place one grew up and the region in general. As we move into discussing life in Green Bay, I ask Sally about her associations with the move.

R: Anything else about, what you associated with moving to Green Bay?
S: The shock of the water, the Bay, being so filthy that you could not swim in it. Um. For some reason, they allowed you to swim in Ashwaubenon,

there was some in Ashwaubenon . . . you could swim there. I don't know why that was cleaner than the tip down here, but it was just down the road from Fort Howard! [Laughing] I mean looking back now, um, they used to have way back when they used to have swimming right at Bay Beach. They used to have swimming, right off, by the University here, that little park, um, Comm-university, they used to have swimming there also. Um, and, the shock of the water being that dirty, it was huge. And, you know they said okay two years, and you say okay I can live with that, two years later it still wasn't clean, and here we are, 2007, twenty years later and it's still not clean. I don't think they ever will have it clean. So.

R: Do you think, as far as your parents moving here. Did they ever mention the water, or um, the change in the quality or anything like that?

S: They were also appalled that you couldn't swim, that the water was so dirty.

R: Uh-huh. Was that something that you all didn't know before you came here?

S: Correct.

R: So perhaps you had an idea that, it would be kind of more of a, resource that you could use?

S: Right. Yeah. Um. We didn't, we just assumed, because we'd, I guess, we did spend a lot of time at the Lake, going swimming down there, and I guess even growing older we'd go down there, if we wanted to go swimming, the hotdog days of summer, we'd go down there. And then living here, you'd want to go swim close by and you couldn't. So it was a shock. And, it – part of me would think, why did the community allow it to get so bad? But, not having lived here in those early years. And there are so many mills here, there are so many mills in the area.

It seems important for Sally to convey her strong views and feelings about the water in Green Bay; the way she communicates this is unequivocal and passionate (in contrast to other participants, such as Victoria, who registers this as matter-of-fact, or Jeff, who notes his shock also when moving from Sheboygan to Green Bay but notes it in an almost jovial way). Early in the interviews, there is a strong association between the move and the "shock of the water" as being so polluted. According to Sally, her parents were "appalled" about the inability to swim in the bay. We also see the beginnings of assigning responsibility in "Why did the community allow it to get so bad?", an expression of disappointment that runs throughout almost all of the participants' interviews. Here it is the community who failed; later in the interviews, it's down to the governmental failure to regulate and how small one feels in relation to such remote powers. There seems to be a lack of comprehension as to how it was allowed to degrade and degenerate so badly. I found her emphasis on the water quality striking, when considering the context of the move and what appears to me as having been a traumatic event on a number of levels. While the focus of the interviews cannot be ignored (indeed are held unconsciously or consciously for the participant), it made me wonder if the water was being used as an object of displacement for the affective responses to the move, which may be otherwise unacceptable to express or even to tolerate (e.g. anger and disgust towards the parents for enforcing the move and putting an abrupt end to childhood innocence and omnipotence). In other words, the severity with which she speaks of the water and her shock seem out of place, considering what sounds like a shocking and traumatic move. Sally was moved in the middle of her junior year, with one year remaining in high school, from a highly developed community and established way of life. She mentions several times the fact she had just earned a high rank in the school orchestra, which had taken years. While much of the content is related in an upbeat and cheerful tone, the facts of the events strike me as painful, sad and about loss. Her account of trying to find the Abbey in Green Bay, soon after the move, and instead ending up at the local prison (correctional institute) conveys this disorientation vividly:

> It was funny . . . We were looking for St Norbert Abbey. We knew it was on Webster and Monroe in that area, you could get it from either side, [Laughing] we kept ending up at the correctional institute! [Laughing] It was hilarious! It's like, is this it? Is this it? This is a huge brick building! It's the correctional institute let's get out of here! So it's kind of funny finding your way around and ending up there. Another place we ended up at was East High. From East High we learned, I don't know why we ended up there, but somehow we always, we'd miss the turn, and we'd always go there, and from there we found our way for a while in Green Bay and all of a sudden you learn the way. Those are just some funny things that I remember about first moving here. Um. [Laughing] Yeah, thinking you're going to St Norbert Chapel and Abbey and you end up at the correctional institute! [Laughs]

I am reminded of what Winnicott has observed about the nature of manic defenses, as a flight from inner reality to outer reality, and the "denial of the *sensations* of depression – namely the heaviness, the sadness – by specifically opposite sensations, lightness, humorousness, etc." (Winnicott, 1935, p. 132). As Sally recounts the circumstances of the move, particularly in the first interview, there remains a brittle lightness, which belies the difficulties she must have experienced. In addition to describing the "shock" of the water, she also acknowledges the culture shock of having grown up around a thriving Mexican population and the relative homogeneity of Green Bay. It is clear she misses Hispanic culture as well, as she mentions piñata parties as a child. As I process the magnitude of this move in Sally's life, I begin to wonder why her parents chose to move at that time and to run a motel business (not even waiting for her to finish her junior year in high school; here my own countertransference is evidence in the experience of anger towards the parents, given her relative lack of affect). In the second interview, I begin to piece together a *gestalt* of the move to Green Bay and revisit the account by feeding back what I have heard and my own queries.

S: They wanted to be their – my dad wanted to be his own boss, he wanted to be in charge instead of being always, you know, an employee for somebody else, he thought it would be great to, to be his own boss and have his own business.

R: Was it something that you all talked about as a family, or was it something they suddenly announced?

S: We all talked about it, but we were the kids, and really, they made the decision that was best for them, and the family.

We see a similar repair as in the opening of the interview, mentioned at the beginning of this case study, in which she says, "Okay, we moved to Green Bay – my parents moved to Green Bay in 1977". Here she begins with "they wanted" and repairs to "my dad wanted" suggesting at least unconsciously that in fact her father was the key decision maker in the family. She tells me, laughing, that she wanted to move in with her aunt, but her aunt then decided to move out of the state so that was no longer an option. This is all relayed in a light, breezy tone, causing me to initially overlook the fact that she had resisted the move and that her one option for staying in Sheboygan was removed. In fact, it took me at least until the second interview to fully grasp the content of what she was telling me, that not only did they move to a new town, but they were all living in close quarters in a motel which was run as a 24/7 business. In the first interview, I am asking her for more information about the lifestyle; I include a lengthy excerpt as it is important for obtaining a sense of what this life was like for her as a teenager. However, there is a notable lack of affect concerning what sound to be difficult circumstances. (This provides a clue as to the 'adaptation and adjustment' theme with regard to environmental issues, to be discussed.)

R: And where did you live?

S: The motel had an apartment upstairs, a three-bedroom, it was really like a house, a ranch house, because you had the kitchen, the living room, a dining area, laundry room, and three bedrooms, with two baths.

R: Was that, um, a step up from where you had been living in Sheboygan.

S: Uhhh . . . only in the fact that it took that many steps to go up there, no. [Laughs] No. They had a ranch home, um, very nice ranch home with a basement, the basement was, they had some area of the basement that was finished off, and we made it into a living room, they had linoleum down, they hadn't hung the ceiling, back then the rage was paneling all over. And um, so they had a nice living area, uh, family area downstairs, um, and a pool table and ping-pong table, we had all that stuff. And back then, having bars in your basement was huge, so they had that, even though they didn't drink that much, you know but when everyone got together they'd all, that was a point of um, hanging out. So part of the basement was done, um, we had the whole first floor or had a ranch home, that was nice, very nice yard with garden and all of that, and um, close to school, close to work, close to everything so it was very nice, nicer than the motel [laughs a bit wryly] so yeah.

There is a brittle, clipped quality to the way Sally is describing this scenario to me, particularly when I ask if she helped out with the work, as if to suggest such a question was ludicrous. It was taken for granted the whole family ran the business. We see Sally surprisingly invoke the topic of the water and access to the Lake, even though we are now speaking about Green Bay – not Sheboygan – so there is some incoherence, and the theme of water and the Lake is still active unconsciously. It is articulated as not accessible due to family pressures and the constraints of running the business. We may view the comment, "We didn't do as much going to the water and to the Lake and things like that" as being about activities associated with *childhood* and life in Sheboygan. Rather, there is no time for playing – "It's just part of your job"; the world of adulthood has suddenly intruded, and one must "do your job". I then ask about what it was like for the family and her parents to adjust to the new lifestyle.

S: So there was a lot more limitations with owning a motel and living there.
R: How did your parents adapt to that, such a radical change in lifestyle and, work life? Given that it used to be your dad putting in a lot of hours at the factory and now, it was totally different kind of situation.
S: [Sighs] Repeat the question . . . [Sounds weary, tired]
R: How did they find the change in work life and lifestyle?
S: It was hard. It was very hard. That's Mavis! [Another cat walks in] I'm glad you came out sweet pea! This is Renee. [I pet the cat, very timid. We both laugh.] She's the curious one, the inquisitive one, always pays attention and knows what's happening.
R: And this one is –
S: The social butterfly! [Laughing]
R: So it was hard –
S: Very hard.
R: – transition

She is struggling to respond to my questions as I try to gain a sense of the level of tension or conflict during this time, and, once she admits how hard it was, she jumps on the change of topic, as her cat walks (conveniently) into the room. I also welcome the diversion, as the topic is becoming more difficult, and I 'jump' to the cat and begin to stroke her, both calming me and conveying a sense of having a relaxed chat. After this initial interruption, we return to the topic, and she opens up more about how hard the transition was – and the importance of being *adaptable*. Understanding how she has responded to the trauma of the move and the difficult circumstances enables me to better understand the theme of *adaptation* that emerges as central in how Sally relates to chronic ecological issues she experiences and is aware of. Here she elaborates on how difficult the transition was and how much she missed her life in Sheboygan; there is now a sense of loss that had not been present previously.

S: Very hard transition. Because we had a very nice life. Um, involved in church, involved in, you know, hey were very involved in their church at that time, they um, we had a full life we had a very nice life. And coming to a motel, a small motel, it's not like a motel where you go and put your hours and then you go home. Um. A small motel, that is your life. That is your, you know, you eat, sleep and breathe that. And um, it was. [Sighs] I don't recommend small businesses, that type of business to somebody unless they are younger and they want to have the 24/7 that they can put into it. It's a lot of hard work. It's a lot of hard work. You find out really how well you work as a family. Um. You know, um, the first two spouses, how they work, because normally one spouse is off to work –
R: Exactly –
S: And work separate times, so you found out how well you work as a couple you find out how well you work as a family. Interesting dynamics. Because, um, you get frustrated, you get upset, um, you're with those people 24/7. You don't, you can't just say at the end of my workday, I'm going home. You already are home! [Laughs heartily] So. That was, that was interesting the dynamics did change a lot. Um. You do adapt because we are, everybody is adaptable. And um, it was just very hard. But the business did well, it um, you know, you work hard put a lot into it, and um, you get a lot out of it too.

In addition to the importance of adaptation is the way the family came together. When I asked her about the mood and if there were tensions in the house, she responds with language that takes me by surprise:

As our family um, we'll all argue, um, you know, complain whatever, but when coming together as a family and working together, and standing united we do that well. So, I mean, if anybody were to attack any one of us we are united force. So. I don't know if that answers your question. We um, always have been a close family. Um, with the excep- – even though my brother has travelled a lot, we still are relatively close family . . . in that kind of thing you learn how to work together, you learn how to get along, you learn how to interact with the other with the other people in your family because otherwise, there'd be constant strife.

Now *three* key themes are emerging with regard to how Sally has creatively negotiated with extremely difficult circumstances: *adaptation*, a sense of one's own limited agency and "coming together and standing united, a united force", the primacy of family unity. The militaristic language employed here denotes a mood of battle and strife, and the allusion to attack was a bit unclear. Who is doing the attacking, and why? Where I was querying internal conflicts and strife, Sally shifts the discourse to one of standing united against external threats. How she articulates the importance of family, in the context of what sounds to be very difficult and trying circumstances – which I would have expected her to feel anger and resentment about – becomes a sort of incantation, to appear throughout the interviews, regarding adaptation and the importance of being a close family. Given Sally's own trajectory and the fact she never, in many respects, 'left home', there is something important here regarding how she chose to respond to these circumstances and how she has subsequently responded to other difficulties, namely the risky drinking water quality, her mother's illness and her awareness of and responses to local and global environmental issues.

Affective relations with water: Love, disgust, threat

What I have heard from Sally up to this point has been an ambivalent account of her object relations with water. As she says of the (polluted) water in Green Bay, "It's still water, and I still love it". However it is clear there is 'good' water (the waters of her childhood Lake Michigan) and 'bad' water (the polluted waters of Green Bay and the contaminated drinking water). (This splitting of good and bad waters has resonance with Donald, for whom the Fox River was 'bad' and Two Rivers is 'good'; one is spoiled by industry and abuse, and the other is protected, pure and pristine, both functioning as internal and external objects.) When Sally tells me she would sit and look out at the Bay and angle her body as to avoid looking at the land or buildings opposite her, it is a poignant and telling metaphor for this ambivalent stance, not able to sever the connection and yet managing it through specific and strategic points of contact. (As we shall see, the ability to calibrate contact with both the 'good' and the 'bad' becomes more evident as she discusses her book, *Our Stolen Future*, to be discussed.) During the second interview, I fed back to Sally what I 'heard' her telling me regarding the difficulty of the move, as a means of both validating with her my own impressions and as a way of building up a rapport and transitioning into a discussion of how she experienced the ecological problems in Green Bay. I was aware that it would be difficult to consciously acknowledge something as subtle and potentially unconscious as how one experiences ecological issues, but I was feeling my way and asking Sally to help me understand how she responded. It is here she expands more fully on the theme of readjustment and elaborates on the importance of adjusting one's expectations, that is, learning to live with disappointments.

S: I guess, I – in one way you readjust, how you do things and what you do. For example, going just right down to the water and going for a swim, there was a bb – there was a beach at Com-University Park and at Bay Beach.

Originally that was a swimming beach. All these, so instead of going to Bay beach, emphasis on beach, going into the water, it became a park and it meant being by the water, not in the water. It meant, going to you know the amusement park at bay beach. Um you could sit and look at the water, but you'd never want to go into it. And it was always in the background, rather than, you know, rather than going into it and playing. Or swimming, not just playing but swimming, or cooling off. Um, going to Com-University Park, you sit there and look at the water. You don't go, you know, on a nice hot summer day you just don't go running into it.

R: Right, right.

S: So it was, getting used to that, and realizing, and then it took a long time, years before we found out about that area where you can go swim, which is ironically just down the road from Fort Howard [Laughing a lot] and that's an approved swimming area.

R: Did you swim in there?

S: Yeah, yeah. When we found out about it, and we were able to drive down there. And with friends I think we would drive down there, we'd go down there with friends, with a youth group, and actually go swimming into the water in addition to the picnic or anything else that was going on. Usually they'd have volleyball and all that other fun stuff. Does that answer your question? You kind of readjust your expectation.

R: Right. I wonder how that colored your experience of living here. I think it's hard to separate out all the other things that were going on –

S: I don't know if it's ss – I don't know, I like your word 'colored' your, feelings, it's just it was just, there were so many changes that you just adapted to the new changes, and okay that's just part of life, and since there were so many of them, it's just, oh, okay.

The irony that Sally is laughing about, of course, is that the area deemed as safe for swimming was just downstream from one of the major paper mills. So even though she went swimming, it was with a group (church youth group) and in dubious waters. The central 'mantra' to emerge from these accounts concern adaptation and adjustment to change. I want to suggest that this same 'mantra' surfaces in relation as well to issues of risky water quality and may have its roots in certain generational familial dynamics which predate the move to Green Bay, as we will see.

The issue of water quality and food purity (e.g. the use of bovine growth hormones in meat and dairy cows) rated high on her radar in terms of key issues in the survey. As I was to learn, Sally had direct experiences with water contamination as relayed through two specific 'incidents'. The first, concerning her narrative about the water smelling like gasoline and how she had to adjust her living conditions to accommodate this mysterious situation, the fact that her cat subsequently died of kidney failure having been given the water; second, her mother's breast cancer and the fact that they learned, retrospectively, that her mother should have been avoiding the drinking water during her chemotherapy treatments. The topic of water quality is also strongly associated with bottled drinking water and her vigilance about drinking tap water, even ice cubes, when out at restaurants. Not surprisingly the topic of water – drinking water, water for swimming, the water in the Great Lakes, the water as home to whales and creatures, water as an industrial site in Green Bay and as a sign of civic inaction and inefficacy – is difficult to 'contain' as discrete and separate topics. Literally and metaphorically, the water 'flows' from one topic to another. Therefore what I wish to focus on in the following section, are the *affective* undercurrents in the discourses concerning water. Specifically, there is a subtle yet palpable *movement* between different affective registers: acceptance, resignation, disgust, anger and sadness. There is also the undercurrent of *disappointment*.

Disappointment

In the second interview, I bring up the topic of industry in the region:

R: What, um, and this is kind of, free association so just kind of whatever comes to mind. What are your feelings about that industry, all those industries being here and the paper mills, and –

S: If you don't think about it, and it's just part of life, it's just oh, that's just part of life, that's how it goes, that's the way the area is. But when you look at the big picture, if you look at, like when you look at the *Weather Channel* and they actually show Canada, and they show kind of the whole nation and you realize, this is the main thing of water, there are other coun–t other states that don't have this much water. And I look at that and I'm surprised at how we allow our water to be polluted.

Sally articulates the complex and uncanny capacity for being both simultaneously aware and unaware of our surroundings – akin to disavowal, the ability to 'know and not know'. Her surprise is registered when she apprehends the significance of the bodies of water that comprise the Great Lakes. She describes the way certain conditions, even those that are distressing or discomforting (e.g. the industry and its degradation of the waters she claims to value strongly) are naturalized: "Just part of life, that's how it goes, that's the way the area is". But when we look at the 'big picture', such as a Geographical Information Survey (GIS) impact of the region on the *Weather Channel*, it becomes quite a different picture; she is able to grasp the magnitude of the situation, the value of the waters and their vulnerability. The affective register returns to what arises in the first moments of our first interview of shock and disappointment. I follow with, "What are your feelings about that?"

S: Oh I dislike it. You know, the, regulations should be stricter. This is the water we are going to be drinking, this is the water that grandkids are going to be drinking. It needs to, they need to clean it up. Water is a limited source. It, it's gotta be, water is one of the things that we need to live by.

R: Hmm hmm. So if you were to describe, emotions associated or affiliated that come up when you think about the industry here in Green Bay. What would those be?

S: Emotions. What emotion would I attach to . . .

R: If you just allow yourself –

S: First thing is disappointment. Ah, disappointment that they're allowing the pollution to continue, disappointment that – I already said disappointment. Well, like I first said when we were all shocked and appalled at how bad the water quality was, I can't think of anything else, I'm trying too hard. [Laughs.]

Disappointment echoes across several other participants, making it a strong thematic undercurrent. What are emotional registers of disappointment; is disappointment an emotion? It is as far as she is able to go in this moment; disappointment is a softening, a blunter edge than anger or outrage, for example. It has a sadder quality, muted, and is entirely livable. We can live with disappointment; one adjusts, as Sally often says. Immediately following this exchange, Sally introduces the topic of water contamination, in telling me that when you have good water you "take it for granted" and how in the nineties, there was a period "when the water was *really bad*. It smelled awful, it tasted awful, I was buying bottled water for a long time". Her parents bought a water filtration unit for the house, as the water smelled like gasoline. I ask her how that was for her:

Um, I'll go to the emotions. Angry. Um. Disgusted, shocked. Um. Because water's what we need to live. You need water to shower, you need water to drink you need water to cook. And um, I wasn't, I had to go buy you know, to do – and you need water to clean. Um. You know we got a, our clothes, our dishes, all of that you need clean water in order to wash all that stuff, because you're going to be eating off it or wearing it. And that type of, you wash water, bad water, you wash clothes in bad water it will smell like the bad water. So. Which, but there's nothing you can do about it, for washing your clothes, you still have to wash your clothes and that's the way it goes. But I purchased bottled water, for cooking and drinking, um, for a number of years.

Listening to this account, I began to experience a sense of indignation and anger myself. I imagined her having to deal with noxious water in her washing and cleaning and asked instinctively if the water department or city had said anything publicly about the situation.

I have to admit – oh publicly? No. But I have to admit every so often, um, the Green Bay water department will send out a little brochure. I don't read it. It's like oh what is this? It's not a bill [Tosses away, laughs] and I never read it. Um. In 2000 my mom was diagnosed with breast cancer. And after she went through the chemo and the surgeries, four surgeries in a year, bilateral mastectomy, all of this – um, we, she actually read, the brochure. And in that brochure, the Green Bay water department, in 2001, had stated, if you are going through chemotherapy do not drink the water. If your immune system is bad, do not drink the water. Yeah. I never knew that, prior to that. Because I never sat and read the whole brochure. You know. I don't think anybody does [Laughs] but now I know that, it, and it was interesting to find out afterwards, if you are, if you have autoimmune disease, if you are very sick, if you are going through chemotherapy, don't drink the water, the local water. And then we had all those scares, um, all the exposés whatever on TV where they were talking about, um, people who are doing bottled water, where are they getting their water from. Is it run-off from the farm-mm, you know farm up above and all the sewage and stuff is running into the water? I mean there were a lot of scandals going on around that for a while, when was that five or ten years ago, something like that. And um, so bottled water isn't even sa- – guaranteed to be safe either. They don't have to say yeah we are at the bottom of the hill and there's a farm at the top of the hill, you know. So how do you know how your water is safe? So. Um. During that time, when did we and then when the Bovine Growth Hormone, when people, when the animals started getting injected with that, we didn't want to drink the milk or eat the meat from there anymore. So we started looking more to the organic meat and more natural meat. So we made that switch around that time. It's a growth hormone, we don't need to have additional hormones in our body. So that's when we started going to Hoaglands Ranch in Algoma and they also sell it at the farmer's market.

There is a negotiation between awareness, shock and disgust and the available modes of response or actions. It moves very quickly to being about protecting the body from the potential contaminants, through the use of filtration, bottled water and organic local meat, although even the bottled water cannot be certain for its safety. The picture is one of increased risk and a move inward, rather than outward, in terms of action. We are presented with a stunning account of her mother's breast cancer and the fact they had unwittingly not read a small pamphlet sent out by the city water department. Sally is laughing, which makes it difficult for me to accurately gauge the magnitude of the story and its affective impacts. However, the content of the story concerns her mother's vulnerability and the lack of effective protection and communication to prevent her from drinking the water. The theme of negligence runs through the interviews and the stories I have collected from Green Bay, notably on account of industry and civic responsibility (a sort of parental protection). We see a hint of guilt arise, in her admission ("I admit") of not seeing the notice and throwing it away but also an acknowledgement of its inadequacy as a form of communication.

Adjusting to conditions: Every body of water has parasites

The of the central themes in the interviews as a whole and in this series of three is the incantation of adjusting to conditions, for it does begin to sound like a mantra or an incantation: when addressing difficult chronic issues, such as the toxicity of the drinking water, or the inertia in cleaning up the Bay, the phrase about adjusting and adapting comes up. We can see this below in the example concerning the incidence of her mother's illness and a possible link to environmental toxicity, where she makes a surprising detour. Sally had mentioned during a phone call to set up the second interview, that she had recalled after our first interview a connection between her mother's illness and the water quality. I asked her to expand on this.

R: You, you, on the phone it sounded like there was a potential connection between the illness and the water. [Referring to earlier phone call.]

S: That's right. There was one point when somebody called my mom and they had mentioned that they were doing a survey and if they could ask her some questions. And, they asked her if, during the nnn mid-90s if they had noticed any little flying planes, if they had noticed if the water had tasted bad or smelled bad during that time. They asked her several different questions. And um, I don't remember all of them, I just remember, mom's surprise when, that they had even asked that. And they wondered if there was a correlation between those items and the cancer rise, because the breast cancer just skyrocketed during that time, it just rose so fast. And a lot of women died from it. And um, but, we didn't actually notice any of those things. I mean, in this area, there's a strip where planes fly over to-to-to the airport all the time. Planes from, where would that be, I don't know, Detroit, Minneapolis, whatever no Minneapolis would be the other way, I don't know. Um. You know it's a, it's a, it's an actual flight, during 911 when all the planes, and everything was grounded for a couple of weeks, it was so quiet it's like 'what's wrong' and then all of a sudden the planes started going away, and it was like okay that's right. Because the planes are going overhead all the time you don't pay attention if they are low-flying planes. You see the helicopters going by once in a while but, so that was very interesting that they had called and asked us those questions and if we had noticed anything during that time.

R: How would you say that affected you?

S: People were aware. People were aware, but you can't really prove that all these things could have caused the cancer.

Sally responds to my question how this affected her by displacement from "you" to the impersonal, "People were not aware". It moves from the personal to the impersonal, to "people" as opposed to herself or her mother, and then undermines the entire narrative in the statement that "you can't really prove" the causal links. It is not an answer to my question; rather, it is a response to an *imagined* question. It is a statement of helplessness; people were aware, e.g. I was not alone in my concerns and anxieties (a validation of her experience and perceptions) and yet it can't be proved, so it moves into the background. People were aware and unaware simultaneously; there is the capacity to make connections and yet an inability to tolerate this awareness (and perhaps feelings of anger, betrayal, guilt, potentially destructive impulses), so it is pushed away, sloughed off. I ask Sally, "I guess what I am wondering is if, that made you feel anxious?" At this point I become extremely interested in the affective register of what Sally is telling me, and my own countertransference experience anxiety at what she is telling me. What I was saying, in effect, was that it was making *me* feel anxious. And yet her tone seems without a trace of perturbation or anxiety.

> [Thinks for few moments.] No. You have to adapt to whatever you have. If the water is bad you have to adapt to it, that's just the way it is.

Here we see the resurgence once again, quite strongly of the repetition of adaptation, which is beginning to feel like a mantra throughout the interviews. Then, Sally supports the mantra of adaptation with an example of a recent holiday with her parents:

> When we went to, for example, when we went to Israel and Egypt and they said when you get to the Nile they said do not put your hand into the water. Every body of water has their own parasites, and your body is, used to the parasites in the water wherever you're at. In the Nile, the, the, parasites, you know they are different parasites, they will enter into your skin and you know it can cause havoc and you can die from it and you can get quite sick from it. So you don't want to go someplace else and just automatically put your hand in the water, because you don't know how contaminated the water is, and your body is not acclimated to those parasites and the things that are there. So I thought that was interesting. Every – every body of water has parasites. [We both laugh a bit.]

When I laugh here, I am partially laughing out of shock, as I listen stunned to this account about parasites and the Nile. Parasites are natural occurrences, and when our physiologies are not adapted or suited to accommodate these foreign bodies, we can become ill. However in the case of Green Bay, the water is not naturally toxic; the water has been contaminated, spoiled by human activities. What seems completely disconnected and distant (the Middle East) has been connected affectively with her experiences of the local water and with how she has managed to relate with it. Sally has effectively gone from speaking of the contaminated water in Green Bay and her mother's potential exposures to toxins and potential links with her cancer, to a story about the water in the Middle East, and you *have to adapt to whatever you have.* Sally's response to my question about her anxiety is a vivid illustration of the ways in which we 'defend' and psychically maneuver around distressing and potentially irreparable circumstances. In telling me about the phone call which raised questions regarding possible toxic contamination and (her perception of) the rise of breast cancer in the region, Sally seamlessly moves into discussing a body of water thousands of miles away and normalizes the threat in making this link: "Every body of water has parasites". Thus the water issues in Green Bay are status quo and to question or challenge this would be to go against the grain of nature.

After the narrative about the Nile, Sally stops and says, "Trying to think if there's anything . . . no, came to a standstill". There is nowhere for her to go from there. I pick up the thread about water and ask about her current filtration practices. Again there is the 'mantra' about her concern and threshold of worry regarding the water, "You know, so I'm not that concerned about it anymore. You have to acclimate, you have to [sighs] get, *accept whatever there is*, otherwise you'll make yourself nuts worrying about it". The ability to acclimate and adjust is a strategy for self-preservation; otherwise one can literally become crazy worrying. This capacity for regulation of knowledge and awareness, combined with the internal mantra regarding acclimation and adaptation, begins to emerge as a rather effective psychic strategy (as well as social, as this is undoubtedly a social process, not limited to individual or intra-psychic processes). We also see Sally exhibit in certain contexts a hyper-vigilance, suggesting a method of choice regarding where the affective investment is channeled. For example, we discuss the quality of drinking water, and she notes that when she is out at a restaurant, she will not drink the tap water because of the ice cubes: "It depends on the taste of the ice cubes, if the ice cubes are old, or if the ice cubes are . . . you take one sip by one sip I know whether I'll drink it or not, and if it's bad I won't. There are some restaurants here in Green Bay where I won't drink their tap water". We also see that Sally will eat only organic meat and hormone-free milk products.

Sally tells me in the first interview, when discussing her cats, that one of her cats had died of kidney failure during the period when the water was dodgy. In the second interview, when discussing her cat's dying of kidney failure in the context of the water quality, she seems to have internalized a sense of blame and guilt. I ask her if she felt the death was connected to the water, and she responds, "Yeah I think so, but can I prove it? No. But I don't know why I didn't you know, sometimes, you're careful and sometimes you're not. And unfortunately I was not thinking clearly . . . yeah I think that may have contributed to her kidney failure". There seems to be an inability to assign anger and aggression towards the source of the problems which were in actuality the fact the tap water was risky and led to the death of one of her cats. The tendency to internalize the guilt I see as a repetition throughout the interview, as she is able to describe alarming instances of transgression and trauma (e.g. the move to Green Bay, in the middle of her junior year, right after she had achieved a high level in orchestra, uprooting her from her community and home) without expressing anger or resentment towards those responsible. It is a remarkable illustration of internalized guilt and resignation.

Negotiating environmental awareness

In the third interview, as with many other participants, Sally is speaking more openly about her environmental concerns and revealing her high level of environmental literacy. There are two instances in which it becomes clear how much Sally has thought about these issues, moments that surprise me. The first concerns her invoking a fantasy author Jean Auel, whose novels are based on traditional indigenous cultures in prehistory. The second is her referencing the book *Our Stolen Future* (Colborn, Dumanoski & Meyers, 1997). What is important in both cases is the coexistence of high levels of affect (energetic investment, involvement) with the incantation regarding powerlessness. This is particularly important if we are interested in exploring whether someone who does nothing to express her or his ecological sentiments is suffering from 'apathy'. In the following excerpt, Sally expresses the irrationality and mystery regarding human destructiveness towards nature and other humans, and she employs Auel's literary worlds to help provide some sort of explanatory schema for this.

> We as humans can do a lot of damage, to the earth, to other animals, to other people. Common sense seems to have died. Um. In the old times, there were the people, you lived off the land, you ate, you killed the animal to eat for that meal or to prepare for the winter. Jean Auel's books are a good example of that. Then there's people who want to trade and you need to have the furs to be able to, cover yourself and some people are not able to, do the hunting, and so there was trading and things like that. So these people would kill extra and so that they would have enough to trade for the supplies that they needed. But then there came those who wanted the ivory for the elephants and just slaughtered the elephants just for the ivory, that's senseless. There was not that big of a need for ivory, didn't need to be that huge, should've remained, when an animal died they were able to get that. Man becomes greedy. In so many different areas. Will that ever ss- stop? No. it just has gotten worse over the years. And um, what can be done about it?

Sally expresses the mantra when discussing the chronic quality of contemporary ecological issues: *What can be done?* I notice a sort of circularity to her narratives (and occasionally incoherence), so that in listening to her I begin to feel almost literally entrapped, or stuck. I suspect this is a countertransferential impression of the sense of 'stuckness' or the lack of agency she may feel in relation to issues beyond the scope of her particular world. She gets "off-track" as she follows these circular expressions of powerlessness, both the acknowledgement of issues and her own sense of impotence.

> Nothing. Very little. Very little. Um. Like for example, when an animal is going to go, they've counted them and they've showed an animal is going

extinct, and you can't hunt that animal anymore, that's as it should be. Find another animal to hunt for meat, or whatever. You know what we have so many [sighs] so many farms and all that who raise the farm fish, raise the chickens, raise the cattle, raise the pork and they keep them in a little stall, just so that they can flood the market with all of this meat. Is that fair to the animals, inhumane treatment for the animal? No. Is there anything that can be done about it? No. Because it's our food supply. [Laughs] Um. I think I got off-track with what you asked me. I guess, it's a complicated thing. You look at things with one hand and you realize you can't do anything, you hear other information about things going in cycles, and all you can do is hope and believe that the cycles is really, is what they found, the research they did is accurate and it really does go in cycles and therefore it gives a person hope.

This passage is a portrait of human greed that is apparently beyond redress: finding ourselves in painful circumstances, but nothing can be done. It is implacable. The last line expresses the desire to believe in "cycles" – both a reference to natural climatic cycles versus human-induced global warming and "cycles" as process of change – as something she wants to believe in, even while acknowledging her need to "hope and believe". There is an underlying quality to the excerpt that reveals a very dark and quite brutal view of life and humanity. If life is basically brutal and dark, then it seems the only options are to withdraw affectively into the domains that have influence (e.g. her music), and "hope and believe" in the existence of cyclical change – change that happens out there, that one is passive to, and not a producer of.

Adaptation as survival: The parents' story

In reflecting back to Sally my observations in the final interview, I connect the preceding notion with the theme of 'adaptation' and ask Sally if there is any connection with her parents' history and perhaps if they helped to instill the need to be adaptable and to accept limitations on what one can do. She then takes a deep breath and begins to relay an extraordinarily detailed account of her parents' life in Berlin; of particular note is the great sense of survival in dangerous and deprived circumstances. I include the excerpt in full due to the level of detail she provides.

Let me go back to my parents' beginnings. My dad was born in '33. And um, my mom was born in 1940 after the war had already begun and she lived in Berlin. During that time with the war, think about it, you're moving along you hear the sirens you have to go into the bomb shelter. You immediately go into safety. You stop everything, immediately survival is the utmost importance. How the war impacted things; the food, the rations, um, what they had or didn't have growing up, and how they survived that, was, um. Interesting because it's really comes down to survival. How you do what you do. Um. Um. After the war dad's, uh step-father had suggested that, okay, we need certain things to um, rebuild some of this stuff, go dig in the rubble and get those things out of there so we can secure our stuff. Um. You know whether it was, um, some kind of shelter you, way back when they didn't have refrigerators or any of that, so they had cellars in the basement where they would keep, that was cooler, where they would keep whatever perishable items they could for food. And, anything else. There's also storage area. So they had to go and repair that. My mom on the other hand, in Berlin, when the bombings and everything came, [inaudible] there wasn't a lot of money. There were times when they didn't have enough food to survive. And they were thankful when a neighbour left them half dried up, half a loaf dried up bread, they were just thankful that they had something to eat. Um. You took, had a small piece of meat, and, ww- what are you going to do, how do you divide that up for a family, a woman and four children? Um. You make a big pot of soup. Take the meat, separate it strand by strand so everybody has a fair share of it. And try to get whatever vegetables and potatoes I think were a good substance of food that you could add to it, so you'd make soup so everybody could have some of the meat. Because if you only had one bite full of meat that wouldn't be enough to satisfy everybody's hunger. So you adapt. The iron breaks, what happens, you can't afford a new iron. Because you can barely afford to put food on the table. My grandma had to learn how to fix the iron. She took it apart and fixed it. Were things a lot simpler then? Yeah. Were they more durable back then? Yeah. We have a disposable society now. They don't make irons that last for 20 or 30 years [laughs] or anything else. So during that time, you had one dress, one pair of underwear. You washed your underwear every night so it was dry in the morning and you could re-wear it. We, we get a hole in our underwear and we throw it away, you know a hole in the sock it's gone and you buy new ones. So adaptability and survival, for my family, my parents, came down to the very basics. Um. And they brought that, you know, that formed and shaped them how they lived their life. Um. Our family's a big thing, you gotta clean off your plate, you can't leave food on your plate when you're done. You take smaller portions but whatever you put on your plate you have to finish because there are starving people in the world [laughs] and at one point, that was them.

There is a great deal of *energy* in Sally relaying this story; she has clearly heard this many times growing up. The account introduces a context for the theme of adaptation and the seeming frivolity of something such as saving the whales. For her parents, adaptability was the basis of survival and has reverberations in Sally's life as well; having moved to Green Bay and finding it abject and disorienting, she had no choice but to 'adapt' – her parents had survived wartime Germany, and she was going to complain about moving to a new city, with a nice school, parks, a home to live? She has remained, in many ways, the dutiful daughter whose more 'wild' explorations have been reigned in; after all, there is nothing one can do, anyway.

Saving the whales

Immediately following the discussion of her foray into the natural foods scene, she mentions her brief yet intense involvement with the Save the Whales campaign. She introduces the topic lightly and with some self-mockery:

S: I was into 'Save the Whales' for a while but then I thought [laughing] you know there's not a whole heck of a lot I can do and just giving my money isn't going to make a difference in the long run . . . It was in the 20s, when I was in my 20s and 30s, I was into, I still have some Save the Whales cards you can mail off to people, I'd buy those, I had 'Save the Whales' t-shirt –

R: Was the whale issue the main one that was concerning you?

S: Yeah, for some reason! I don't know why! [Laughing a lot with clear amusement]

In the laughter and comment about her money, Sally is distancing from the issues and the emotions they may relate to; in a sense, we can see in terms of how she perceives her capacities for real effect (for reparation).

Those things are important, but in the whole scheme of life, donating money to the cause, is it really going to the cause or is it going to the overhead? [Laughs] you know is it going um, somebody's wages or is it really going to help? You know. The rainforest or the whales. And [laughs] how will my money help the whales? [Laughs a lot] I mean when you look at it from a different perspective.

I press on, wanting to acknowledge what I perceive as a form of concern; in other words, I am resisting the collusion with the part of her self that is denigrating this activity.

R: It makes me wonder what happens to the concern though. The concern is still there. And you realize that, well I'm not sure that this is the best way of taking action by giving my money –

S: Correct. Because now, I'm looking at, I have to admit, I'm looking at how much, I didn't go full-time in my job until 11 years ago. I didn't put anything in my retirement until then. Is giving money to, to save the whales, or putting my money in an IRA more important, or 401K. And I have to say, retirement is a higher focus of, you know, to me, then saving the whales right now. You know. I have a lot, I have a lot of catching up to do on that [laughs]. When I see how much it costs to live, and I'm thinking, how long am I going to be living and how much do I need, and I like to travel, you know. So. Financial resources are not to save the whales anymore but . . .

This is a common litany with regard to why people do not support environmental advocacy: the perceived dichotomy between self-interest (retirement, 401K) and altruistic concern. Concern (Winnicott's concept of reparation) develops when the infant feels herself to be able to *contribute* (Winnicott, 1963, p. 77). The perception of "nothing I can do" exists in dialectic with the energies mobilized for practice; however, it does not necessarily correspond with the level of concern or care that may be present.

R: I'm wondering, there is the financial aspect of it, but there's the initial concern of wanting to help something. You know what I mean?
S: Yeah that's always there.
R: Where does it go, is it in your mind or do you just kind of, other things take over? Or,
S: You never want to see an animal go extinct. [Measured voice] You never want to see, um, Save the Whales, you have to save the whales, part of it is saving the water and making sure the water is healthy so the whales and all the creatures in the water will be well. I'm concerned about the fish and the virus that is going through the Great Lakes right now. And you can't eat the fish out of there anymore. I'm concerned about it, I'm aware of it, there's nothing I specifically can do for it. The states around the Great Lakes, somebody has to pass legislation, well the virus they can't do anything to stop, but like the pollution things like that, that, something has to be done on there, but all these things going through, to get approved or disapproved through congress, you never know what will be approved or what won't be. It's dependent on what they attach it to. Um like, the bill that they wanted to do for military, for our troops. Um, they were attaching so many other little things on to that, that's the reason the money didn't get approved because of all these other things they were trying to sneak along in, you know, it's like, were they trying to save the whales at the same time, I'm just using that as an example, as, at the same time as they were trying, needing to fund the troops? That shouldn't be in the same bill. So it all comes down to congress and how they're going to pass legislation to protect these things. And there's not really a lot I can do. You can do political action committees and things like that, I do political action committee for where I work, and um, that, they will try to push through things that will benefit my job. Um. But, is that answering your question?
R: Sort of.
S: The concern is there, but it's also dependent on who and how they try to pass the bill and how they try to get the legislation passed.
R: It sounds like there is a recognition of limits of what you can do.

The narrative becomes incoherent in the free associations with the whales, the Great Lakes, the fish virus, the military and troops and how it comes down to congress and legislation. It feels muddled, and the sense is that these issues *are* muddled internally. I get the sense of her experience as a 'little person', someone who has very little impact on the world and its forces, so best to withdraw one's vital energies and focus on what one *can* effect. The phrase "There's not a lot I can do" is what stands out amongst the muddle. There is a great sense of disappointment and anger that degradation has been allowed to go "so far", as seen in this narrative about the fish virus in the Great Lakes. What this emerges to be about is the issue of containment, the lack of protection, of immunity, of quarantine. "They" should have stopped it.

> When I heard about the virus and that it was in Lake Erie, it's like I hope it doesn't come into Lake Michigan. And when they say, when they said that they found it and that it had already been here, that it's already here, I was disappointed and angry that it was allowed to be, allowed to go that far. That somebody wasn't able to do something about it. Is there anything I can do about it? No. um. Giving money is the only solution a lot of people will say. It's like I don't have the training, I don't have the authority in any way shape or form, to try to have stopped that. That should have been stopped before it even entered into the Great Lakes or as soon as they found it, it should have been isolated.

As mentioned, the topic of water 'flows' in the interviews: we started with a discussion about her involvement with the Save the Whales campaign, which moved into a discussion of the virus in the Great Lakes. The associations can be traced: water, creatures, protection, invasion, risk, vulnerability and acute lack of control. There is a sense of betrayal and disappointment in those who should have been 'minding the store'. In this incantation, I hear echoes of potential disappointments that go back to the move; did Sally's parents let her down in moving her at a crucial time in her development, as an adolescent establishing her sense of bearings in the world?

Sally free-associates to a recent story of man who had contracted tuberculosis but had ignored the doctor's advice to not leave the country, thereby putting thousands of people at risk. In this excerpt is the repeated theme of permeability, of lack of containment and protection, running throughout the interviews:

> Yes that's the word. Quarantine. There is no more quarantine. People are not, people high up are not willing to quarantine and take a tough stand and say, okay, um you know, this area is quarantined, period. I mean it has to be really bad before they do that. Like that guy with the T.B. who left the country, they didn't quarantine him. They should have. Until they knew exactly what they did. But they don't do that any more. Is there any way that they could, um, with the deer, the wasting disease, that should

have been quarantined and eliminated immediately. You know, tested it and taken care of – but nobody followed through on it. There wasn't enough funding, there wasn't enough money, whatever. You know. So. What was your question, am I off-track. . . .

Well you can see I have strong opinions on it, and I do pay attention, I do w-watch for all of this stuff. And I'm frustrated that they don't do the quarantine, they don't do the, take stronger measures. Unfortunately, I don't have, I'm thinking of the Mad Cow Disease and all of that, can you imagine if you are a farmer and one cow gets infected. It's possible the other cows are carrying it. A carrier but not necessarily infected. But they could infect others [laughs] I'm watching my cat stare at you, that's why I'm chuckling. Technically that should have been all quarantined and killed but then you'd wipe out that man's living. So they don't do that anymore. So how do you justify all of that? How do you regulate, how do you take care of the problem without putting some people's business, or their livelihood, how do you So then you just have to step back and say there's nothing I can do, [breathes out, sighing] let it go. Does that answer your question?

It is an iteration of the previous dynamic of a harsh and senseless world, in which people will do what they wish, and of the impotence in the face of such conditions. It is an extremely painful position to occupy and yet Sally appears to be negotiating this through her brittle and quite resilient capacity to almost 'slough' off the painful affects of sadness or heartache.

Possibilities for creativity and participation: The 'little realms'

After a brief foray in the natural foods scene in Green Bay, revolving centrally around the co-op, Sally found she did not identify with the "lifestyle" it seemed to promote.

There are those who are environmentalists and how they live and what they choose and how they do things, there are those um who are totally into the natural foods and everything organic and all of that. And you live within that realm. . . . Getting to know the organic group and people, was very interesting, they also have a slightly different lifestyle. They are in their own little realm.

Thus the route to identify with a particular group does not work for Sally, as with Donald and Howard, who perceive environmentalists to be fanatic and totalizing in their adherence to a particular view and way of life. It is a closure to something, these "little realms", not openings into new possibilities for reparation and creativity. So where does Sally find expression for reparation, and how does she express her creativity? I see this taking place in a number of ways.

First and perhaps most obvious is her enthusiasm towards participating in the interviews and her subsequent phone calls to set up the meetings and to ensure I did not forget or overlook her. Each time she rang me (three times), she iterated her desire to participate and also took the opportunity to include reflections since our prior interviews; e.g. after the first interview, she tells me by phone she remembered something about her mother's illness and the survey about low-flying planes. She also tells me with some enthusiasm, as Howard does, in our second interview how she spoke with her brother to share memories and as a means of corroborating her own recollections. Sally was excited about participating in the interviews; by the end of the three meetings, she tells me how much she benefited from the experience and how she is now considering donating to the Healing Our Waters project (which was not my intention, as I had explained).

Second, when we view how Sally chooses to engage in the issues and her contact with the water and local ecology and specifically her love of Lake Michigan, we see how certain objects are employed affectively: the poster above her bed, of the waves, connects her with the wildness and open horizon of the Lake Michigan of her childhood; the Save the Whales T-shirts and cards she has kept all these years; and the frozen organic meat she shows me in her freezer and her retrieval of the card for the ranch. Primarily what I view as her creative response is in the form of how she has filled up her life and her time with busyness and activity; as she describes in the narrative about the Save the Whales in the final interview, she has chosen to turn to music as a way of channeling her creativity, energies and desires. It affectively (and effectively) fills up, takes the space of, other competing concerns which, by her own admission, "would drive you nuts" if you were to focus too much on them. What we can see then is a carefully calibrated capacity for 'contact' and engagement. It would be incorrect to see Sally as not engaged or connected with these issues, but rather on closer analysis, a finer grain emerges. The texture of this engagement is complex, full of ambivalence and contradiction, and it reveals the way she has been able to stay with and yet hold at a distance the issues which she finds troubling: the quality of the water, the issue of health and safety, responsibility and accountability, and the trustworthiness of those deemed 'responsible', e.g. the city and regulatory bodies.

Fantasies of immunity: The golden ring

Two vignettes convey a powerful longing for protection, immunity and omnipotence (power). The first concerns a long narrative in the second interview, following the discussion of the contaminated water and her cat's death. She tells me of her brief foray into the natural foods lifestyle and how she once spent much money and time at the local co-op (which has since been closed). She then makes one of her surprising free associations to a talk she had been to the night before at a church group; she says she thought they were going to be talking about baking with coconut flour but instead the speaker was addressing the topic of the immune system. She begins to describe the speaker and the topic with great excitement, almost breathlessly. The story concerns how the speaker and his wife are opposed to the use of vaccinations and how they will expose their child to someone who has the chicken pox or mumps: "let them go through the whole process and build up immunity, because if we get the virus and our body fights it off, one at a time, we have permanent immunity from that disease. Life-long immunity. That's the right word. Immunity". It strikes me that this conveys her wishes and desires for "life-long immunity" and protection. It seems her reparative efforts towards her own health and quality of water and meat are ways of expressing this desire, in however limited a capacity possible.

The second vignette takes place during the third interview, and Sally is telling me about a nature program she has seen about weather patterns and the cyclical nature of freezes. On account of the program, she says,

> Therefore I don't worry as much. Because based on that, the freezing will come back. If it doesn't we are going to be in trouble.

Immediately after this statement, there is a rather extraordinary association to a science fiction story and a magic ring:

S: There was a science fiction fantasy type book that I read many years ago. And um, this one man was, had a lot of problems with his health and his body and he finds this gold ring. And this gold ring takes him to another world. And the world had just, um, it was getting hotter and hotter. Like with the global warming, and everything, this guy was way ahead of every-thing that's been going on. With this gold ring he was able to wield power and make things better and right. But the world on its own just kept getting hotter and hotter, the water supply by book three or four, had dried up and all this stuff, but he was able to rectify some of that. And, I lost my train of thought, somehow with the global warming and all of that it reminded me of that book, and that could happen to us, if what they say about global warming is true.

R: What was it about the story that was compelling for you? That he had like –

S: He had the ability to change the negative effects and rectify some of the things that had gone wrong. And then he'd be there for a while, he'd fix the planet and then he'd be back, in his modern time, and the ring also made him healthier while he was there. And then when he came back it had no effect on him, because he was in our time [laughs a bit] whatever. And that author, just two weeks ago I read someplace he's come up with another book. So, it was, but it it showed me that it kind of, seeing that science fiction thing, fantasy thing, showed me, it uh, when you read a book you picture things along in your mind. Um. If the global warming really does happen, something like that could happen to our earth. Where the water would all dry up or it's so polluted it's not usable. And where do we get fresh supply of water. So. It was interesting. [Laughs]

Both of the stories – the ability to have lifelong immunity through the exposure to dangerous viruses, and the magic gold ring that endowed the character with health and the capacity to "make things better and right" – convey powerful reparative fantasies and wishes. In her account of the character with various health problems (recall Sally is recovering from surgery during our interviews) and his magical healing, as well as the planet's healing, we see deep desires to be able to heal, restore and be well. She is unable to make a coherent connection between the story and global warming, except to say that the story allows her to "picture things in your mind" and the image of what the earth could look like if it got hotter (and there was no savior with a magic ring in sight). She is both comforted by the idea of cyclical weather patterns and is acknowledging the real threats the planet faces if these patterns are not stabilized.

In many ways, these accounts take us to the heart of what is affectively taking place with regard to Sally's own sensitivities, awareness of issues and recognition of her own lack of agency and efficacy. As we see in the narratives about her involvement with the Save the Whales campaigns, she wishes to make reparation but is able to do so only with a remote region (the world's oceans) and with far away, almost mythical creatures (the whales). It concerns water but is (safely) far from the troubled waters of the Great Lakes and Green Bay. And yet, as she tells me, laughing, what could her money possibly do to protect the whales? The idea of *her having impact on this issue* strikes her as ludicrous, so she laughs. Her family thought it was "hilarious" that she was so passionately involved with the issue, and yet decades later she still has the T-shirts and cards, transformational objects which connect her with this time, the concern and the belief she had that she could become involved in something larger than herself to make reparations.

Managing affect, negotiating awareness

At the end of our third interview, as with all participants, I presented Sally with the image of the "Girl on the Beach" advert (Figure 1.3). I asked her to take her time and look at the image and to share with me whatever comes to mind, her feelings and thoughts. She began with presenting a sort of caveat regarding her tendency to 'modulate' her information intake, as much of it is distressing and negative. She then reflects, in a stream–of–consciousness manner, why she responded to the survey and the fact that often she is so exhausted from her work and activities she collapses into bed most nights. I find this part of the interview quite moving, as she is feeling her way through what may have motivated her to participate and reflects on her own desires and needs that may have come through (in this being a time of reflection and re-evaluation, due to being off work to recover from the injury).

S: Again. We're polluting our water. Ahh – and it, I, I really like the ad, I like the way they laid it out, I like the way they presented it, it is so true it covers all the things, and they even give you access to where you can go and um, and you know, I'm going to check out that website and I hope it's still there and valid. Before we had this interview, how would I have, how would, how I would have reacted. I'd have probably just read it, and agreed with it and thought, yeah. Actually by having our interviews it's made me, kind of, re-brought to the surface a bit more. I have to admit I don't know why I chose to do that survey. Um. They send a lot of surveys out, sometimes I don't have time, I don't always check my email every day. And there are some days I work, come home, shower and change and out the door and I left at 6:30 and I get home at 10 o'clock and I'm exhausted and I go back to sleep. So I don't get, some days I don't get to do a lot. But. I was surprised that I actually did that environmental survey and as I was filling it out I thought, wow I haven't thought about these things in a really long time, what do I think about this? (Yeah.) So I had to put a lot into it. I like the ad. I like the way they presented it. Prior today, prior today would I have done anything about it? Probably not. I would have looked at it and said yeah I agree with that. And would have continued on with my day-to-day busy life.

R: Right. Right. But you're not busy at the moment. I wonder if that has something to do with it as well.

S: That could be. [We both laugh.] And, I look at this time as an opportunity to re-evaluate, re- you know, reassess, because you get into a routine and you just keep doing the same old, same old so this is an opportunity to, how am I going to do things differently after I can get back into everything. And I haven't quite figured that all out yet. But. So this came at a really appropriate time.

R: Hmm. Well you did, I called you and then, you called me back, and you were concerned that I might have dropped the ball or something or you had scared me off because you had mentioned your parents may be doing it –

S: Yeah [laughing]

R: I did wonder, I thought it was important that you were enthusiastic about it. It made me wonder what it was about this, that was drawing you, in some way. Especially considering the fact that in the survey you did not rate high in terms of your environmental concern –

S: No. [We both laugh; she laughs a lot here.]

R: Something obviously must have, um,

S: I don't even know. It's just one of those, really bizarre things that just, I can't explain it. I guess because it was there a long time ago. And other things just kind of, I don't know. Was that website dot org?

It seems Sally is describing how her daily practices and lifestyle serve as effective 'defenses' against experiencing certain affects and anxieties. She is so exhausted she literally doesn't have time or energy to contemplate these issues.

And yet she has taken the time and energy to participate in the survey and the interviews, and it is clear there is often considerable reflection on our discussions between the meetings. She seems genuinely interested, curious and energetic, despite her being quite 'defended' with regard to the painful content of some of the material shared. There is evidence that the experience of participating in the interviews – and indeed, beginning with the survey – was productive for Sally and enabled her to process and think through material that had been latent for quite some time. She states this at the end of the third interview.

> I have really enjoyed doing this. It has made me think about things I haven't thought about in a long time, personal and environmental and you know. The whole thing. And, um, I've really enjoyed . . . In a way you've challenged me. [Hmm hmm.] Just by asking neutral questions and making me think about what are my responses, what do I think now, what did I think then? How do I, you know, and like you were just asking, how does it all fit in now, from this to now. And um, will it overwhelm and overtake my life? The environmental issues and causes? No. Music is my passion and that's where my heart, emotions and energy goes into. But. There are other things that you can add into your life. And I'd like to add a litt- that a little bit more into it again. So I've really enjoyed this. And I hope I've helped you. I know you've kind of made me think, and um, whenever I walk away after you leave, I still think and dwell over everything that we've discussed and everything, the questions you've asked me, and sometimes I think, was that the answer I wanted to give? Yeah. [Laughs] So. Thank you.

Reflections

Sally's first articulation about moving to Green Bay is the "shock of the water" at how polluted it was. I was interested in what about her life story can help me understand the nature of her relationship with ecological issues, namely those concerning water. Looking at the narratives concerning childhood and life in Sheboygan, it is evident that the time playing in the "pure sand" of the dunes with her family (without the father) is very much associated with a time of innocence, safety and feeling the world is safe. It's about containment. Her lamentation about the loss of the sand, due to the overgrowth of reeds and grasses, suggests to me a loss of the sands and the purity of the dunes and the wild, clean waters of the Lake Michigan. I perceive that in fact life in Sheboygan at the time of the move was at a high point for Sally, at least this is how she *represents* this – socially, musically and in terms of establishing autonomy. The Lake had receded in her life after their move across town. As she says, "the world revolves around you" as a teenager; we see how the busyness of life becomes potentially an effective strategy for negotiating the transition between childhood and adult life.

The interview opens with the "shock" of the water, and "shock" appears primarily in relation to her affective response to pollution. However, the affect feels bound up with the "shock" of the move, the disorientation and the sense of abjection that may be bound up in life living in a motel, all crowded together, the loss of clean water and air, and metaphorically, the loss of childhood and sense of safety and protection. This we can see that it is impossible to separate out internal and external object relations, as they are imbued with psychic meanings and associations, and, precisely as Winnicott (1975) and Bollas (1992) have suggested, there is an excess that cannot be expressed and for which we draw on and use our material work, e.g. the environment functions as an 'objective correlative', a concept coined by T. S. Eliot that has particular salience here.

There are currents of care and concern and expressions of reparation – even if they may not be channeled or directed in forms that are easily recognizable (in terms of environmental advocacy). Reparation (and concern) are expressed in her desire to do the interviews and her eagerness and enthusiasm; her vigilance about drinking water and organic meats, which ties directly to her mother's illness and links with environment and contamination; and the need to protect the boundaries of one's body as the only site of actual control. Sally goes out to look at the water but angles her body so she cannot see the industrial buildings. This is a metaphor for how she has gone about coping with the move and the loss of something vital in her life.

The move also signals a potential loss of agency, the experience of oneself as an agent that can influence change, in that it suggests that in fact she is not omnipotent, her parents have control and power, and perhaps this occasions a form of resignation or a way of negotiating the events that leads to the central theme, or 'mantra' of the interview, which concerns *adaptation, adjustment* and *survival*. These are underlying themes that can be seen in dynamic relation with the biographical narratives shared concerning her parents' survival in wartime Berlin. If we want to explore the themes of adaptation and adjustment more closely, we can look to her parent's survival and their highly detailed accounts of surviving in poverty and deprivation in Berlin 1940s, as well as their subsequent exodus to the New World, and we may begin to appreciate how getting involved in Save the Whales seems frivolous. At the same time, we can see this involvement with Save the Whales as a way of connecting with water and large vulnerable creatures in a way that may have captured Sally's imagination and affective relationships but was safe in that it was very far from Green Bay's polluted waters and quite mythical, almost like a fairy tale.

Viewed through these underlying, unconscious dynamics, we can view Sally's discourses about water, global warming and other issues in the interviews in a new and enriched light. She says we all need water to live and expresses disgust at the way the drinking water and Lakes have been degraded. She recounts a time when their water smelled like petrol and her cat died of kidney failure (and her mother ended up with cancer). Then she presents a very curious story about the water in the Nile and how "all bodies of water have parasites", a resurfacing of the theme of adjusting to life's circumstances. She gets close to anger on several occasions but then retreats into a story and discursive style (laughter, quick speech) that smoothes the edges. This also appears in her account of watching a documentary about weather on television and how climates have been changing for millions of years – a comforting thought in the face of growing evidence of human-made climate change.

In summary, the material illustrates the complexity of these issues and problematizes simplistic notions of what environmental concern or care is or how it manifests. My interpretation is that the event of the move to Green Bay was so traumatic and registered a loss on such a scale that it led Sally to withdraw into a smaller world and to accept a level of resignation and 'adaptation' as a way of life. She is not able to openly critique or express anger towards her parents or even the City of Green Bay, just laughs it off, and *creates* a full and active life, in arenas where she has impact (music). Further, biographical contexts, such as her parents' experiences as immigrants from Germany, may inform a particular worldview that is conductive to certain forms of agency and what positions of action are possible. In both the case studies and across the data material, I detect underlying formative, unconscious and yet social themes concerning the importance of survival, adaptation and 'getting on with things', a mode of existence commensurate with a particular formation of immigrant experience and subjectivity that is both historically situated and psychically animated and expressed. Understanding what positions for response – indeed, the expression of protest, of anger, of indignation – must be viewed in light of the social, cultural and political contexts for the participants and their relations, as well as the individual processes of negotiation and affective investments.

Sally's case study surfaces the following themes. The loss of childhood spaces, and specifically spaces in nature, constitutes a key theme in these interviews and across the participants, manifesting in different ways of negotiating their relationships with these lost places. In light of understanding environmental responses to degradation, it is important to contextualize these relations and appreciate their psychic and material dimensions. How loss is processed and negotiated then leads to issues of mourning, melancholia and how pain and loss are managed; in this sense, if loss does not find a 'home' to process, e.g. social forms of acknowledgement or support, it may go underground or become expressed in more defensive ways, such as filling up space to avoid any sense of loss or impotence. Second and related themes of survival and 'getting on with life' in response to difficulties inform and complicate notions of 'agency' and 'action' in terms of asserting that, where there is no 'action', there may be apathy. In this case study, there is evident concern, anxiety and affective investment in degraded ecologies. At issue is not a lack of concern or care but rather how responses to losses and risk are socially and psychically managed. In this sense, the background of the parents' survival in wartime Germany may provide some clues for understanding political acts of protest or resistance. Third, certain environmental objects appear to function as "objective correlatives" (Eliot, 1921) in the sense that the qualities of innocence, childhood or abject may be introjected into the environment; one can never return to the innocence and purity of childhood (cannot protect, restore or repair the Lakes). This may have bearing on how environmental action or response to degradation or threat is conceptualized and responded to, on a symbolic, psychic level.

References

Bollas, C., 1992. *Being a Character: Psychoanalysis and Self Experience.* London: Routledge [reprint 1997].

Colborn, T., Dumanoski, D., & Meyers, J., 1997. *Our Stolen Future.* New York: Plume.

Eliot, T. S., 1921. *The Sacred Wood: Essays on Poetry and Other Criticism.* New York: Alfred A. Knopf.

Winnicott, D. W. (1935) [1958]. The manic defence. In Winnicott, D. W., *Collected Papers: Through Pediatrics to Psychoanalysis.* New York: Basic Books.

Winnicott, D. W., 1963. The development of the capacity for concern. In *The Maturational Process and the Facilitating Environment.* London: Karnac.

Winnicott, D. W., 1975. *Through Paediatrics to Psychoanalysis.* New York: Basic Books.

Screening questions

Demographic Parameters
> 18 years of age
Exclude environmental professions if possible (sciences OK, but not specific to environment)

Basic Demographic Information to Collect:
Occupation
Age
Education level
Length of time living in Green Bay or in a Great Lakes region
What part of Green Bay do you live in (choice of regions)
Would you be willing to be interviewed over 3-4 sessions, in your own home or at Matousek and Associates?

Level of Environmental Awareness/Consciousness Screen:

1. I think about environmental problems (including local issues, or those in other parts of the world)...

☐ never
☐ rarely
☐ occasionally
☐ seasonally
☐ depends on events
☐ frequently
☐ not sure

IF ANSWER NEVER/NOT SURE, TERMINATE.

1a. What specific 'issues' come most to mind for you?
(e.g. climate change, water quality in Lakes, threat to species far away, local biodiversity, etc)

_____

(FILL IN BLANK)

2. Are these topics ever discussed in your family?
☐ Yes
☐ No
☐ Rarely
☐ Not sure

3. Are these topics ever discussed among your friends, or colleagues (e.g. work, church, etc)?
☐ Yes
☐ No
☐ Rarely
☐ Not sure

4. If you answered yes to questions 2 or 3, can you please give a brief example of such a discussion or exchange?

_____(FILL IN THE BLANK)

Media Screen:
How do you get your news and information? [GENERAL IS OK]
[Check all that apply]

☐ Books
☐ Magazine articles (what magazines)
☐ Scientific articles
☐ Newspapers (which ones)
☐ Radio (what stations)
☐ Television (what stations/news programs)
☐ Videos
☐ Courses/Training/Workshops
☐ Own observation and experience
☐ Friends
☐ Memberships in interest groups (which ones?)
☐ Movies
☐ Internet
☐ Discussions with friends and other people
☐ Rallies or political demonstrations
☐ Spending time by or near the water
☐ Council hearings
☐ Other (please specify)

Short Answer Questions:

1. Can you recall the most recent occurrence of hearing about an environmental issue? What was the issue? Where was it? What were you doing?

2. If your feelings or behavior towards the environment have changed over time, what has influenced these changes? Please rate the extent to which the following sources of information or events may have changed your feelings about the environment:

☐ Books, magazines, articles, newspapers (please provide details)
☐ Radio and television (please provide details)

☐ Courses
☐ Conversations with friends or family (please specify)
☐ Local events, incidents (please specify)
☐ First-hand experience (please specify)

3. Off the top of your head, what issues do you think are most pressing for residents in Green Bay? This does not have to include the environment.

Survey responses: 9 participants

(See following pages for individual survey responses.)

Victoria

Occupation	Housewife
Involved in a science-related field	No
What area of science do you specialize in?	—
Age	45–54
Education	Associates degree
Length of time Green Bay area	11 or more years
Part of Green Bay	DePere
Willing to participate	Yes
Frequency of thinking of environmental issues	Rarely
Discussed with family	Rarely
Discussed with friends/colleagues	Rarely
Can you please give a brief example of such a discussion or exchange.	—

How do you get your news and information?

✗ Books	✗ Courses/ Training/ Workshops	✗ Memberships in interest groups	✗ Rallies or political demonstrations
✗ Magazine articles			
✗ Scientific articles		✗ Movies	
✓ Newspapers	✗ Own observation and experience	✗ Internet	✗ Spending time by or near the water
✗ Radio		✗ Discussions with friends and other people	
✓ Television	✗ Friends		✗ Council hearings
✗ Videos			✗ Other

Magazines read	—
Newspapers read	greenbay press gazzet
Radio stations	—
Television stations	5
Interest groups	—

Thinking about the most recent occurence of an environmental issue, please answer the following questions:

What was the issue?	Global warming
Where was it?	everywhere
What were you doing?	nothing
Have your feelings or behavior towards the environment changed over time?	No
What has influenced these changes?	—

Rate Impact:

Books, magazines, articles, newspapers	4
Radio and television	5
Courses	2
Conversations with friends and family	3
Local events, incidents	4
First-hand experience	7

Off the top of your head, what issues do you think are most pressing for residents in the Green Bay area?	cleaning up the fox river
If you were asked about environmental issues, which specific environmental issues come to mind?	water pollution, air pollution, landfills

Sally

Occupation	Tradesman/Laborer
Involved in a science-related field	—
What area of science do you specialize in?	—
Age	45–54
Education	Some college
Length of time Green Bay area	11 or more years
Part of Green Bay	City of Green Bay
Willing to participate	Yes
Frequency of thinking of environmental issues	DependsOnEvents
Discussed with family	Yes
Discussed with friends/colleagues	Yes
Can you please give a brief example of such a discussion or exchange.	if it comes up at work. I share what I think

How do you get your news and information?

✘ Books	✘ Courses/	✘ Memberships in	✘ Rallies or
✔ Magazine articles	Training/	interest groups	political
✔ Scientific articles	Workshops	✘ Movies	demonstrations
✔ Newspapers	✔ Own observation	✘ Internet	✔ Spending time by
✔ Radio	and experience	✔ Discussions with	or near the water
✔ Television	✘ Friends	friends and other	✘ Council hearings
✘ Videos		people	✘ Other

Magazines read	womans day, O oprah, real simple,
Newspapers read	green bay press gazette, herbal newspaper also
Radio stations	102.7, 91.5, 90.5, 88.1, 89.3,104.3 FM 1280am
Television stations	abc, nbc, cbs, cnn, cnbc
Interest groups	—

Thinking about the most recent occurence of an environmental issue, please answer the following questions:

What was the issue?	water contamination for bottled water
Where was it?	several places
What were you doing?	trying to figure out which brand of bottled water I could drink
Have your feelings or behavior towards the environment changed over time?	Yes
What has influenced these changes?	unable to drink the brand of bottled water I used to drink due to contamination

Rate Impact:		
Books, magazines, articles, newspapers		5
Radio and television		5
Courses		1
Conversations with friends and family		5
Local events, incidents		5
First-hand experience		5

Off the top of your head, what issues do you think are most pressing for residents in the Green Bay area?	wires being buried. A person does not know if these wires are in your back yard or the neighbors yard. If they are up above you can see and avoid living there.
If you were asked about environmental issues, which specific environmental issues come to mind?	pollution in water, dioxins, growth hormones to all animals being raised for food consumption

Howard

Occupation	Tradesman/Laborer
Involved in a science-related field	—
What area of science do you specialize in?	—
Age	45–54
Education	High school graduate
Length of time Green Bay area	11 or more years
Part of Green Bay	DePere
Willing to participate	Yes
Frequency of thinking of environmental issues	Depends on events
Discussed with family	Yes
Discussed with friends/colleagues	Yes
Can you please give a brief example of such a discussion or exchange.	we have talked about using less water for normal household chores and the fact that all the water that rains down in city and suberbs doesn't drain through the soil to replenish the water supply but is piped directly to the rivers.

How do you get your news and information?

✗ Books	✗ Courses/	✗ Memberships in	✗ Rallies or
✓ Magazine articles	Training/	interest groups	political
✓ Scientific articles	Workshops	✗ Movies	demonstrations
✗ Newspapers	✓ Own observation	✓ Internet	✓ Spending time by
✗ Radio	and experience	✗ Discussions with	or near the water
✓ Television	✓ Friends	friends and other	✗ Council hearings
✗ Videos		people	✗ Other

Magazines read	popular science
Newspapers read	—
Radio stations	—
Television stations	history channel, hgtv,home,public broadcast,discovery,national channels,ect
Interest groups	—

Thinking about the most recent occurence of an environmental issue, please answer the following questions:

What was the issue?	recyling
Where was it?	home
What were you doing?	cleaning out my car with all my water bottles that needed to be recyled
Have your feelings or behavior towards the environment changed over time?	Yes
What has influenced these changes?	general public awareness

Rate Impact:	
Books, magazines, articles, newspapers	5
Radio and television	4
Courses	2
Conversations with friends and family	4
Local events, incidents	4
First-hand experience	4

Off the top of your head, what issues do you think are most pressing for residents in the Green Bay area?	pcb clean up of fox river
If you were asked about environmental issues, which specific environmental issues come to mind?	clean drinkable water, recycling, clean energy, pollution of all types

Survey responses: Frequency breakout

I think about environmental problems (including local issues, or those in other parts of the world):

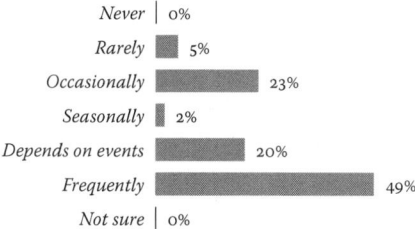

Are these environmental issues you shared above ever discussed within your family?

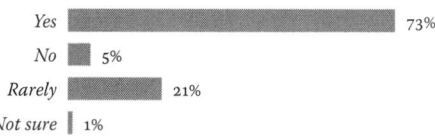

Thinking about those same environmental issues you shared above, are these issues ever discussed among your friends or colleagues (e.g. work, church, etc.)?

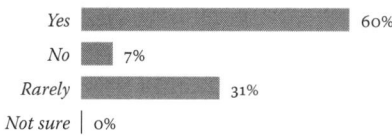

Thinking about those same environmental issues you shared above, are these issues ever discussed among your friends or colleagues (e.g. work, church, etc.)?

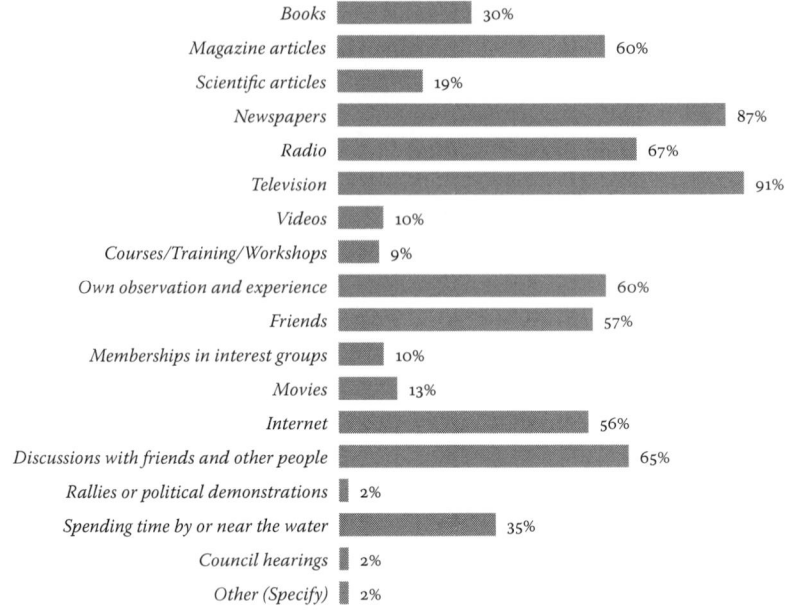

Books — 30%
Magazine articles — 60%
Scientific articles — 19%
Newspapers — 87%
Radio — 67%
Television — 91%
Videos — 10%
Courses/Training/Workshops — 9%
Own observation and experience — 60%
Friends — 57%
Memberships in interest groups — 10%
Movies — 13%
Internet — 56%
Discussions with friends and other people — 65%
Rallies or political demonstrations — 2%
Spending time by or near the water — 35%
Council hearings — 2%
Other (Specify) — 2%

Using a 1 to 7 scale with 1 being 'No Impact at All' and 7 being 'Very Strong Impact', how much impact do the following sources of information have on your feelings or behaviors towards the environment.

Books, magazines, articles, newspapers:

3%	5%	7%	21%	25%	19%	18%	1%
1	2	3	4	5	6	7	Don't know

Radio and television:

1%	5%	7%	22%	24%	17%	23%	1%
1	2	3	4	5	6	7	Don't know

Courses:

26%	11%	7%	10%	7%	9%	4%	25%
1	2	3	4	5	6	7	Don't know

Conversations with friends and family:

2%	6%	17%	22%	20%	17%	12%	4%
1	2	3	4	5	6	7	Don't know

Local events, incidents:

3%	2%	6%	15%	28%	15%	25%	4%
1	2	3	4	5	6	7	Don't know

First-hand experience:

2%	4%	2%	14%	17%	20%	35%	6%
1	2	3	4	5	6	7	Don't know

Which of the following categories best describes your occupation?

Professional- Technical	18%
Upper Management / Executive	2%
Middle Management	10%
Sales / Marketing	5%
Clerical / Service Worker	15%
Tradesman / Laborer	6%
Agriculture / Farmer	1%
Education	9%
Other (Please Specify)	34%

Are you involved in a science-related field?

Yes	16%
No	84%

Please indicate which of the following age categories you fall in (select one):

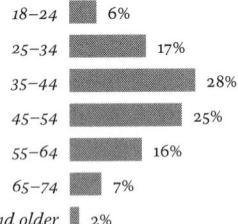

18–24	6%
25–34	17%
35–44	28%
45–54	25%
55–64	16%
65–74	7%
75 and older	2%

Which of the following categories best describes the highest level of education you have completed? (Select one)

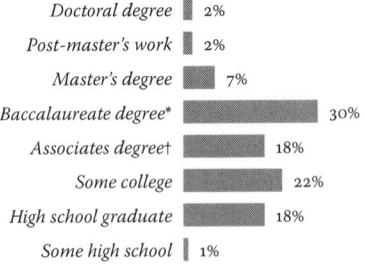

Doctoral degree	2%
Post-master's work	2%
Master's degree	7%
Baccalaureate degree*	30%
Associates degree†	18%
Some college	22%
High school graduate	18%
Some high school	1%

* 4-year college   † 2-year technical college / vocational school

Which of the following categories best describes the length of time in which you have lived in Green Bay or in the Great Lake region?

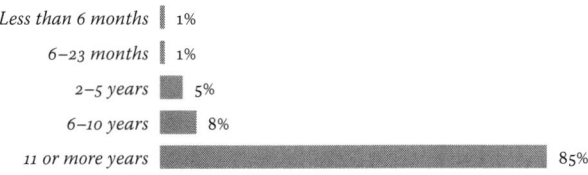

Less than 6 months	1%
6–23 months	1%
2–5 years	5%
6–10 years	8%
11 or more years	85%

What part of Green Bay do you live in?

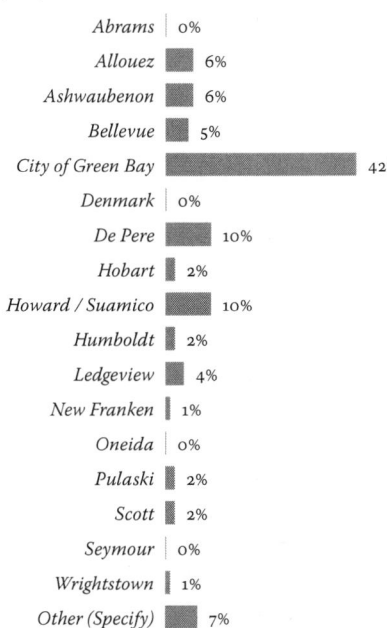

Abrams	0%
Allouez	6%
Ashwaubenon	6%
Bellevue	5%
City of Green Bay	42%
Denmark	0%
De Pere	10%
Hobart	2%
Howard / Suamico	10%
Humboldt	2%
Ledgeview	4%
New Franken	1%
Oneida	0%
Pulaski	2%
Scott	2%
Seymour	0%
Wrightstown	1%
Other (Specify)	7%

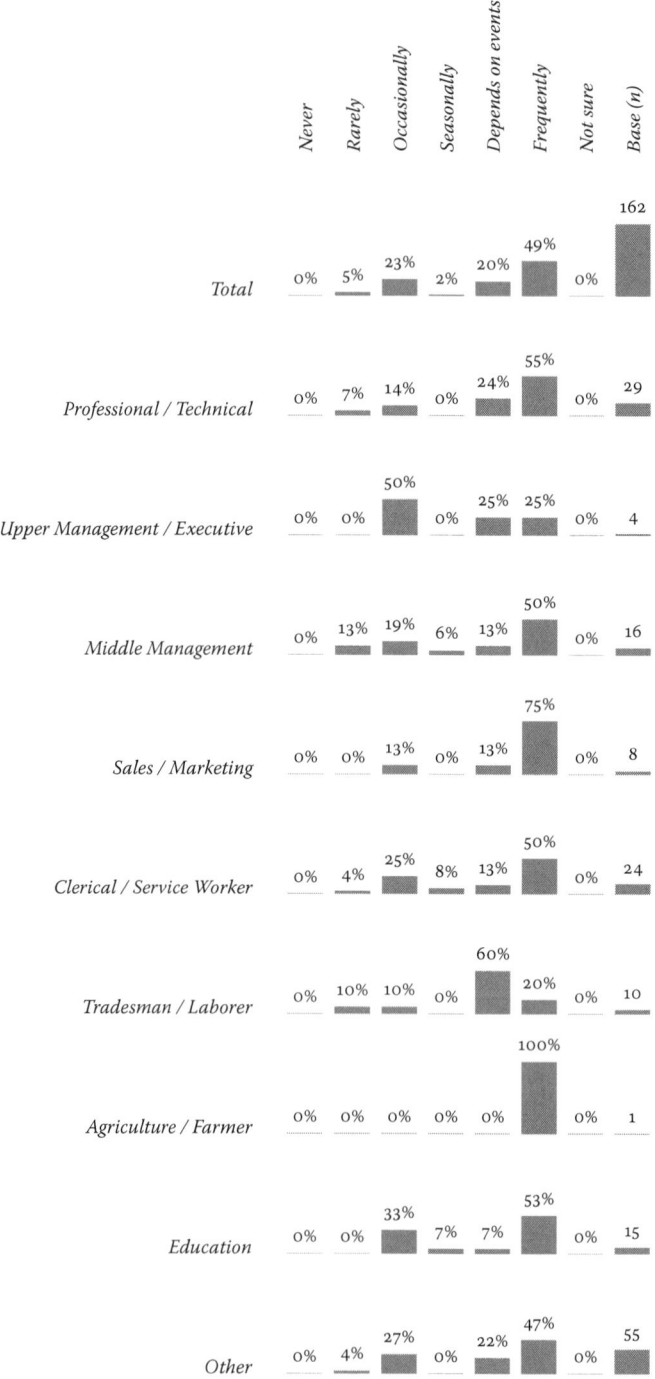

Donald: Tables of environmental objects

Note: The following tables are examples from my personal data analysis and notes, in terms of applying object-relational analysis for understanding the simultaneous and specific meanings and relationships associated with these particular 'environmental objects'. It also demonstrates how, when interviews are conducted over time – in this case, three interviews – the meanings shift, and new revelations can appear.

Baird's Creek

Interview 1	Interview 2	Interview 3	Notes
Walking with aunt, falling in water, happy memory, privately shared (between them).	Walking with aunt, special occasion because she lived far from us.	Development of Baird's Creek: "well it's built up, there are a lot of homes".	Initially a containing holding environment; experience with aunt special, falling into water, their own private joke. Later it's a place of separation, autonomy from family, parents, and yet it's containing – evidenced in being rescued by a frantic mother who drove in the middle of the night along winding roads to get them. No shame about this rescue. Sees Baird's as wilderness but close to city; registers sense of loss, not a place can go back to. Flat affect when discussing development (no anger).
Group (teenagers) would go out, sometimes do overnight camping, just enjoy the outdoors.	Going to Baird's creek with group of young men, take our bikes, 'do whatever young boys in the forest do'.

Camping in rainstorm with friends (boys) and getting rescued by friend's mother, "parental protection at its greatest!" | It's still there, just a little bit.

"I'm at a dead end with Baird's Creek" (in terms of what to talk about). | |

The Farm

Interview 1	Interview 2	Interview 3	Notes
Every summer as a child (pre-siblings) would spend two weeks at relative's farm, "always a thrilling thing to do", learning about farm life, before they used machines, horses and wagons, hay, being around relatives, away from parents. Very positive association.	—	—	The farm comes up early in the first interview, as important for Donald when he was young (presumably between ages of 4–6 before his sister was born). Signals sense of autonomy early on in his forays away from parents with a more exciting and exotic farm life. Brought Donald first-hand into contact with a working farm. Again like Baird's Creek, it was about adventure and being away from parents/siblings.

Bay Beach

Interview 1	Interview 2	Interview 3	Notes
A *fond* memory, very young years, going to Bay Beach with father, learning to swim, walking out on very nice sandy bottom, to raft. Don't have specific memory of when it closed. They just shut the whole thing down . . . Going to Bay Beach, enjoying the rides, recreation, etc.	After the closure, we swam in very tiny little pools and you'd pretend you were swimming by hanging on to the bottom and walking across the pool. Describes large municipal pool; sighs when saying that's where the swimming now revolved.	—	Very positive memory with father of learning to swim. When talking about closure and replacement of recreation, I start to feel bored and sleepy; there is a lack of affect in this account. Suggest perhaps a closure or an affective flattening as it was such a pleasurable place, but closure was when he was quite little. Contrast of Bay Beach with pools striking.

Fox River

Interview 1	Interview 2	Interview 3	Notes
The "tooth incident". Donald lost his front tooth when playing with boys down on the riverbank. One of his primary associations with the river, comes at the very end, with some humour but associated very strongly with the Fox River.	It isn't seen as a river in the sense that it was a recreational opportunity; we were much aware of that, because my father would tell me he used to swim in the Fox River. Nothing called us to the Fox River; there were other bodies of water, the Green Bay, of course Baird's Creek, that called to us. Even at its most polluted days, you could use it, because you didn't have to go in it; But I guess you could say we didn't see it as a river, and I would say, the Fox River is an important part of the whole Green Bay scene. I mean, you could see, not that we went down there, but you could see solid matter floating on the water. And so there was not an attraction, nothing that called us to the Fox River.	Canoe trip: Donald remembers story of paddling in a canoe with a friend down the Fox River about 20 years ago. "I had totally forgotten about it." Took the same canoe we canoed the Lakes, not the lakes but the rivers in Northern Wisconsin. We just wanted to see if we could do it. I don't have any memories of it, other than understanding that we were on a polluted body of water. It doesn't have the same impact as if had been on that body of water for the first time (naturalized to it) It was just something we needed to try one time, and accomplished it and that was enough. He then switches abruptly back to previous topic about how the interview is going. Just sort of stuck that memory in, in a disjointed way.	The Fox River seems to have a menacing association with it. Relationally it connects with a traumatic accident where he loses his front tooth (and has to live with it permanently) and his father's accident although that does not come up directly in relation to the Fox River, until I ask directly about it.

Two Rivers

Interview 1	Interview 2	Interview 3	Notes
Bought cottage on property 23 miles away, on the west twin river that flows into Lake Michigan, Two Rivers; use to hike, walk and have enough water in river to fish, "enjoyed the area for all of these years, nurturing our kids out there, they have enjoyed it, to the point where when they come back home, that is one place they wish to go." Unique geography, rocks, woods, water. Affectionate story of how they first found it, going to the property, being attacked by mosquitoes and then having it cleared up and falling in love with it.	Familiar with the land through friend; because of work, didn't have much time off, so the land was close enough to use and enjoy year-round easily (accessible). It had all the things cherished as a young person and even into that stage of life where he could get outdoors and recreate He wanted to share that with my family and kids		New place, new memories, new associations. Replacing Baird's Creek of childhood and young adulthood with Two Rivers, starting over. *Terra Nova*. The place is a locus for the family, to return to and provides continuity (contrast with Victoria, sense of fragmentation). For Donald, the children live far away, but the land seems to act as a hub or a focus. It's remained relatively unchanged; hence it's outside of progress, industry, tech, etc.

Paddle to the Sea (book)

Interview 1	Interview 2	Interview 3	Notes
—-	As he grew older, he became aware of Green Bay as a port, commerce, business and all that; became aware these bodies of water served a great purpose for the development of the Green Bay area. "I was given a book that I cherished as a young person . . ." "A very neat little story about an Indian boy who was given by his father a little carved out canoe . . ." Aunt gave him book, she is someone interested in stories and books, associated with nature on his walk in Baird's Creek. Gave it to oldest grandson but then asked for it back. Understood from the stories what impact the Great Lakes has on commerce and business, and how fortunate we are to have water resources that we do in the Great Lakes basin. Leads into discussion of value of the Great Lakes, environmental ethics.	Book is "respected but well used". Mother would read it to him from time to time, then started reading it himself. Teaching about activity/commerce in Great Lakes: forest fires, beaver dams, logging, shipping "You weren't sure the little guy would survive at all." Paddle never made it to Green Bay; sort of works out why he didn't and if he did, he would have gotten "stuck". Book suggests/ shows some carelessness in illustrations (bottle, etc.). Being aware that Green Bay is a small part of a very large system.	Good object relation: respected and well used, which are phrases he uses in connection with the Great Lakes (wishing people would use but respect). Book suggests a bridge or way to connect positively with the goodness of the region, seeing Green Bay as part of larger system, helping make coherent its significance in the face of senseless brutality with father's accident perhaps. Great deal of affection tied up in this object; relationship with aunt and mother, and with the locale. Also *Paddle* is the boy going out into the world, it's a coming of age story and also about transition from boy to man. He seems strongly identified with the boy and with the figure. In his recall, the boy was given canoe by father. In the actual story, the boy carves the canoe himself and sends it out into the world so he can stay at home and help father with work. Significant error in recall (it is serving something for Denis to see it as father giving to son, wishful phantasy?)

Green Bay Industry, Fort Howard

Interview 1	Interview 2	Interview 3	Notes
Father was machine tender, injured at work, broke both legs. Company made sure he was mended and then told him they didn't need him. "Nearly destroyed the man, emotionally shattered, great upheaval, betrayal." Donald worked at auto- motive factory with father briefly between accounting school and work in Green Bay cannery.	Father never talked about anything that may have bothered him. Not a great communicator. "One of the things I think about the old Fort Howard (now Georgia Pacific), when I walk down the trail, I'm kind of aware that they filled in parts of the river in order to make land for their operation. Also aware that they have lagoons and which they discharge their effluent and just opened gates and let it flow into river. Then they stopped that. Also aware because of recent knowledge that the treatment of wood was one of the big polluters in our system. But again I think as I matured I became involved in business, recognized what the paper industry has meant to this city. We are not a one-horse town." "I knew my father had been wronged. He had been terribly wronged by that company. Was never able to talk with dad about what happened." "I was laying the groundwork for trying to find something where I had a little better control of my destiny than my father did . . ."	"We were put here for a purpose and that is to enjoy and use the land. But does that need to spoil it? In my mind, I don't think so." "I can accept we modify the things around us, for our own comfort, I can't accept is why my forefathers had such a terrific, terrible impact on the water and the land." "I think about, this is a total environment not just waterways, I think about what has happened to it and I get upset. We don't respect it [environment]."	Interesting movement between anger, resentment, even disgust at paper mill and then quickly moves into "what the paper industry has meant to this city". (Cannot tolerate this critique, or perhaps is able to hold both the good/bad, destroying and nurturing mother). He is able to distance from the traumatic events with father and how he feels about the presence of industry in the city. At once it's positive, "appreciating", and on the other he is aware of the damages they have done to the land, the water and his own family, in the brutality expressed by this company. It's a disregard that upsets him so much. And yet he lives close by and seems to manage this and not allow it to become focused or fixated too much on the industry itself, as it's the industry which has made Green Bay what it is (good place to live etc).

Great Lakes

Interview 1	Interview 2	Interview 3	Notes
Renting uncle's boats with father, fishing on Green Bay. Adolescence, going with friends on fishing trips, became less of an attraction because of pollution. A group of friends after high school went up to Boundary Waters north of Lake superior, "one week or ten day excursions, came back home and enjoyed more of this local area . . ."	Great Lakes in relation to *Paddle to the Sea* – how book has helped his awareness, appreciation, connecting him with the larger system, commerce, business. Sadness at the fate and issues facing the Great Lakes.	Disappointed that Paddle doesn't get to Green Bay, indicating something about GB in relation to the Great Lakes (important, etc). GB as overlooked, forgotten? Travels to Lake Superior with wife in recent years. Great concern, worry about the fate of the Great Lakes, especially issue of exporting water.	He is able to extend and generalize his own connection with Green Bay (it's always been home) with the larger system of the Great Lakes. This seems to come about due to his early experiences with father, relatives, fishing and swimming around the waterways, and with the introduction of *Paddle to the Sea*, which helped Donald articulate or conceptualize GB in relation to the excitement and significance of the Great Lakes systems. Worries a lot about its future, but from a distance.

Index

Note: Italicized page numbers indicate a figure on the corresponding page.